SPECIAL EDUCATION

A Practical Approach to Educating Children with Special Needs

Dr. Umadevi, M.R.

Professor of Education

Dept. of P.G. Studies in Education

Davangere University

Karnataka.

NEELKAMAL PUBLICATIONS PVT. LTD.

EDUCATIONAL PUBLISHERS

(EXPORTERS & IMPORTERS)

NEW DELHI HYDERABAD

SPECIAL EDUCATION
A Practical Approach to Educating Children with Special Needs

Dr. Umadevi, M.R.

Edition : 2019
(Hardback)

ISBN : 978-81-8316-215-9

NEELKAMAL PUBLICATIONS PVT. LTD.
Sultan Bazar, Hyderabad - 500 095.
✆ 24757140, 24757197, 24757951, +91 80199-18182
Delhi Office:
4764/1, 23, Ansari Road, Daryaganj, New Delhi-110 002,
✆ 011-23244237, +91 98118-28953
e-mail : neelkamalbooks@gmail.com
website : www.neelkamalbooks.com

Published by ***Suresh Chandra Sharma*** for
Neelkamal Publications Pvt. Ltd., New Delhi, Hyderabad
and printed at ***Sri Vinayaka Art Printers,*** Hyderabad, India.

Preface

This text is about exceptional learners and Special Education. The term exceptional refers to Physical, Social and Intellectual uniqueness; the term learners refers to individuals who are waiting to be taught; and the term Special Education refers to adaptations of typical teaching approaches made to accommodate the uniqueness of the exceptional learner. In the chapters that follow, exceptional learners and their unique learning characteristics are discussed in detail. Also policies and practices in education of disabled children are dealt with and educational approaches and strategies to educate exceptional children and tips for teachers in remediating their problems are also discussed. Exceptional children are those who require Special Education and related services if they are to realize their full human potential. Disabled children must have access to regular schools which is a declaration of UNESCO and UN to provide inclusive education to all children with or without disabilities.

This text was written with a commitment to educate teachers, students and parents associated with the education of exceptional children. Its intention was to realize the mission of "education for all" in the regular schools. Thus achieving the goal of universlization of elementary education.

For the convenience of the readers the text has been divided into two parts. Part I presents the foundations of Special Education, so that the reader can gain insight about the concept of exceptionality, comprehend the process of Special Education, be aware of the various approaches to Special Education and assessment procedures adopted in Special Education. Part II presents the characteristics and education of the different categories of exceptional children, such as; gifted, mentally retarded, learning disabled, visually impaired, hearing impaired, communication disorders, behavior disorders, autistic, ADHD, and physically impaired.

Chapter 1 addresses the issues relating to the policies and practices and education of disabled children from Indian and International perspectives.

In Chapter 2 a number of categories of exceptional learners have been identified and been typically classified based on their uniqueness. The reader is able to understand normality and the special characteristics of exceptional children, so that appropriate educational and vocational placement can be prescribed.

Special Education services are addressed in detail, clearly and precisely in Chapter 3. So that the reader understands the different approaches to Special Education and this knowledge helps him to create a compatible classroom climate or environment to cater to individual needs of the exceptional learners.

Chapter 4 contains a framework on the assessment approaches in Special Education to help the reader to familiarize with common assessment practices to make decisions about Special Educational services that could be provided to exceptional learners.

Chapter 6 defines students who are gifted and talented and discusses their characteristics as a background for providing special programmes in educating them. This chapter also describes gifted underachievers, their identification, and educational programmes for overcoming their underachievement.

Chapter 7 provides indepth knowledge about definition, classification, characteristics, functional programming and education of mentally retarded children. This chapter also defines slow learners and discusses their identification and educational interventions.

Chapter 8 describes learning disabilities and focuses the difficulties faced by learning disabled children in various areas of learning and educational interventions to remediate them.

Chapter 9 and 10 is devoted to students with sensory disabilities (visual and hearing impairments) and deals with the types, causes, characteristics, identification of sensorily impaired children and highlights interventions to assist children with sensory disabilities.

Chapter 11 focusses on communication disorders and deals with types of communication disorders, characteristics of children with communication disorders, their assessment and educational provisions provided to them.

Chapter 12, 13, and 14 covers Behavior Disorders, Autism, Attention Deficit Hyperactivity Disorder. Detailed description of the terms is provided in these chapters respectively. Identification, causes, classification, characteristics and intervention strategies to children of each of the categories is also provided.

Chapter 15 provides key information about children with physical and neurological impairments, their identification, treatment and educational provisions. This chapter covers children with orthopedic impairments, cerebral palsy and epilepsy.

This book is designed to be used by students who are taking their course in Special Education. It is also written for practicing teachers who want to broaden their knowledge and skills in diagnosing and remedial techniques, intervention strategies of exceptional children. This book also provides the necessary information for in-service teachers to incorporate the intervention strategies in regular classroom to provide inclusive education.

Umadevi M.R

(Umadevi, M.R.)

Special Education

A Practical Approach to Educating Children with Special Needs

PART I

FOUNDATIONS OF UNDERSTANDING SPECIAL EDUCATION

PART II

❖ ❖ ❖

Part-I

Foundations of Understanding Special Education

Policy Perspectives in India and Abroad

1.1 Special Needs Policy in India

1.1.1 Introduction

There was a sea change in attitudes and global initiatives on equalization of opportunity, and education for all in the recent years. This change was mainly because of a growth in the understanding of children with disability, resulting in a change in attitude towards children with disabilities and stressing the paramount importance of integrating them in appropriate environments, suited to their special needs. This was followed by various Acts of Parliament which were later strengthened by fiscal support ensuring implementation. Today the new approach recommends access to a common schooling for all children, with access to a curriculum appropriate for all pupils.

During the British period, primary and mass education did not receive any serious attention. It was only in 1953, at a National Policy level, with the creation of the Central Social Welfare Board that the Government started playing a role on a broader scale. Between 1960 and 1975, several national committees were appointed by the government to look into child welfare activities and these recommended that a comprehensive national policy was needed to take an integrated view of the needs of children in socially disadvantaged areas (Sood, 1987; Verma 1994). In 1974, The National Policy for Children declared "children as a supremely important asset of the nation whose nurture and solicitude are the responsibility of the nation", and the National Children's Board came into existence. It was with the Fifth Five Year Plan (1974) that a major breakthrough was made for the provision of early childcare by the State for children in socially disadvantaged areas with the launching of the Integrated Child Development Scheme (ICDS), the largest preschool programme in the world.

In 1960, the Ministry of Education, which had been responsible for the education of disabled children, was bifurcated and the Ministry of Social Welfare was created, now known as the Ministry of Social Justice and Empowerment. The MSW was entrusted with the responsibility for the vulnerable and weaker sections of society, with rehabilitation as the main objective. The weaker sections included the schedule castes and tribes, women and children, and the disabled, the argument being that the weaker sections of society needed welfare and rehabilitation. Children with disabilities were not a part of the programmes that were created for the other weaker segments. The priority of education was not spelt out.

In 1968, reviewing the status of educational development for disabled, Sargent reiterated that 'few people in these days would deny that provisions for those children who are physically or mentally handicapped should form an essential part of any national system of education' (Sargent, 1968).

1.1.2 Historical Context

A Pre-Independence Overview of Education for the Handicapped

Historically, organised attempts to educate blind children were made in India when Christian missionaries established schools. The first school for blind children was established by an English missionary known as Annie Sharp in Amritsar in 1887. Interestingly enough, throughout the nineteenth century, an unknown number of blind children were casually integrated with sighted children, picking up whatever they could from oral repetition, which was the major tool of pedagogy. Priscilla Chapman remarked on a blind girl in Calcutta in 1826, who 'from listening to the other children got by heart the Gospel' (Chapman, 1839, as mentioned in Miles, 1996).

Due to insufficient documentation, researchers in the past 50 years, both Indian and foreign, are poorly informed about India's Special Educational needs and disability issues in the nineteenth century. Until about 1947, the then provincial governments had taken sporadic interest in the education and training of the handicapped, usually by giving adhoc grants to schools and other institutions for the handicapped, and it emerges that it was voluntary effort that played a pioneering role in the field of education and social service (Gupta, 1984).

In 1944 in England, the Education Act or the Butler Act was passed universalising education. At about the same time in India, in 1944, the Central Advisory Board of Education (CABE) published a comprehensive report on the post-war educational development of the country, popularly known as the Sargent Report. In this report, provisions for the handicapped were to form an essential part of the national system of education and were to be administered by the education department. Whenever possible, the report stated, handicapped children should not be segregated from normal children. Only when the nature and extent of their defect make it necessary, should they be sent to special schools (Sargent Report, 1944: Chapter IX, pp. 76-82). The CABE Report goes on to point out that governments in India, whether central or provincial, had shown little interest in this subject and had left it almost entirely to voluntary effort.

— Provision for the mentally or physically handicapped should form an essential part of a national system of education and should be administered by the education department.

— Hitherto in India, governments have hardly interested themselves at all in this branch of education; what has been done has been due almost entirely to voluntary effort.

— Wherever possible, handicapped children should not be segregated from normal children. Only when the nature and extent of their defect make it necessary, should they be sent to special schools or institutions. Partially handicapped children should receive special treatment at ordinary schools.

— Particular care should be taken to train the handicapped, wherever possible, for remunerative employment and to find such employment for them after-care work is essential.

— In the absence of any reliable data it is impossible to estimate what would be the cost of making adequate provision for the handicapped in India; 10 percent of the total expenditure on basic and high schools has been set aside for special services, which include such provision, and it is hoped that this will suffice (Sargent Report, 1944: Chapter 9, p. 82).

We see, therefore, that the board was guided by the fundamental principle that children with disabilities should not, if it can possibly be helped, be segregated from normal children; only when the nature or extent of their defect makes it necessary should they be sent to special schools or institutions.

1.1.3 Post-Independence Scenario

1.1.3.1 The Kothari Commission, 1964-1966

In 1964, the Kothari Commission was the first education commission which brought up the issue of children with special needs in the Plan of Action (Gupta, 1984; Jangira, 1995) and again gave strong recommendations for including children with special needs into ordinary schools.

The education of handicapped children has to be organised not merely on humanitarian grounds of utility. Proper education generally enables a handicapped child to overcome largely his or her handicap and make him a useful citizen. Social justice also demands it. It must be remembered that the Constitutional directive on compulsory education includes handicapped children as well.

There is much in the field that we could learn from the educationally advanced countries which in recent years have developed new methods and techniques, based on advances in science and medicine. On an overall view of the problem, however, we feel that experimentation with integrated programmes is urgently required and every attempt should be made to bring in as many children in integrated programmes.

The Commission further recommended

The Ministry of Education should allocate the necessary funds and NCERT should establish a cell for the study of handicapped children. The principal function of the cell would be to keep in touch with the research that is being done in the country and abroad and to prepare materials for teachers.

Therefore, while reviewing Government of India documents created during the post-Independence period, one finds that services for children with special needs seem to have followed the pattern of segregation, although statements of intent show otherwise The rhetoric remains on paper and not in practice.

Examining what has been the practice during the 53 years since Independence, three policies of the Government of India have been analyzed.

a) Policy of Assistance to Voluntary Organisations, Ministry of Welfare

b) Policy of Integration, Ministry of Human Resource Development

c) Policy of Integrated Child Development Scheme, Ministry of Human Resource Development

a) Policy of Assistance to Voluntary Organisations, Ministry of Welfare

In June 1964, work concerning the education, training and rehabilitation of the handicapped was transferred from the Ministry of Education to a newly created Department of Social Security. This department became the Ministry of Social Welfare (GOI, 1965). This happened despite the CABE Report and the Report of the Kothari Commission which had recommended that children with disabilities should be a part of the mainstream system. The Ministry of Welfare as it became known in the 1980s was entrusted with the responsibility for the welfare of the scheduled classes, other backward classes, drug addicts, cancer patients, those affected with leprosy, women and children, and children with special needs – a heterogeneous group of people who constitute the most vulnerable and weakest segments of the population, and form over half of India's population.

Since the commencement of the Second Plan (1956-1961), the union government continued the same paternalistic practice of the provincial governments of the pre-Independence period of doling out grants to voluntary organisations. Thus, government policy towards children with special needs was, and still is, principally dependent on voluntary organisations to deliver minimal micro-level services.

Today major work is done by the voluntary sector. There are over 2,500 organisations in the field. About 450 of these organisations get grants from the Ministry of Welfare towards their operational costs (GOI, 1990; Gupta, 1984; Jangira, 1995). Special schools exist for the blind, deaf, cerebral palsied, mentally handicapped and slow learners, very similar to what was happening in England in 1944 when there was rigid labelling and categorisation of disabled people. A larger number of NGOs sustain activities through their own funding efforts and in partnership with international partners.

The government's assistance in the way of grants-in-aid to voluntary organisations has become officially the accepted state policy as far as children with special needs are concerned, with no direct link between the state and the child. ..no obligations, no rights.

b) Policy of Integration, Ministry of Human Resource Development

In 1975, the government introduced Project Integrated Education for the Disabled (PIED). This scheme, previously with the Ministry of Welfare, was transferred to the Ministry of HRD, under the IEDC Scheme. Children in the age group 5 to 14 with not so severe impairments as determined through medical assessment were to be eligible for admission in regular schools. Through PIED, integration of a large number of children has happened.

Aggarwal, reviewing current developments in education, writes that 28,000 children spread over 6,000 schools are presently receiving benefits under this scheme. A much larger number are receiving indirect benefit through special teachers and other learning materials (Aggarwal, 1992).

According to Miles (1985), the number of children with special needs in ordinary schools far exceeds the number of children with special needs in special schools. The fact that there are states which do not have any special schools has no doubt helped 'casual integration' to take place.

On the whole, the findings indicate that India has the largest number of children with special needs integrated into ordinary schools in the Asia region and, due to the paucity of special schools round the country, an amount of casual and unplanned integration is already taking place, though no major study has been done about the efficacy of this integration (World Bank, 1994). This undoubtedly will help the question of inclusive education.

Again, of late there has been a significant trend towards integration. India has been a signatory to the Salamanca Conference held in Spain on 'Education for All'. In June 1994, representatives of 92 Governments and 25 international organisations signed a resolution which was a dynamic new statement on the education of all disabled children. In pursuance of the Salamanca Conference 'Education for All', the Government of India has launched the District Primary Education Programme (DPEP) where children with special needs are to be integrated into ordinary schools. The DPEP is expected to examine teacher training, curriculum modification, resource room support and teacher support. The Ministry of Social Justice and Empowerment, in the Indian Eighth Five Year Plan, 1991-1996, increased the budget for children with impairments by more than five times (DPEP Programme, 1993). With the establishment of the DPEP programme, India has taken a step forward in its policy of inclusion. However, the finding shows that the issue of integration is sporadic and based on individual initiatives, and not taking place as an organised programme of the state. The continuance of state-supported special schools certainly brings sharply into focus the contradictory government approaches in maintaining special schools as well as in attempting to integrate children with special needs into the regular school system in a piecemeal fashion.

c) Policy of Integrated Child Development Scheme, Ministry of Human Resource Development

In 1974, the government launched the Integrated Child Development Scheme. This programme is supposedly the world's largest package of services for the most vulnerable sections of the population (Swaminathan, 1992).

Since the ICDS works in the slums, the tribal and rural areas, it is the most appropriate service to include disabled children, who are mainly amongst the most vulnerable sections of society.

The policymakers too are aware of the critical 0-5 years and a large resource allocation has been made to the ICDS; yet children with special needs are not included in this so-called integrated package concerning even basic needs such as health, nutrition and preschool facilities.

Clearly such a major social policy in the country has left out disability from their agenda. The argument usually preferred by policymakers is that the para-professional workers are overloaded and have no knowledge of how to handle a handicapped child.

Therefore, although provisions are made for the scheduled castes, the poor, women and children, the disabled get identified as a separate category and remain marginalized.

The policy implementation process operates continuously, involving many levels of people on the central government level, on local government level, concerning local policy and priorities; or at the level of administrators and professionals (Criacher et al., 1988; Hill 1993).

1.1.4 Programmes of Inclusive Education in India

1.1.4.1 Centrally Sponsored Scheme of Integrated Education for Disabled Children (IEDC) (1982-83)

i) Accordingly, with the objective of providing educational opportunities for disabled children in common schools so as to facilitate their retention in the school system, the Department of Education has been implementing a centrally sponsored scheme of Integrated Education for Disabled Children (IEDC) since 1982-83. The scope of the scheme includes preschool training for disabled children and counselling for parents. Under the scheme, 100 percent financial assistance is provided, as per prescribed norms, for education of disabled children. This includes assistance towards:

   a) facilities for disabled children like books and stationery, uniform, transport allowance, readers' allowance for blind children, escorts' allowance for severely handicapped children and boarding and lodging charges for disabled children residing in hostels;

   b) setting up of resource rooms;

   c) resource teacher support in the ratio of 1:8 in respect of all disabled children except those with locomotor disabilities;

   d) survey for identification of disabled children and their assessment;

   e) purchase and production of instructional material;

   f) training and orientation of resource teachers and school administrators; and

   g) salary of an IEDC Cell at the state level to implement and monitor the programme.

ii) The scheme is implemented through education departments of the state governments/union territories, autonomous organisations of statutory and voluntary organisations. Presently, 24 states/union territories are implementing the scheme and over 50,000 disabled children in 12,292 schools have been covered so far.

iii) In addition, the Project on Integrated Education for the Disabled (PIED), with UNICEF assistance, was introduced in 1987 to strengthen the implementation of the IEDC scheme. This project was tried out in selected blocks in ten states of Haryana, Madhya Pradesh, Maharashtra, Mizoram, Nagaland, Orissa, Rajasthan and Delhi. A block was taken as a project area and all the schools in the block were converted into integrated schools. The teachers under this project were given three types of training: a general one-week training (Level I) to all primary teachers in the project area; a more intensive training (Level II) to some teachers in each school to equip them to handle children with disability; and the multi-category training (Level III) of one year's duration provided by the colleges of NCERT. The teachers with Level III training were placed in the project block to function as resource teachers for a cluster of schools.

An external evaluation of this project in 1994 showed that not only the enrolment of disabled children increased considerably, but the retention rate among the disabled children was very high (95 percent), much higher than that of normal children in the same blocks. It created a greater awareness about education of disabled children in general schools and even the teachers acknowledged that they were becoming better teachers by teaching disabled children. Over 6,000 disabled children have been covered in 1,382 schools under PIED.

iv) The NCERT is providing technical and academic support to the programme. It has;

1. developed print material such as identification checklists, an assessment schedule, a handbook for teachers, a functional assessment guide, and source books in modular form for various types of impairment like hearing and visually impaired;
2. developed non-print material such as video films on IEDC and films on the special needs of parents;
3. trained master trainers under the Education for All Project, in handling special needs of children in normal schools. A multi-site action research programme has also been launched in 23 DIETs and four regional institutes of education;

4. under manpower development, NCERT organised a number of training programmes for teachers as well as IEDC workers for early identification of disabled children and Multi-Category Training (MCT) programmes for resource teachers. Based on the feedback received, the MCT programme is being reviewed to enable trainees to acquire working knowledge about the nature and need of children with visual, hearing, orthopaedic or mental disability. Orientation programmes for parents, community, administrators and teacher educators of DIETs have also been organised between 1988 and 1994; and
5. undertaken a project entitled 'Examination Procedure for Children with Special Needs at the Elementary and Secondary Levels'. It is also working in the area of providing suitable classroom strategies and curriculum adaptations for these children.

v) Due to financial constraints only an amount of Rs. 250 million was allocated for this scheme during the Eighth Plan period. With the given allocation, the coverage was expected to reach 50,000 disabled children by the end of the Eighth Plan. This has been achieved. The main problems in implementation of this scheme have been lack of financial resources, trained teachers and specialised aids, and inadequate priority by the state governments.

1.1.4.2 National Policy on Education, 1986 and Its Programme of Action

The National Policy on Education (NPE), 1986 brought the education of this group of children under the Equal Education Opportunity Provision. It envisaged:

- education of children with locomotor disability and other mild disabilities in general schools;
- special schools for severely disabled children at district headquarters;
- reorientation of teacher training programmes by including a compulsory Special Education component in pre-service training of general teachers;
- provision of vocational training for the disabled; and
- involvement of NGOs in this work.

The Programme of Action (POA) states the placement principle: a child with disability who can be educated in the general school should not be in the special school. Even those children who are initially admitted to special schools for training in daily living skills plus curriculum skills should be integrated in general schools, once they acquire daily living skills, communication skills and basic academic skills. The POA, 1992 not only reiterated the principle of integration but also made it an integral component of all basic education projects: non-formal education, adult education, vocational education and teacher education schemes, funded by the central government.

1.1.4.3 The Persons with Disability Act (PDA) 1995

What is significant, however, is that a new direction is noticeable. Global initiatives mentioned earlier have influenced India. A new legislation was enacted in 1994 known as The Persons with Disability Act which states that disabled children should, as far as possible, be educated in integrated settings.

This proposed Act was introduced in pursuance of India being a signatory to ESCAP, which had adopted a proclamation on the full participation and equality of people with disabilities in the Asian and Pacific Region.

The PDA is a landmark legislation in the disability movement in the country. It presents a vision for people with disabilities, people who have for centuries been victims of prejudice, neglect, ostracism, treated as lesser beings and consigned to the bottom heap of humanity.

The intent of the proposed legislation is extremely laudatory as it is the first time that India recognises persons with disabilities as equal human beings. However, no rights have been conferred on them in the event of non-compliance by the state, nor is there any enforcement agency or fiscal support.

The Ministry of Welfare is the nodal ministry for the welfare of the handicapped. The special schools' sector is dealt with by the Ministry of Welfare whereas integrated education is being dealt with in the education sector. At present, only about 60,000 children receive education in about 1,400 special schools and about 50,000 disabled children are in the integrated education programme. This is against the estimated 10-15 million children with disabilities that require educational facilities.

As the present coverage of disabled children under the umbrella of education is not more than I percent, the Working Group for the Welfare and Development of Persons with Disabilities has suggested systematic efforts to provide education to all of them by 2010 AD. Insofar as integrated education is concerned, it has recommended extension of this approach to 500 additional blocks in the Ninth Five Year Plan.

The Persons with Disabilities (Equal Opportunities, Protection of Rights and Full Participation) Act, 1995 has also come into force recently. It has identified seven categories of disability, both physical and mental. Chapter 5 of the Act pertains to Education. It enjoins upon the government –

— Every child with disability shall have the right to free education till the age of 18 years in integrated or special school set up.

— Appropriate transportation, removal of architectural barrier and restructuring of examination system shall be ensured for the benefit of children with disabilities.

— Children with disabilities shall have the right to free books, scholarships, uniform and other learning material.

— Special schools for children with disabilities shall be equipped with vocational training facilities.

— Non-formal education shall be promoted for children with disabilities.

— Teacher training institutions shall be established to develop requisite power.

The Act places responsibility on the 'appropriate government' for implementing its various provisions. The onus, therefore, is apportioned between national, state and local governments. At the national level, the Ministry of Welfare is the nodal ministry for the welfare of the disabled. The chapter on 'Education' has relevance to this department. In this sector, while the special schools come under the purview of the Ministry of Welfare, the Department of Education has been making efforts to provide integrated education to disabled children with mild and moderate handicaps in normal schools. Since education is a concurrent subject and is under the administrative control of the state governments, the primary responsibility for education of the disabled has to be taken by the state government. The central government's role is to provide a catalyst and support the endeavours of the state government. The local bodies, the NGOs and all others concerned with education are equally responsible for implementation of the provisions of the Act.

1.1.4.4 National Trust Act 1999

National Trust Act is meant for the Welfare of Persons with Autism CP, MR Multiple Disabilities. The objectives of the Trust Act are as under:

- To enable and empower persons with disabilities to live as independently and as fully as possible within and as close to the community to which they belong.
- To strengthen facilities to provide support to persons with disability to live within their own families.
- To extend support to registered organizations to provide need- based services during the period of crises in the family of person with disability.

- To deal with problems of persons with disabilities who do not have family support.
- To promote measures for the care and protection of persons with disability in the event of death of their parent or guardian.
- To evolve procedure for the appointment of guardians and trustees for persons with disability requiring such protection.

1.1.4.5 National Policy for Persons with Disabilities

The National Policy for Persons with Disabilities was released by the Ministry of Social Justice & Empowerment in February 2006. The major highlights of the Policy document with regard to the education of persons with disabilities are the Constitution of India ensures equality, freedom, justice and dignity of all individuals and implicitly mandates an inclusive society for all including persons with disabilities. In recent years, there have been vast and positive changes in the perception of society towards persons with disabilities. It has been realized that a majority of persons with disabilities can lead a better quality of life if they have equal opportunities and effective access to rehabilitation measures.

1.1.4.6 Action Plan for Inclusive Education of Children and Youth with Disabilities August 20, 2005

The Ministry of Human Resource Development is currently in the process of developing a Comprehensive Action Plan on the Inclusion in Education of Children and Youth with Disabilities. A statement spelling out the areas of action was made in the Rajya Sabha by Arjun Singh, Minister for Human Resource Development on the 21 March, 2005. Since then, the Ministry has been interacting and consulting with experts, NGOs, Disability Rights Groups, Parents Groups, Government bodies etc.

The following framework of the Action Plan and list of activities has been developed as a result of the initial consultations. The plan covers the inclusion in education of children and young persons with disabilities. The different sectors to be covered in the plan are 1) Early Childhood Care and Education 2) Elementary Education 3) Secondary Education 4) Higher and Technical Education 5) Vocational Education.

The different departments at the Central level are in the process of developing their work plans. Roles and responsibilities for implementing agencies and their partners, the roles of NGOs, parents groups are also being drafted. Monitoring guidelines, success indicators etc are also being reviewed. The role of special schools, special educators and other support professionals are being assessed within the changing scenario.

The main objectives of the Action Plan will be:

- To ensure that no child is denied admission in mainstream education.
- To ensure that every child would have the right to access an Anganwadi and school and no child would be turned back on the ground of disability.
- To ensure that mainstream and specialist training institutions serving persons with disabilities, in the government or in the non-government sector, facilitate the growth of a cadre of teachers trained to work within the principles of inclusion.
- To facilitate access of girls with disabilities and disabled students from rural and remote areas to government hostels,
- To provide for home-based learning for persons with severe, multiple and intellectual disability,
- To promote distance education for those who require an individualised pace of learning,
- To emphasize job-training and job-oriented vocational training, and
- To promote an understanding of the paradigm shift from charity to development through a massive awareness, motivation and sensitization campaign.

Under this plan, the first level of intervention will be through the Integrated Child Development Services Programme. The ICDS Programme reaches out to all children in the age group of 0-6 years. The Anganwadi workers will be trained to detect disabilities early at an early stage by the Department of Women and Child Development, which will use the training modules prepared for this purpose by the National Institute of Public Cooperation and Child Development (NIPCCD) and other such agencies with the inputs of the Ministry of Social Justice & Empowerment. ICDS workers will be trained to motivate parents of children with disabilities. The ICDS Programme itself will provide for supplementary material to be used in the centers.

Our Constitution provides for free and compulsory education of all children up to 14 years. The Ministry is separately working on legislation on this subject. Through the Action Plan the Ministry will monitor the enrolment in schools of disabled children. The Sarva Shiksha Abhiyan provides for district-based educational planning and implementation for all children of the age group 6 to 14 years. It will be ensured that district level plans focus on all aspects of the education of children with special needs, including enrolment, support through assistive devices and the availability of trained teachers. Appropriate Special Schools in the non-governmental sector would increasingly become resource centers to assist with teacher training and supply of training material, and ensure retention of enrolled children with disabilities within the mainstream schools. These resource centers will support non-formal education as also home-based learning activities. Under the Sarva Shiksha Abhiyan State Governments are given 'earmarked' funds for undertaking special activities aimed at every single identified child with special needs. Utilisation of these funds will be closely monitored.

The Persons with Disabilities Act, 1995 provides for access to free education in an appropriate environment for children with disabilities till they attain the age of 18 years. The educational needs of disabled persons between the ages of 14 and 18 will be covered through a range of interventions including a Revised Plan for Inclusive Education of Children and Youth with Disabilities (IECYD) at an enhanced outlay of Rs. 1,000 Crores. Whereas under the Scheme of Integrated Education for the Disabled Children (IEDC) as it stands at present, children with disabilities are placed in a regular school without making any changes in the school to accommodate and support diverse needs. The revised IECYD will, in contrast, modify the existing physical infrastructure and teaching methodologies to meet the needs of all children including Children with Special Needs.

The Persons with Disabilities Act, 1995 further provides for 3 % reservation in all institutions receiving funds from Government for persons with disabilities. The implementation of these provisions in educational institutions will be taken up as a priority activity under the Action Plan. The fulfillment of the reservation in schools admissions will however not be a criterion for denial of admission of other children with disabilities.

All the schools in the country will be made disabled friendly by 2020 and all educational institutions including hostels, libraries, laboratories and buildings will have barrier free access for the disabled. Special attention will be given for the availability of study material for the disabled and Talking Textbooks, Reading Machines and computers with speech software will be introduced progressively in addition to an adequate number of Braille books. An adequate number of sign language interpreters, transcription services and a loop induction system will be introduced for the hearing handicapped students. Taking into account the special transportation needs of disabled college students, universities will be encouraged to introduce special shuttle services for the disabled.

To support the entire process of inclusive education we are also required to address issues of curriculum and pedagogy. The NCERT is addressing this issue and has set up a group under the National Curriculum Framework Review to examine the pedagogic inputs and classroom reorganization required for the education of Children With Special Needs.

Sensitizing teachers to the requirements of Children with Special Needs will be ensured by regular in-service training of teachers in inclusive education at the elementary and secondary level. In addition a Disability element in the syllabus of pre-service courses such as B.Ed., M.Ed will be strengthened. Towards this end, an MOU has been signed between the National Council for Teachers' Education (NCTE) and the Rehabilitation Council of India leading towards a convergence so as to ensure that all teachers and other resource persons will be enabled to address the diversity of children in the classroom to ensure enrollment and retention. Selected schools will be converted into a Model Inclusive Schools in order to demonstrate what is necessary and possible; this exercise will then be extended to schools across the country. Suitable trades and training institutions will be identified for vocational education of the disabled with the help of NCERT and other training mainstream institutions, and the Ministries of Labour, Rural Development and Urban Employment and Poverty Alleviation.

To provide a special focus on disabled students in higher education, all universities will have a Disability Coordinator who will act as a one stop shop for the disabled students and assist them in all their needs. The UGC will assist all universities to establish a separate Department of Disability Studies including modules on foundations of inclusion and on inclusive practices, research and discourse. We also propose to set up a Chair of Disability Studies in the Central Universities, in different Departments as appropriate. We will also examine the possibility of affiliating our leading national institutes working in the area of disabilities with an apex University.

The National Institutes and Special Schools that exist all over the country would enhance their capacities to match the demand that is placed on them by the Ministry of Human Resource Development. The Ministry of Social Justice and Empowerment will put in place a phased programme of transition for the Special Schools, enabling them to draw on their huge experience in working with children with disabilities and act as agents of change in all schools and to be external partners on physio, rehabilitation and speech therapy, and support on aids/ devices.

The Ministry of HRD will assume nodal responsibility to monitor, guide, facilitate and coordinate the new Action Plan. The Ministry will also be responsible for making an assessment of the additional funds required and for making the appropriate recommendations in this regard. A person/persons with deep experience of inclusive education practices will be nominated to the Central Advisory Board of Education (CABE) and will, in addition, assist the MHRD and ensure proper implementation of the new action plan. The Ministry will also devise methods to make the implementation of the Action Plan transparent, measurable and accountable and will involve non-governmental experts in monitoring this area of work.

1.1.5 Sarva Shiksha Abhiyan

Sarva Shiksha Abhiyan (SSA) is the national flagship programme launched in 2001-02 for achieving the goal of Universalisation of Elementary Education (UEE) through a time -bound approach in partnership with States and local bodies. It is also an attempt to provide an opportunity for improving human capabilities of all children (6-12 years age), through provision of community-owned quality education in a mission mode.

What is SSA doing for children with disabilities ?

The thrust of SSA is on providing inclusive education to all children with special needs in regular schools. It also supports a wide range of approaches, options and strategies for education of children with special needs. This includes education through open learning system and open schools, non formal and alternative schooling, distance education and learning, special schools, wherever necessary, home based education, itinerant teacher model, remedial teaching, part time classes, community based rehabilitations (CBR) and vocational education and cooperative programmes.

The following activities are undertaken:

- Identification of children with special needs through surveys.
- Assessment of each identified child.
- Provision of aids and appliances to those requiring assistive devices.
- Sensitization of teachers through specific training modules to the needs of CWSN.
- Parental training and community mobilization.
- Removal of architectural barriers in schools and providing an enabling environment for CWSN.
- Special emphasis for girls with disabilities.

- Convergence with activities of Ministry of Social Justice and Empowerment, State Departments of Welfare, National Institutions and NGOs.

26.36 lakh Children With Special Needs (CWSN) have been identified, of which 23.68 lakhs have been covered through enrolment in regular schools. EGS/AIE centers and home-based education. 8.46 lakh children with special needs have been provided with assistive devices. 16.75 lakh teachers have received 3-5 days training on inclusive education. 5.72 lakh schools have been provided with ramps and handrails, facilitating barrier free access.

SSA's Policy on Inclusion: "Education is the fundamental right of all children" and "Universalisation of education" is meaningful only when all the children in the age group of 6-14 are in school and get education. In this context, different programmes for different children with different abilities need to be organized to enroll and retain them in schools. SSA ensures that every child with special needs, irrespective of the kind, category and degree of disability, is provided meaningful and quality education. Hence, SSA has adopted a zero rejection policy. This means that no child having special needs should be deprived of the right to education and taught in an environment, which is best, suited to his/her learning needs. These include special schools and home-based education.

1.1.5.1 Objectives

- To provide access to schooling to all children with special needs.
- To achieve 100% enrolment and rehabilitation of children with special needs.
- To provide necessary supporting services to the children with special needs in the context of education.
- To reduce the gaps between the normal children and children with special needs in the context of education.
- To involve parents and community in the process of educating the children with special needs.
- To empower the teachers and parents to manage the children with special needs (CWSN) in the process of education.
- Establishment of resource persons and resource centers at block level to handle the children with special needs.

1.1.5.2 Components

The Following Activities could form Components of the Programme

a) **Identification:** A concerted drive to detect children with special needs at an early age should be undertaken through PHCs, ICDS, ECCE centers and other school readiness programmes. Identification of children with special needs should become an integral part of the micro-planning and household surveys.

b) **Functional and formal assessment** of each identified child should be carried out with a team constituted at every block to carry out this assessment and recommend most appropriate placement for every child with special needs.

c) **Educational placement:** As far as possible, every child with special needs should be placed in regular schools, with needed support services.

d) **Aids and appliances:** All children requiring assistive devices should be provided with aids and appliances, obtained as far as possible through convergence with the Ministry of Social Justice and Empowerment, State Welfare Departments, National Institutions or NGOs.

e) **Support services:** Support services like physical access, resource rooms at cluster level, special equipment, reading material, Special Educational techniques, remedial teaching, curricular adaptation or adapted teaching strategies could be provided.

f) **Teacher training:** Intensive teacher training should be undertaken to sensitize regular teachers on effective classroom management of children with special needs. This training should be recurrent at block/cluster levels and integrated with the ongoing in-service teacher training schedules in SSA. All training modules at SCERT, DIET and BRC level should include a suitable component on education of children with special needs.

g) **Resource support:** Resource support could be given by teachers working in special schools. Wherever necessary, specially trained resource teachers should be appointed, particularly for teaching special skills to children with special needs. Wherever this option is not feasible, long term training of regular teachers should be undertaken.

h) **Individualized Educational Plan (IEP):** An IEP should be prepared by the teacher for every child with special needs in consultation with parents and experts. Its implementation should be monitored from time to time. The programme should test the effectiveness of various strategies and models by measuring the learning achievement of children with special needs periodically, after developing indicators.

i) **Parental training and community mobilization:** Parents of children with disabilities should receive counselling and training on how to bring them up and teach them basic survival skills. Strong advocacy and awareness programmes should form a part of strategy to educate every child with special needs. A component on disability should be included in all the modules for parents, and community.

j) **Planning and management:** Resource groups should be constituted at State, district levels to undertake effective planning and management of the programmes in collaboration with PRIs and NGOs. An apex level resource group at the national level to provide guidance, technical and academic support to children with special needs under SSA may be constituted.

k) **Strengthening of special schools:** Wherever necessary, special schools may be strengthened to obtain their resource support, in convergence with departments and agencies working in that area.

l) **Removal of architectural barriers:** Architectural barriers in schools will be removed for easy access. Efforts will be taken to provide disable-friendly facilities in schools and educational institutions. Development of innovative designs for schools to provide an enabling environment for children with special needs should also be a part of the programme.

m) **Research:** SSA will encourage research in all areas of education of children with special needs including research for designing and developing new assistive devices, teaching aids, special teaching material and other items necessary to give a child with disability, equal opportunities in education.

n) **Monitoring and evaluation:** Ongoing monitoring and evaluation should be carried out to refine the programme from time to time. For this, appropriate monitoring mechanisms should be devised at every level and field tested at regular intervals.

o) **Girls with disabilities:** Special emphasis must be given to education of girls with disabilities.

1.1.5.3 Programmes Implemented

1. **Inclusive education resource teachers:**

   - Continued in-service training should be provided to prepare Integrated Education Resource Teachers (IERT) in each block for the educational and supportive services of the children with special needs. These teachers are the regular teachers who have put in experience in the regular classroom transaction and with 90 days of training in the distance mode.
   - These teachers conducted survey of children, functional assessment, medical camp and trainings to teachers and parents, planning of inclusive education activities at the block and cluster level depending on

the local situations providing guidance and conducting awareness programmes for the parents of CWSN, community and other children. Totally 606 Resource Teachers appointed.

2. **Functional assessment camps:** The children were identified after screening at the block level. The department converged with health department, women and child development and NGOs working in the field in this activity. A total of 53539 children attended medical camp with their parents.

3. **Providing aids and appliances:** After functional assessment, required aids and appliances were provided to the 18,360 children identified in the camps.

4. **Teachers training:** All the districts have conducted short-term training for 18957 general teachers at block level and long-term training for 1229 teachers through Rehabilitation Council of India (RCI) recognised study centers, affiliated to MP, BHOJ University through distance mode.

5. **Awareness programme:** The awareness programmes are conducted at state, district, block level and cluster levels. The state level programmes are organised through NGOs who conducted awareness camps at 30 blocks of 10 districts. In each block 8 schools were selected. The objective of the programme is to change the attitudes of people. The theme of the programme was "We too have ability, we are capable and we are educable". This programme was conducted by a group of children with special needs and normal children.

6. **Parents training:** The districts have conducted training for 22467 parents and counseling sessions to educate parents regarding the effective management of their children and activities to be adopted.

7. **Barrier free environment:** Barrier free environment was created in 3501 existing schools during 2006-07 and it is made mandatory to provide ramps in new school buildings. Totally 17967 schools have ramps with handrails and the coverage is 41%.Till now 54,855 schools are made barrier free.

8. **Resource centers:** It was proposed to establish one resource center in each block to use them for teacher training and teacher empowerment programmes. These centers will help the teachers in handling the children in their schools, and the materials to be provided and use the centers for their children. Action has been initiated to establish the resource centers in 202 blocks.

Karnataka is putting earnest and honest efforts to implement the policies and the programmes – Sarva Shiksha Abhiyan mission on inclusive education.

1.1.6 District Primary Education Programme (DPEP)

A programme called the District Primary Education Programme (DPEP) was launched in 1995 by the government, supported by the World Bank, with the aim of working out curricula, teacher training, etc., for early childhood care, including disabled children. The most significant change proposed is that the district primary schools in the state would be held responsible for all children, including disabled children. India was aiming to reach 'Education for All' status by the year 2000. The District Primary Education Programme (DPEP) was started in 14 states of India. This is the first time that primary education has been delinked from the state. The primary objectives of the DPEP are to support Government of India's efforts towards universalisation of elementary education; address the issue of dropouts, out-of school children and early marriages by starting primary schools in every village; provide extensive teacher training; address gender issues and create programmes for the empowerment of women. Convergence of different government agencies and NGOs at various levels would be promoted actively; teachers would receive regular in-service training through the District Institute of Education and Training (DIET) and the State Council of Educational Research and Training (SCERT); case studies and statistics showing enrolment, retention, dropouts and gender-wise specifications would be compiled annually; alternate schooling would be promoted with a focus on flexible curriculum, informal evaluation criteria, flexible timings and other issues of adult illiterate persons; and, following world trends, integrated or inclusive education of children with mild to moderate disabilities would be promoted.

1.1.7 Schemes for Disabled Children

1.1.7.1 Integrated Education for Disabled Children (IEDC)

In 1974 the Government of India launched the scheme under the Ministry of Social Justice and Empowerment, which was later shifted to Ministry of Human Resource Development. The scheme intends to provide educational opportunities to students with disabilities in regular schools and facilitate their retention through resource support in the schools. Children with disabilities in the age group of 15-18 years are provided free education under the following heads:

I. A disabled child may be given the following kinds of facilities at the rates prevalent in the State/UT concerned. The facilities should, as far as possible, be given in kind. In case similar incentives are not being offered by the state government/UT Administration under any other scheme, the following rates could be adopted.

a) Actual expenses on books and stationery up to Rs. 400 per annum.

b) Actual expenses on uniform up to Rs. 200 per annum.

c) Transport allowance up to Rs.50 per month. If a disabled child admitted under the scheme resides in the school hostel within the school premises, no transportation charges would be admissible.

d) Reader allowance of Rs. 50 per month in case of blind children after class V.

e) Escort allowance for severely handicapped with lower extremity disability at the rate of Rs. 75 per month.

f) Actual cost of equipment subject to a maximum of Rs. 2000 per student for a period of five years.

II. In the case of severely orthopaedically handicapped children, it may be necessary to allow one attendant for 10 children in a school. The attendant may be given the standard scale of pay prescribed for class IV employees in the State/UT concerned.

III. Disabled children residing in school hostels within the same institution where they are studying may also be paid boarding and lodging charges as admissible under the State Government rules/schemes. Where there is no state scheme of scholarships to hostellers, the disabled children whose parental income does not exceed Rs.5000 per month may be paid actual boarding and lodging charges subject to a maximum of Rs. 200 per month. However, disabled children should generally not be placed in hostels unless the required educational facilities are not available in the nearby schools.

IV. Severely orthopaedically handicapped children residing in school hostels may need the assistance of a helper or an ayah. A special pay of Rs. 50 per month is admissible to any employee of the hostel willing to extend such help to children in addition to his / her duties.

1.1.7.2 CBSE Relaxation for Disabled Children

The facilities extended by the board to the disabled candidates (Dyslexic, Blind, Spastic and Candidate with Visual Impairment) are as under:

- The persons with disabilities (Dyslexic, Blind, Spastic and Candidate with Visual Impairment) have the option of studying one compulsory language as against two. The language opted by them should be in consonance with the overall spirit of the three language formula prescribed by the Board. Besides one language they can offer any four of the following subjects: Mathematics,

Science and Technology, Social Science, Another Language, Music, Painting, Home Science and Introductory Information Technology.

- From the 2002 Examination, alternate questions in lieu of questions requiring special skills based on visual inputs have been provided in Mathematics and Science for Sec. School Examination (Class X).
- Blind, Physically Handicapped and Dyslexic Students are permitted to use an amanuensis. The amanuensis must be a student of a class lower than the one for which the candidate is taking the examination.
- The visually handicapped students appearing from Delhi were provided questions papers with enlarged print for 2003 Examination.
- Disabled candidates are allowed additional one hour (60 minutes) for each paper of external examination.
- Board does not give relaxation in minimum marks prescribed by it.
- Exemption from Examination in the third language.
- The Board considers the physiotherapic exercises as equivalent to physical and Health Education course of the Board.
- Centre Superintendents have been instructed to make arrangements for the conduct of the examination of such candidates on the ground floor as far as possible.
- Physically challenged children will specifically indicate their category and also state whether they have been provided with a writer in the columns provided in the main answer book.
- Answer books of such candidates are evaluated by the Regional officers at one Nodal Centre.
- The Centre Superintendents have been requested to send the answer books of such candidates in the separate envelope to the Regional Officer concerned.
- Separate question papers in Science & Mathematics at Secondary (Class X) level have been provided for blind students w.e.f. 2003 Examinations.
- Assistant Superintendents for the blind are teachers from the schools where the blind are studying. As far as possible, teachers of the same subject are not allowed to be appointed on the day of examination. One invigilator is from outside the school.
- Assistant Superintendents supervising the physically challenged children who have granted 60 minutes extra time are paid remuneration @ Rs.50/- + Rs. 20/-

- Amanuenses are paid @ Rs.100/- per day / paper daily by the Centre Superintendent from the centre charges amount.

1.1.7.3 Scheme of Assistance for Purchase/Fitting of Aids and Appliances

The main objective of the scheme is to assist the needy disabled persons in procuring durable, sophisticated and scientifically manufactured, modern, standard aids and appliances that can promote their physical, social and psychological rehabilitation and reduce the impact of disabilities and enhance their economic potential. The aids and appliances supplied under the Scheme should be ISI/BIS marked or approved. The scheme is implemented through the implementing agencies which provide financial assistance for purchase, fabrication and distribution of standard aids and appliances. The implementing agencies take care of/make suitable arrangements for fitting and post-fitting care of the aids and appliances distributed under the Scheme.

1.1.7.4 National Scholarship Scheme

The object of this scheme is to provide financial assistance to students with disabilities for pursuing higher and technical education. They are also supported for acquiring special aids and appliances. 500 scholarships are available for pursuing higher and technical education. The rate of scholarship ranges from Rs.400 to Rs.1000 for diploma to PhD level for dayscholars and hostellers. The scholarship awardees are also reimbursed the course fee subject to a ceiling of rupees ten thousand per year.

1.1.7.5 National Handicapped Finance & Development Corporation (NHFDC)

Loans are available up to Rs. 5 lac for persons with disabilities under the schemes for setting up small business in service/trading sector, for, purchase of vehicles for commercial activity, for setting up small industrial unit, for agricultural activities, to promote self-employment amongst persons with mental retardation, cerebral palsy and autism, and loan for education/training to persons with disabilities.

1.1.7.6 National Institutes

In consonance with the policy of providing complete welfare services to the physically and mentally handicapped individuals and groups and in order to effectively deal with the multidimensional problems of the handicapped population, the following National institutes have been set up in each major area of disability:

1. National Institute for the Visually Handicapped, Dehradun.
2. National Institute for the Orthopaedically Handicapped, Kolkata.
3. AL Yavar Jung National Institute for the Hearing Handicapped, Mumbai.
4. National Institute for the Mentally Handicapped, Secunderabad.

These Institutes are apex level organisations in the field of education, training, vocational guidance, counselling, research, rehabilitation and development of suitable service modules for the handicapped. The institutes also serve as premier documentation and information centres in their respective areas of disability. Development and standardisation of aids and appliances and preparation of community awareness materials, both for the electronic and the print media are also included in their activities.

1.1.7.7 Facilities, Concessions, and Allowances available to Persons with Disabilities

Travel concessions: Travel concessions for journey by train are up to 75 percent available to the persons with visual, locomotor, hearing and mental retardation. Similarly, by air, concessions up to 50 percent are admissible to persons with visual and locomotor impairment.

Postage: 'Blind Literature' are exempted from the payment of postage.

Tele-communication: For the blind persons there is a provision for 50 percent rental rebate on telephone connection.

Preference in allotment of STD/PCO: Educated unemployed persons with disabilities are given preference in allotment of STD/PCO booths.

Customs concessions: Aids, appliances, devices such as braillers, canes, calipers, wheel chairs etc. are exempted from custom duty for individuals as well as institutions.

Conveyance allowance: Special conveyance allowance is admissible to persons with visual impairment and locomotor impairment working in government organizations.

Children's educational allowance: Provision has been made for the reimbursement of tuition fee of children with disabilities to the parents working in government organizations.

Income tax concessions: Persons with disabilities can claim rebate on the Income Tax under relevant clause as applicable to persons with disabilities.

Award of dealership agencies by oil companies: Reservation has been made for the award of dealership of kerosene, LPG etc for persons with disabilities.

1.1.7.8 Reservation of Jobs and other Facilities

i) *Three percent reservations in grade government jobs*: Three percent jobs are reserved for persons with disabilities (1 percent each for the hearing impaired, locomotor impaired, and visually impaired) in government jobs.

ii) *Posting of handicapped candidates:* As per the decision of the Government of India, persons with disabilities should be posted as near as possible to their native place.

1.2 International Policy and Practice in the Education of Disabled Children

On the international platform there have been a number of encouraging pronouncements in recent years, regarding the education of disabled children. The messages supporting inclusive education have never been stronger.

1.2.1 UN Convention on the Rights of the Child 1989

The 1989 UN Convention on the Rights of the Child has been ratified by 177 countries worldwide. There are several general Articles in the Convention which lead up to Article 23, which is specifically about disabled children.

The Convention includes statements such as: 'all rights shall apply to all children, without discrimination on any ground including disability. In all actions the child's best interests shall be a primary consideration and they should develop to the maximum extent possible'. The Convention also states the right of the child to express an opinion and to have that opinion taken into account.

But it is Article 23 that covers disabled children saying the child's education shall lead to the fullest possible social integration and individual development, including his or her cultural and spiritual development. He or she shall have the right to enjoy a full and decent life, in conditions which ensure dignity, promote self-reliance, and facilitate the child's 'active participation in the community'. Article 23 also states the right of the disabled child to special care, education, healthcare, training, rehabilitation, employment preparation and recreation opportunities.

Furthermore, Articles 28 and 29, covering all children's education' generally, say it shall be on the basis of equal opportunity; and that it should develop them to their 'fullest potential'. Education, says Article 29, should prepare a child for an 'active and responsible' life as an adult.

There are many values expressed by the UN Convention relevant to the struggle for inclusive education.

1.2.2 UN Standard Rules

The UN Standard Rules on the Equalisation of Opportunities for Persons with Disbilities (1993), set an international standard for policy making and action covering disabled people. They give powerful support for the development of inclusive education for disabled pupils worldwide. In order to implement inclusive education, countries should have a 'clearly stated policy' that is understood at a school level and in the wider community. States should recognise principles of equal educational opportunities for children, young people and adults with disabilities, in integrated settings. Rule 6, covering education, says that states should ensure that the education of disabled people is an integral part of the education system and it calls for

1. buildings to be accessible,
2. interpreter and other support services,
3. parents and organisations of disabled people to be involved in the education process,
4. a flexible curriculum plus additions and adaptations for disabled pupils, and
5. ongoing teacher training.

Where ordinary schools cannot yet make adequate provision to include disabled children, Rule 6 calls for 'special school education aimed at preparing the students for inclusion in the mainstream'.

1.2.3 UNESCO Salamanca Statement (1994)

In 1994, UNESCO, the UN's Education Agency, published the Salamanca Statement, a declaration on the education of disabled children, which called for inclusion to be the norm. Representatives of 92 governments and 25 international organisations agreed on it.

UNESCO's statement is unequivocal in asking the international community to endorse the approach of inclusive schooling: 'We call upon all Governments, and urge them to adopt as a matter of law or policy the principle of inclusive education, enrolling all children in regular schools, unless there are compelling reasons for doing otherwise.'

Disabled children 'must have access to regular schools' and it adds.

Regular schools with this inclusive orientation are the most effective means of combating discriminatory attitudes, creating welcoming communities, building an inclusive society, and achieving education for all.

Moreover, they provide an effective education to the majority of children and improve the efficiency and ultimately the cost-effectiveness of the entire education system.

The Salamanca Statement asks all governments to undertake a variety of actions, India included. It wants governments

- to give the highest policy and budgetary priority to improve education so all children can be included, regardless of individual difference or difficulties;
- to develop demonstration projects and encourage exchanges with countries which have inclusive schools;
- to ensure organisations of disabled people, along with parents and community bodies, are involved in planning and decision making; and
- to make early identification and intervention strategies a priority as well as vocational aspects of inclusive education and to ensure that both initial and in-service teacher training address the provision of inclusive education.

The Salamanca Statement calls for action from:

- UNESCO itself,
- UNICEE
- the UN Development Programme, and
- the World Bank.

As the UN agency for education, UNESCO was specifically asked in the report to use its funds up to 2001 to create an expanded programme for inclusive schools and community support projects, thus enabling the launch of many pilot projects.

Salamanca says: 'In those countries with few or no special schools those countries should establish inclusive ordinary schools -not special schools, to serve disabled children.' And to finish this part on the Salamanca Statement, there is a quote in the report from a Swedish Member of Parliament, Mr Bengt Lindqvist:

The challenge now is to formulate requirements of a school for all. All children and young people of the world have the right to education. It is not our education systems that have a right to certain types of children. It is the school system of a country that must be adjusted to meet the needs of all children.

1.2.4 Public Law (P.L.) 94-142

1.2.4.1 The Individuals with Disabilities Education Act

In 1975, the United States Congress Passed Public Law 94-142, originally called the Education for all Handicapped Children Act. Shortly after its passage, P.L. 94-142 was called "block buster legislation" (Goodman 1976) and hailed as the law that will probably become known as having the greatest impact on education in history.

P.L. 94-142 is directed primarily at the states, which are responsible for providing education to their citizens. Each state education agency must comply with the law by

a) Locating and identifying all children with disabilities.

b) Identifying and placing handicapped children by means of testing and evaluation procedures that do not discriminate on the basis of race, culture, or native language.

c) Developing an individualized education program (IEP) for every handicapped child in the state.

d) Educating each handicapped child in the least restrictive environment.

e) Protecting the rights of handicapped children and their parents by ensuring due process, confidentiality of records, and parental involvement in educational planning and placement decisions.

❖ ❖ ❖

Exceptional Children

2.1 Understanding Exceptional Children

There are individual differences among children; the differences among most children are relatively small enabling them to benefit from general education programme. The physical attributes and/or learning abilities of some children however those we call exceptional children differ from the norm (either below or above) to such an extent that an individualized programme of Special Education is required to meet their needs. The term exceptional children includes both children who experience difficulties in learning and children whose performance is so superior that Special Education is necessary to help them fulfill their potential. Thus exceptional children is an inclusive phrase that refers to children with learning and /or behaviour problems, children with physical disabilities, and children who are intellectually gifted (William and Orlansky 1992).

The term exceptional children refers to children whose needs are very different from those of the majority of children in society. These children deviate from average children to the extent they cannot receive classroom instruction in regular schools. This was the belief prevalent for several years. At present it is appropriate to define exceptional children as those who differ from the average to such a degree in physical and psychological characteristics that the traditional school programme does not allow all around development and progress for them. They need Special Education or special ancillary services to grow according to their ability.

Students are considered exceptional when they

1. Meet the criteria for being classified as exceptional.
2. Require a modification of school practices, or Special Educational services to develop to maximum capacity.

Exceptional Children are those who require Special Education and related services if they are to realize their full human potential. The exceptional child is different in some way from the hypothetical average youngster. He may have problems or special talents in thinking, seeing, hearing, speaking socializing, etc. More often than not he may manifest a combination of special abilities or disabilities. However most of Special Education is focused on education of students with disabilities.

2.1.1 Definition by Kirk

The exceptional child is defined as the child who deviates from the average or normal child in mental characteristics, in sensory abilities, in neuromuscular or physical characteristics, in social or emotional behaviour, in communication abilities, in multiple handicaps to such an extent that he requires a modification of social practices or Special Educational services, in order to develop to his maximum capacity.

2.2 Impairment, Disability and Handicap

Several terms have been used to describe exceptionality, subnormal, handicapped, disabled, exceptional, special, impaired etc. The World Health Organisation (WHO 1976) defines a disability as any restriction or lack (resulting from an impairment) of ability to perform an activity in the manner or within the range considered normal for a human being. UN standard rules on the equalisation of opportunities for persons with disabilities (1993), defines disability from a perspective that emphasises social conditions which disable a group of individuals by ignoring their needs of accessing opportunities in a manner conducive to their circumstances. In simple words, disability is one that affects daily functioning in two or more of the following areas.

- Capacity for independent living
- Economic self-sufficiency
- Learning
- Mobility
- Receptive and expressive language
- Self-care
- Self-direction

The WHO (1999) has estimated that between 7 and 10 percent of the world's population has some type of disability and that 80% of these live in developing countries, out of which one third are in India.

The World Health Organization has clearly distinguished the use of three terms: *Impairment, Disabilities* and *Handicap.*

- **Impairment** means abnormalities of body structure and appearance and organ or system function resulting from any cause in principle. Impairment represents disturbances at the organ level WHO (1976).
- **Disability** reflects the consequences of impairment in terms of functional performance and activity by the individual WHO (1976).
- **Handicap** on the other hand refers to disadvantages experienced by the individual as a result of impairments and disabilities; handicaps thus reflect interaction with an adaptation to the individuals surroundings WHO (1976).

These terms are based on an organic model having functional interrelationship.

Impairment ⟶ Disability ⟶ Handicap

2.2.1 Interrelationship among the Three

1. A child with a fingernail missing has malformation, a structural impairment or ear pinna missing has malformation, a structural impairment but this does not interfere with functioning of hand or ear, there is no disability or handicap.
2. A myope or a diabetic suffers from functional impairment but can be corrected with drugs or aids; he may not necessary be disabled but he may be handicapped to play some games.
3. An individual with colour blindness has an impairment but it would be unlikely to lead to activity restriction: whether the impairment constitutes a handicap would depend on circumstances. If he was an agriculturist he might well be unaware of his impairment, but would be at a disadvantage if he was to drive a railway engine.

E.g.: Subnormal intelligence is an impairment; if his occupation does not demand normal intelligence it may not be a handicap. A learning disabled child may not be identified at all if he is a labour.

A disability results from a medical, social or learning difficulty that interferes significantly with the students normal growth and development -such as the ability to profit from schooling experiences or the ability to participate successfully in work activities.

Disability refers to reduced function or loss of a particular body part or organ. A disability limits the ability to perform a certain task (e.g., to see, hear, talk, walk) in the same way that most non-disabled persons do. A disabled person is not handicapped, however, unless the physical disability leads to educational, personal, social, vocational or other problems.

E.g.: If a child has lost a leg, he can learn to use artificial limb and thus function in and out of school without problem.

Handicap refers to the problem a person with a disability or impairment encounters in interacting with the environment. A disability may pose a handicap in one environment but not in another. The term handicapped children is more restrictive than exceptional children and does not include gifted and talented children.

Exceptional children are more like other children than they are different. All children are unique individuals who require individual attention, nurturing and caring.

2.3 Statistical Standards

Many human behaviours and characteristics fall into a pattern of distribution that forms a bell shape. This symmetrical distribution is called the normal curve. The shape of the normal curve is exactly the same on either side of its midpoint, so we can predict the area between points on the curve. The midpoint is the Mean (arithmetic average) of the curve. The degree to which occur-rence of a behaviour characteristic differs from the Mean is expressed in Standard Deviations (SD) units, each of which contains a fixed percentage of cases above and below the Mean.

2.3.1 Normal Probability Curve

The normal curve gives us a numerical basis for making decision about the probability that a behaviour or characteristic will occur. Special educators use these standards in defining exceptionality, focusing on the small percentage of cases at either side of the curve. For ex: the definition of mental retardation (MR) is based on the idea that intelligence is normally distributed (meaning that it follows the normal curve) in the general population. In this context. IQ scores that are 2 Standard Deviations below the average on intelligence tests are used to identify students with retardation. Giftedness also is defined in terms of performance on intelligence tests. Here scores 2 Standard Deviations above the mean indicate exceptionality; when these criteria are applied, we can expect that about 2 percent of the population will be identified as gifted and about 2 percent mentally retarded.

In Medicine normally means presence of normal signs or the absence of disease symptoms.

E.g.: Normal temp 98.6

Normal blood sugar 90-120

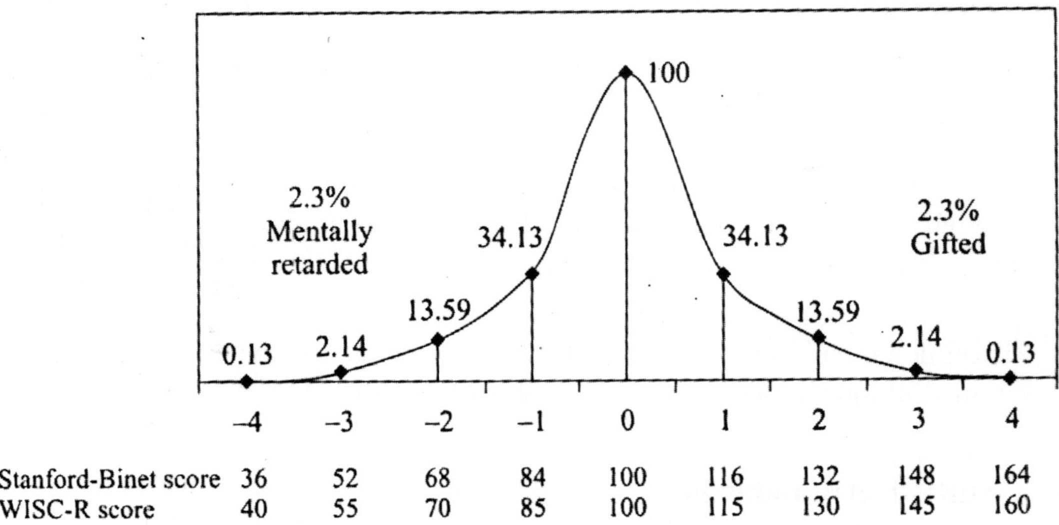

Fig-2.1: Normal Probability Curve showing the Distribution of Intelligence

Heartbeat, respiration rate, pulse rate are used to determine physical well being. Genetic abnormalities, prenatal problem, infection, physical trauma can cause special learning needs. Genetic abnormalities may cause Downs Syndrome, M.R. Measles, encephalitis, also can cause developmental retardation or delays. Anoxia (insufficient oxygen at birth) destroy brain cells, producing general palsy, M.R., Learning disability. Malnutrition, poisoning, physical trauma increase risk of M.R. and learning difficulties.

Sociologists, psychologists, anthropologist and educators often define normality in terms of societies code of behaviours. Certain behaviours are expected from normal schooling. Many of there behaviours are written down or otherwise classified in the form of explicit rule. For e.g.: students are generally expected to demonstrate competence in basic skills (reading, writing and math) by the end of 3rd grade. Not being able to read or write is accepted as a form of exceptional behaviours.

2.4 Labeling and Classifying Exceptional Children

Some educators argue that, even today, the classification of exceptional children functions to exclude them from normal society. Others argue that a workable system of classifying exceptional children (or their exceptional learning needs) is a prerequisite to providing the Special Educational programmes. These children require Special Education if they are to be integrated into normal society.

No other aspects of Special Education have been more widely debated during the past two decades than classification and labeling. Classification is a complex issue involving emotional, political, and ethical considerations, in addition to scientific and educational interests. Research sheds little light on the problem; studies that have been conducted to assess the effects or labeling have produced inconclusive, often contradictory, evidence and have generally been marked by methodological weakness (MacMillan, 1982).

As with most complex questions, there are valid arguments on both sides. Here are some of the reasons for and against classification and labeling of exceptional children.

2.4.1 Possible Benefits of Labeling

- Categories can relate diagnosis to specific treatment.
- Labeling may lead to a "protective" response in which non-labeled children accept certain behaviours of handicapped peers more fully than they would accept those same behaviours in "normal" children (MacMillan, 1982).
- Labeling helps professionals communicate with one another and classify and assess research findings.
- Funding of Special Education programs is often based on specific categories of exceptionality.
- Labels allow special interest groups to promote specific programmes and spur legislative action.
- Labeling helps make exceptional children's special needs more visible to the public.

2.4.2 Possible Disadvantages of Labeling

- Labels usually focus on a child's negative aspects, causing others to think about the child only in terms on inadequacies or defects.
- Labels may cause others to react to and hold low expectations for a child based on the label, resulting in a self-fulfilling prophecy.
- Labels that describe a child's performance deficit often mistakenly acquire the role of explanatory constructs (*e.g.* "Sheila acts that way because she is emotionally disturbed".)
- Labels tend to suggest that learning problems are primarily the result of something wrong within the child, thereby reducing the systematic examination of instructional variables as the cause of performance difficulties.

- A labeled child may lead peers to reject or ridicule the labeled child.
- Special Education labels have a certain performance: once labeled "retarded" or "learning disabled", a child has difficulty ever again achieving the status of being "Just another Kid".
- Labels often provide a basis for keeping children out of the regular classroom.
- A disproportionate number of children from minority culture groups have been inaccurately labeled "handicapped" especially as educably mentally retarded.
- Classification of exceptional children requires the expenditure of a great amount of professional and students time that could better be spent in planning and delivering instruction.

2.5 Categories of Exceptional Children

Exceptional children have been classified into the following subcategories

a) Gifted and talented

b) Mentally retarded

c) Learning disabilities

d) Emotional and behavior disorders

e) Communication disorders

f) Visual impairment

g) Hearing impairment

h) Orthopedic impairments

i) Attention deficit hyperactivity disorders

j) Autism

k) Other health impairments and multiple handicaps.

In separate chapters, we will examine the defining characteristics and educational implications of each of the categories.

Special Education

3.1 Background of Special Education

The concept "Children with Special Educational needs" is of British origin. Prior to 1944 provision of education was made on the basis of a specific handicap i.e., usual hearing impairment, essentially through charitable initiatives. The emphasis was more on training than on education. Originally, provision for children with sensory and physical disabilities and mental handicaps was made and subsequently extended to those with emotional and behavioural problems.

After World War II an increasing amount of research was directed at children with Special Education needs, particularly in the USA. The current definition of Special Educational needs is widely considered to constitute a major change from the previous framework based on educational handicap. The concept of Special Education Needs (SEN) is more positive as it is concerned with everything – as well as resources and constraints.

The early history of Special Education started with hearing handicapped as early as 1555 when Spanish monk taught children to read write, speak and learn academic subjects.

Jnan Publo Bonet 1620 developed one-handed manual name alphabet used even today. Helen killer and Graham Bell worked tirelessly for the deaf.

Education of blind began in France in 1784 by Valantin Hany. Louie Braille (1809-1852) blind from childhood himself developed the system of Braille using raised dots to represent letters of alphabets.

Education of children with MR began by French Physician Dr Itard (1775-1855) to educate an 11 year boy found living as savage in woods. This technique was followed by Maria Montessori 1870-1952 in Italy. Special Education expanded rapidly after World War II both in numbers and types of children served.

First school for hearing impaired started in Bombay in 1885 followed by Visually Impaired in Amritsar in 1885. By 1974 India had just 32 schools for blind. By 1980 it rose to 170, Now there are 243 schools.

3.1.1 Need for Appropriate Education for Exceptional Children

In a democratic nation when the development of the abilities and skills of each person is considered a human right, it becomes the duty of the nation, society and parents that they should provide Special Education for those children who have exceptional abilities and potentialities. The Article 45 of the Indian Constitution says that free and compulsory education should be provided for all children including those who are physically, mentally and socially handicapped. Exceptional children cannot be benefited by normal classes in regular schools. They need special teachers. If these children are not paid proper attention at the right moment, they may become problematic, antisocial, mentally ill, maladjusted, useless and a burden to society. These children have the capacity to learn but in a different way, hence it is the duty of the educationists, parents, and teachers to understand the abilities, deficiencies of exceptional children and provide Special Education appropriate to suit their needs such that they too become self-confident, independent and productive citizens of the nation.

3.2 Defining Special Education

- Special Education means specially designed instruction which meets the unique needs of an Exceptional Child.
- Special Education is instruction designed for students with disabilities or gifts and talents who also have special learning needs. Some of these students have difficulty learning in regular classrooms; they need Special Education to function in school. Others generally do well in regular classrooms, but they need Special Education to help them master creative skills to reach their full potential in school.
- Special Education has been defined as that additional services, over and above in the regular school programme, that is provided for an exceptional child to assist in the development of his potentialities.
- Special Education is an individually planned, systematically implemented and carefully evaluated instruction to help exceptional children achieve the greatest possible personal self-sufficiency and success in present and further environment.
- Special Education is the individually planned and systematically monitored arrangement of teaching procedures, adapted equipment and materials,

accessible settings and other interventions designed to help learners with special needs achieve the greatest possible personal self-sufficiency and success in school and community.

Students with special needs, such as learning differences, mental health issues, specific disabilities (physical or developmental), and giftedness are those whose needs are addressed within the classroom setting.

3.3 Who Receives Special Education?

Students considered exceptional in today's classrooms are those with disabilities and those who are gifted and talented. Using the various standards for defining normality and abnormality, educators and other professionals have established that some students require more and some require less instruction to master the content mastered by their non- exceptional peers. Sometimes they need different instruction than their non-disabled peers. Sometimes they need instruction in environments that are different from general education classrooms.

The similarities between exceptional and non-exceptional students far exceed their differences. Some of the differences are central to success in school, and so form the basis for the concern of teachers, parents, and students themselves.

Today, most states organize their Special Education departments along categorical lines. A category is simply a name assigned to a group of exceptional students. Although the names of the categories vary slightly from state to state, Special Education generally is provided to students within each of the following groups.

a) **Visual Impairments:** These students have special learning needs in areas requiring functional use of vision. (The word functional refers to the way an ability is actually used in daily life). Of the school-age population 0.04 percent is classified in this category.

b) **Hearing Impairments:** These students have special learning needs in areas requiring functional use of hearing. Of the school-age population 0.11 percent is classified in this category.

c) **Deaf and Blind:** These students have special learning needs in areas requiring functional use of hearing and vision. Less than 0.01 percent of the school age population (the number is so small that it is listed as 0.00 percent of the population in the 1993 report to Congress) is classified in this category.

d) **Orthopedic Impairments and Other Health Impairments** These students have special learning needs in areas requiring functional use of hands, arms, legs, feet, and other body parts. This category may also include students who have serious illness or medical conditions (for example, heart conditions). Less than 1 percent of the school age population is classified in these two categories (0.09 percent for orthopedic impairments and 0.10 percent for other health impairments).

e) **Mental Retardation:** These students have special learning needs in areas requiring functional use of intelligence and adaptive behaviors. About 0.96 percent of the school age population is classified in this category.

f) **Gifted and Talented:** These students have special learning needs in areas requiring functional use of intelligence and adaptive behaviour. About 0.96 percent of the school age population is classified in this category.

g) **Specific Learning Disabilities:** These students have special learning needs in areas requiring functional use of listening, speaking, reading, writing, reasoning, and arithmetic skills. This is the largest category in Special Education with about 3.9 percent of the school age population. Half of all students with disabilities are considered learning disabled.

h) **Speech and Language Impairments:** These students have special learning needs in areas requiring functional use of language and communication skills. Often, the many varieties of speech and language disabilities are called communication disorders. About 1.73 percent of the school age population is classified in this category.

i) **Multiple Disabilities:** These students have special learning needs in more than one area requiring functional use of skills. Less than 1 percent of the school age population (about 0.17 percent) is classified in this category.

j) **Traumatic Brain Injury:** These students have brain injury caused by an external physical force or by an internal occurrence such as stroke. It does not include children born with brain injuries or who suffer brain injury as a result of birth trauma. The number of students classified in this category is so small that it is listed as 0.00 percent in the 1993 Annual Report to Congress.

k) **Autism:** Autism is a specific developmental disability that significantly affects communication and social interaction. About 0.01 percent of the school-age population is classified in this category.

3.4 The Special Education Process

The provision of Special Education involves a three-step process.

a) Determining eligibility.

b) Delivering Special Education.

c) Evaluating whether Special Education has brought favorable outcomes.

3.4.1 Determining Eligibility

The eligibility decision requires that a child study team find that the student.

1. Has special learning needs
2. Meets the criteria for a particular Education Category

This Process begins from

Pre-referral to Referral: When a student progresses usually quickly or slowly at school or home, when the teachers feel that the student can't learn in a regular classroom setting without special help.

Interventions may be often used in the regular classroom to improve students functioning. These are often called pre-referral interventions because they take place before the student is referred for formal evaluation.

Records are kept of student's performance. If the student's progress is unacceptable a referral is made. The teacher requests for Special Education services. In response, a team of professionals using several data gathering tools both formal to informal assess the scholar, gather information and uses it to decide the student's eligibility.

The Intervention Assistance Team: IAT is a group of teachers who help regular educators solve problem with individual student's help in determining eligibility.

A child study team which includes teachers, other school personal, representatives of school district and child's parents is responsible for determining eligibility for Special Education. They determine measurable discrepancy between ability level and performance.

3.4.2 Delivering Special Education

Once a student is declared eligible he or she moves to second step -the delivery of Special Education . The student receives Individualized Instruction from trained professionals. Also Special Education professionals may work with general education personnel to design intervention for use in the regular classroom. This phase is guided by a formal document called Individualized Education Programme (IEP) developed by the child study team in association with other professional.

Fig-3.1: A child study team meets to develop an IEP and then reviews and revises the IEP at least once a year

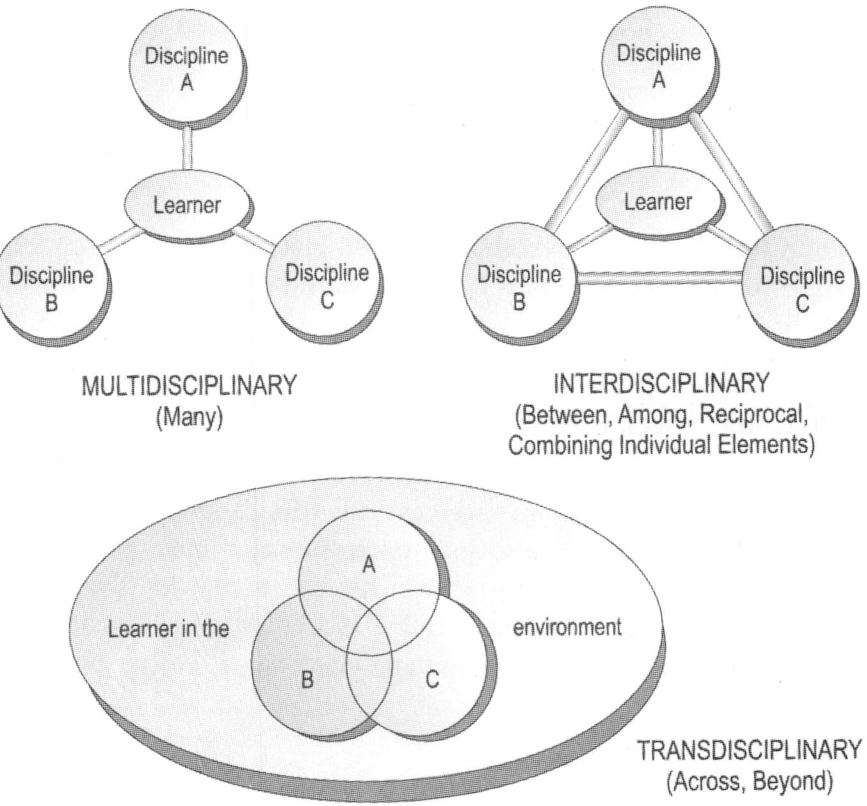

Fig-3.2:

3.4.3 Evaluation

The final step of Special Education process is evaluation. The student's progress is evaluated to determine the need for continuing, changing or concluding special services. A student with a disability must be evaluated at least once a year. Every two or three years formal reevaluation is necessary to determine if a student is still eligible for special services; students can be removed from special programme any time they show sufficient progress.

3.5 Special Education Services

There are three types of assistance generally available to exceptional children.

1. **Direct Services:** These are provided by working with students themselves to correct or compensate for the conditions that have caused them to fall behind in school or to enrich or accelerate the progress they are making in school. Teaching a student who is deaf to use sign language, a student with a learning disability to read using a special method of instruction or a gifted 4th standard child to do algebra are direct services provided by teachers.
2. **Indirect Services or Consultative Services:** These are provided to classroom teachers and others who work with exceptional children over a period of time to help meet the needs of the students. Helping the teachers identify the best method for teaching a student with L.D to read or showing a teacher how to reposition a student with physical disabilities are indirect services provided by teachers or other professionals to parents.
3. **Related Services:** These are provided by specially trained personnel directly (to students) or indirectly (to those who work with exceptional students). Related services include psychological testing and counseling, school social work, educational/occupational therapy, adopted physical education, school health services and transportation portion related services may also include assistance technology, which means equipment designed to improve or maintain the functional abilities of students with disabilities. *E.g.* The provision of electronic communication aids.

3.5.1 Continuum of Services

Exceptional children, their teachers, and their families may need a wide range of Special Education and related services from time to time. Today, most schools provide a continuum of services that is, a range of different placement and services options to meet students' needs. The continuum is often symbolically depicted as a pyramid, with placements ranging from least restrictive (regular classroom placement) at the bottom to most restrictive (special schools or institutions) at the

Fig.-3.3: Special Education Classroom

Fig.-3.4: Resource Room in Regular School

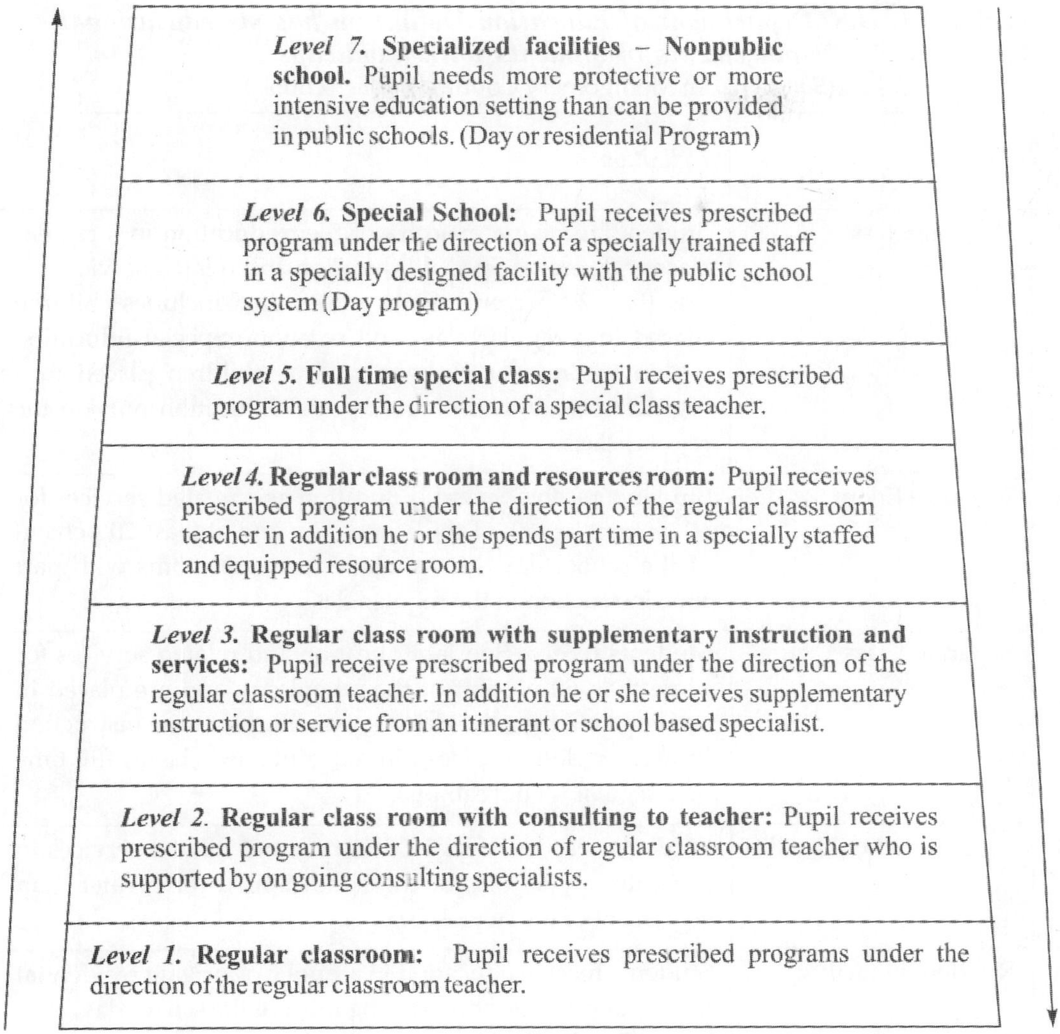

***Level 7.* Specialized facilities – Nonpublic school.** Pupil needs more protective or more intensive education setting than can be provided in public schools. (Day or residential Program)
***Level 6.* Special School:** Pupil receives prescribed program under the direction of a specially trained staff in a specially designed facility with the public school system (Day program)
***Level 5.* Full time special class:** Pupil receives prescribed program under the direction of a special class teacher.
***Level 4.* Regular class room and resources room:** Pupil receives prescribed program under the direction of the regular classroom teacher in addition he or she spends part time in a specially staffed and equipped resource room.
***Level 3.* Regular class room with supplementary instruction and services:** Pupil receive prescribed program under the direction of the regular classroom teacher. In addition he or she receives supplementary instruction or service from an itinerant or school based specialist.
***Level 2.* Regular class room with consulting to teacher:** Pupil receives prescribed program under the direction of regular classroom teacher who is supported by on going consulting specialists.
***Level 1.* Regular classroom:** Pupil receives prescribed programs under the direction of the regular classroom teacher.

Fig.-3.5: Continuum of educational services for students with disabilities
(*Source:* from Montgomery county public schools)

top. The fact that the pyramid is widest at the bottom indicates that the greatest number of exceptional children should be served in regular classrooms, and the number of children who require more restrictive, intensive and specialized placements gets smaller as we move up. As we have already noted, the majority of children receiving Special Education services have mild mental retardation, for example, is far greater than those who experience severe retardation. Likewise, children with mild or moderate behaviour disorders greatly outnumber those with severe behaviour disorders. As the severity of the disability increases, the need for more specialized services also increases, but the number of students involved decreases.

Table-3.1: U.S. Department of Education Definition has six educational placements of students with handicaps
(*Source:* From Montgomery Country Public Schools)

Sl. No.	*Placement*	*Definition*
1.	Regular Class	Students receive a majority of their education in a regular class and receive Special Education and related services for less than 20 percent of the school day. Includes children placed in a regular class and receiving Special Education within the regular class as well as children placed in a regular class and receiving Special Education outside the regular class.
2.	Resource Room	Students receive Special Education and related services for 60 percent or less of the school day and at least 20 percent of the school day. May include resource rooms with part time instruction in the regular class.
3.	Separate Class	Students receive Special Education and related services for more than 60 percent of the school day and are placed in self contained special classrooms with part time instruction in regular class or placed in self contained classes full time on a regular school campus.
4.	Separate School Facility	Students receive Special Education and related services in separate day school for the handicapped for greater than 50 percent of the school day.
5.	Residential facility	Students receive education in a public or private residential facility at public schools during most of the school day.
6.	Homebound/hospital environment	Students placed in and receiving education in hospital or homebound programs.

Source: Adapted from Twelth Annual Report to Congress on the Implementation of the Education of the Handicapped Act, PP. 18-19, 1990, Washington, DC: U.S. Department of Education.

It is worth noting that of the seven levels of services depicted in figure below the first five are available in regular public school buildings. Children at levels 1 through 4 attended regular classes with non-handicapped peers: supportive help is given by special teachers who provide consulting to the children's regular teachers or in special resource rooms. A resource room usually has a specially trained teacher who provides instruction to exceptional students for part of the continuum of educational services for students with disabilities in school day, either individually or in small groups.

Children at level 5, who require full-time placement in a self – contained class, are with other exceptional children for all or most of the school day, but they may still have the opportunity to interact with non-handicapped children at certain times, such as during recess or on the bus to school. Although this alternate provides less integration than the regular classroom, it provides much more opportunity for interaction than placement in a residential institution or a special school attended only by children with disabilities. Self-contained classes in regular school buildings are gaining acceptance as an appropriate placement for many children with severe and multiple disabilities.

Placement of an exceptional child at any level on the continuum of services should not be regarded as permanent. Teachers, parents and administrators should periodically review the specific goals and objectives for each child. New placement decision can be made: in fact, the continuum concept is intended to be flexible, with children moving from one placement to another as dictated by their current educational needs. A child may be placed in a less integrated setting for a limited time; then, when a performance review shows that certain goals have been achieved, the child should return to a more normalized setting as soon as possible.

Current interpretation of the least restrictive environment, based on recent court cases, is that a child should be removed from the regular school programme only to the extent that there is clear evidence that removal is necessary for the child to receive appropriate educational services. The child's parents must be properly informed if removal from the regular classroom is being considered so that they can either consent or object to the removal and can present additional information if they wish. No removal from the regular school programme should be regarded as permanent; there should be a plan for returning the child to as normal a setting as possible, as soon as certain needs or educational experiences appropriate to that child's special needs and as similar as possible to those that a non-handicapped child would have.

3.6 Objectives of Special Education

The fundamental goal of schooling is to help students develop the skills they need to function in society. Those skills relate to content areas like reading, mathematics, writing, science, language and arts to specific jobs, and to affective or social behaviours (developing trust, building relationship, coping with frustration and steers handling joint decision and inter-personal conflicts) Teachers and others working in schools help students develop these skills.

Instruction in regular education is designed to help students achieve competence in a variety of broad areas of knowledge. The goals and objectives of regular education reflect societies values when parents, teachers or other professionals themselves believe students need help to meet these broad educational goals. Special Education is one option. The broad goals of instruction in Special Education are the same as for regular education; the specific goals may be different.

Within any classroom some students already have developed the skills being taught, others need help developing those skills, and still others need to be taught a set of prerequisite skills before they can learn the content.

When teachers need help in accommodating a student with special learning needs they can turn to Special Education, because the objectives of the instruction in Special Education focus on meeting the needs of students who are exceptional.

3.6.1 Objectives of Special Education Instructions

Objectives of Special Education Instructions are:

- Development Instruction
- Enrichment Instruction
- Acceleration
- Remediation Instruction
- Compensation Instruction
- Prevention

3.6.1.1 Development Instruction

The process of teaching students a set of progressively more difficult skills to enable them to demonstrate the complex skills or abilities necessary to meet instructional objectives are called developmental instruction. Developing the basic skills and cognitive skills.

3.6.1.2 Enrichment Instruction

Students make very rapid progress in regular classes. They are able to read, write, do math, language, earlier than their peers. These basic skills of learning are more developed then their classmate; they may possess special talents in art or music. To meet the special needs their teachers adjust instruction; for this enrichment is the simplest approach. Classroom teachers enhance the educational experiences of these students by adding materials and activities to the curriculum. The educational setting remains the same.

3.6.1.3 Acceleration

Acceleration is another way to meet the needs of students who are gifted and talented. In accelerated programme, students progress through a curriculum at a faster pace than their peers. They may spend less time drilling and practicing or they may skip one or more grades to accumulate their heightened academic skills.

3.6.1.4 Remediation Instruction

When students don't make expected progress in regular classes they receive Remediation Instruction designed to repair or correct basic problems or difficulties. In much the same way that doctors treat patients with medication, teachers give their students remedial instruction. A student can be taught specific skills such as reading, writing or math skills to remediate deficiencies in skill development, or specific deficits in abilities (memory, perception of sounds) can be addressed in remediation. The process of going back to remedy skills deficits is the kind of instruction that takes place in resource rooms or in regular classroom.

3.6.1.5 Compensatory Instruction

Instruction can also be compensatory. The word comes from compensate which mean "to make up for". *E.g.*: If you don't own a car you may compensate by taking a bus, train, bike. People who do not have legs compensate by getting around in wheel chairs; those who have lost eyes read using Braille. Compensatory treatments are used only when it is impossible to remediate a condition or when its easier to compensate for the condition than to remediate it. Many Special Educational methods are compensatory – blind using Braille, deaf using sign language and finger spelling, child without arm writing with toes or using head equipment with pencil, arranging student who has difficulty reading and writing to take oral exam, taperecording lectures for blind etc. Compensatory Instruction is designed to help students overcome the effects of disabilities that cannot be corrected.

3.6.1.6 Prevention

The final objective is prevention. Researchers have indicated the reasons why students fail to achieve. They have identified individual student's characteristics, home and family characteristics, teaching and school factors. When school personnel know which academic skills and social behaviors a student must have developed and when they know what interferes with skill development they are in a position to develop curriculum and intervention to prevent failure in school.

A good example of prevention intervention is Headstart program. Headstart is a well recognized early intervention for children. It is a preschool program to recognize failures among children, and provide intensive preschool instruction in an attempt to alleviate later problem.

These six objectives are more evident in Special Education program than in regular school program. These help to prevent learning problems to reduce dropouts, wastage and stagnation.

3.6.2 General Objectives of Public Law on Special Education

- A free appropriate public education must be provided for all children with disabilities.
- School systems must provide safeguard to protect the rights of children with disabilities and their parents (Due process)
- Children with disabilities must be educated with non- disabled children to the maximum extent possible (Mainstreaming Integration)
- An individualized education programs (IEP) must be developed and implemented for each child with disabilities.
- Parents of children with disabilities are to play an active role in the process of making any educational decision about their children with disabilities.
- The State and central government meeting the requirements to help offset the additional costs incurred in providing Special Education Services.

1. **Free appropriate Public Education must be provided** for all children with disabilities is based on the principle of zero exclusion. Zero exclusion means not to put any disabled child in the regular classroom without any special provision. It means every child irrespective of exceptionality must be provided free appropriate public education to his level of functioning. All students between the ages 3 to 18 have the right for appropriate education depending on their disabilities. These students should be identified and must be placed in regular classroom whenever possible or other appropriate Special Education must be provided.

2. **School system must provide safeguards to protect the rights of children with disabilities and their parents.**

   The due process provision brings parents into the system; they give parents an opportunity to be involved, to understand and question what the school is doing with their child. (Earlier, practice of testing for placement in Special Education service was followed without the knowledge of parents)

Whenever the school proposes or refuses to change identification, evaluation or placement of child, the parents have the right to challenge schools decision. The right to educational placement is based on the principle on non-discriminatory testing, and to protect children from inappropriate classification. At a due process hearing, parents have the right to consult experts in Special Education, right to present evidence, cross examine the Special Educator.

3. **Children with disabilities must be educated with non-disabled** children to maximum extent possible. This is based on the principle of mainstreaming and principle of least restrictive environment. Mainstreaming is the process of integrating exceptional children into regular schools and classes i.e., students with disabilities should be educated in settings with students who are not handicapped. Much discussion and controversy have led to the confusion of mainstreaming.

   However depending on the severity of the handicapped, education in integrated settings can be achieved with the use of supplementary services. Some parents strongly support mainstreaming; some are against it because of the fear of segregation.

4. **An Individualized Education Program (IEP) must be developed and implemented for each child with disabilities**.

   An IEP is a written document that summarizes a learning program tailored to a specific child.

   The contents of IEP are:

   a) The statement of the child's present level of educational performance including academic achievement, social adaptation, prevocational and vocational sills, psychomotor skills, and self-help skills.

   b) A statement of annual goals describing the educational performance to be achieved by the end of each school year.

   c) A statement of short-term instructional objectives presented in measurable and intermediate steps.

   d) A statement of specific Special Educational services needed by the child.

   e) The starting date and excepted duration of services should be mentioned.

   f) The statements of needed transitional services for students including the interagency linkages before the child leave the school setting.

g) A description of the extent to which the child will participate in regular education program.

h) A justification for the type of educational placement.

i) A list of individuals who are responsible for implementing the individualized education program.

j) Objective credentials for monitoring progress and evaluation procedures and schedules of determining whether the short-term institutional objectives are achieved.

5. **Parents of children with disabilities are to play an active role** in making educational decision about their children with disabilities. This is based on the principle of parent participation. Parents must give acceptance in placement decision by giving written consent prior to testing and evaluation. They must provide the necessary support to utilize the facilities available to bring about progress in their child.

6. **The state and central government should contribute** in meeting the requirements to help overcome the additional costs incurred in providing Special Education services. The government should sanction funds and remove taxes on learning material of exceptional children.

The least restrictive environment supplicates that to the maximum extent handicapped children, including children of public or private institutions and other special schools are educated with children who are not handicapped and that special classes, separate schooling or removal of handicapped children from the regular educational environment occurs only when the nature of severity of the handicap is such that education in regular classes with the use of supplementary aids and services cannot be achieved satisfactory. Thus L.R.E. is continued to be the setting that closely parallels a regular school program and also meets the child's educational needs.

3.6.3 Specific Objectives of Special Education

1. Fair testing and evaluation
2. Least restrictive environment. (Mainstreaming)
3. Early intervention.
4. School to adult life transition.
5. Special Education-regular education relationship.

6. Increasing the availability and quality of Special Education program for gifted and talented students.
7. Developing teaching strategies that enable students with severe handicaps to generalize namely learned skills to other settings.
8. Reducing the number of Special Education students who drop out of school.
9. Applying advances in high technology to greatly reduce or eliminate the handicap effects of physical and sensory disabilities.
10. Improving the behaviour and attitudes of non-handicapped people toward those with disabilities.
11. Opening up more opportunities for individuals with disabilities to participate in the full range of residential employment and recreational option available to non-disabled persons.
12. Preventing and combating the causes that effect learning development and success in school.

Approaches to Special Education

Special Education is a complex system for meeting the special learning needs of exceptional children.

Special Educational services which are designed to help handicapped/ exceptional children are mainly given in two ways.

1. Integrated Education (Mainstreaming)
2. Segregated Education (Institutionalization)

4.1 Integrated Education

4.1.1 Integration

Integration is the process of including exceptional children into regular schools and classes which is also termed as mainstreaming. Exceptional children attend regular classes with non-handicapped peers but with supportive help by special teachers in special resource rooms. Regular classroom teacher provides most of the instruction and the special teacher provides intermittent instruction to the student and in consultation with regular teachers, the student is integrated except for brief instructional sessions. Students with visual impairment or physical disorder and mild learning disabilities can be integrated with regular students.

Integrated Education refers to the temporal, instructional and social integration of eligible exceptional children with normal peers. It determines educational needs, assessment requiring classification, and responsibility for coordinated planning and programming by regular and Special Education administrative, instructional and support personnel (Kauffman).

The term mainstreaming is used to mean an integration of regular and exceptional children in a school setting where all children share the same resources and opportunities for learning on a fulltime basis.

Integrated approach was first started in America in 1930. This approach was introduced in India in 1960 by Batlibai. But this approach was not successful in India untill 1986 when the new education policy was introduced. NCERT and DSERT took up this approach more seriously. DIETs took up an inservice programme to train the teachers in primary schools. During this programme provision for impaired children were discussed. The resource teacher will be paid Rs. 150 extra salary to help exceptional children.

Integration cannot be reduced simply to an educational issue or an employment issue. Its achievement will require the successful co-ordination of a whole series of transitions for the handicapped, ranging from early identification, to early intervention, to school programmes, to community, jobs and finally to community living.

An approach to integration that takes the individual needs of the special child into full consideration may result in:

- *Physical integration* i.e. planning for the location of the special programmes in school buildings with regular education programmes.
- *Social integration* -it means planning for regular personal interactions between students who have handicaps and those who do not.
- *Academic integration* i.e., planning to ensure students with and without handicaps simultaneously using school resources.
- *Societal integration* i.e., planning designed to enable students with moderate and severe handicaps to work, live and spend leisure with their fellow non-handicapped citizens.

4.1.1.1 Integration Means

- Providing special services within the regular school.
- Supporting regular teachers and administrators
- Having students with disabilities follow the same schedule as non-disabled students.
- Involving disabled students in as many academic classes and extra curricular activities as possible including music, art, fieldtrips, assemblies and exercise.
- Arranging for disabled students to use library, playground and other facilities at the same time as non-disabled students.
- Encouraging, helping and building relationships between disabled and non-disabled students.

- Arranging for disabled students to receive their education in regular community environments when appropriate.
- Teaching all children to understand and accept human differences.
- Providing appropriate individualized programmes.

But it should also be kept in mind that integration does not mean dumping students with disabilities into regular programmes without preparation or support or placing too much demand on teachers and administration or isolation of children with disabilities in regular school etc. Mainstreaming is a workable process. It needs a comprehensive support system for its success in the school. Mainstreaming aims at bridging the difference between milder consideration of disability and normal peers by providing access to equal educational opportunities under the least restrictive environment.

4.1.2 Types of Integration Approach

These are 3 types of Integration Approach.

1. Resource Approach
2. Itinerate Approach
3. Cluster Approach

4.1.2.1 Resource Approach

Eight children with impairment are grouped together and education is given before or after classroom in consultation with general teacher. These children are taken to the resource room for education depending upon their deficiencies and requirements.

4.1.2.2 Itinerate Approach

Children from various classes are put together in this system and education is given to them, by visiting Special Educators. The class resource teacher is also consulted during Special Education classes. The visiting teacher moves from one school to another and should spend at least 150 minutes in the school, she visits.

4.1.2.3 Cluster Approach

In this approach 42 days in-service training is given to regular teachers to teach children with impairment of all types.

4.1.3 Merits of Integration

- Children are not taught in special schools; hence they have an opportunity to live with parents.
- Children have the chance to compete with normal children also.
- They can show their talent, through performance.
- Also children are provided opportunity to mix with other members of society and make adjustments in society.
- The feeling of exceptionality can be removed.

4.1.4 Limitations/Demerits of Integration

- It is difficult to teach different types of impaired children in regular classes.
- Regular teachers can teach only by normal methods for normal children but the exceptional child does not benefit from this.
- Teacher will look at children with pity and just promote him.
- Teacher may show negligent attitude towards that child.
- There is problem of labeling
- The exceptional children may not get facilities at a proper time.

4.1.5 The Role of Class Teacher

The regular class teacher where a child with special needs has been admitted should:

— Learn about the student's handicapping condition.

— Its common characteristics.

— The child's expected performance.

— Common difficulties the disabled child will experience.

— Learn about the appliances and special materials the child uses. E.g.: Pushing a wheel chair up or downstairs, storing wheelchairs etc.

— Determine if any special methods, techniques or adaptations are needed for the disabled child to function more independently and successfully.

— Meet the Special Education teacher to determine specific strengths, weakness and needs of the handicapped students.

— Prepare the classroom, remove obstacles, and make necessary adaptations to furniture. Rearrange furniture to help the special needs students and so on.

— Conduct class activities in ways to encourage student interaction.

— Collect and record data to evaluate student progress.

— Develop a feedback system that will furnish continuous data to students, teacher and parents.

— Use evaluation data to assess the attainment of goals and to set new goals. Just as the resource room/special teacher, the regular teacher and other staff members have specific roles to play for successful mainstreaming, the special and regular students are no less important.

4.2 Segregated Education

Some children who have a severe problem cannot be integrated with normal children and taught in normal school setting; so these children are separated from normal children and taught in special schools, which are specially designed for them.

Students receive prescribed program under the direction of specially trained staff in a specially deigned facility which is usually organized for a specific category of exceptional students and may contain special equipment necessary for their care and education. Their students return to their homes during non – school hours.

In special classes students receive Special Education and related services for more than 60 percent of the school day and are placed in self-contained special classrooms with part-time instruction in regular class or placed in self-contained class fulltime on a regular school campus. A specially trained teacher or special educator provides all or most of the instruction. Children spend the whole school day segregated from their non – disabled peers, although sometimes they are integrated with non – disabled peers during part of the day (perhaps for physical education music or other activity in which they can participate well); students with severe or profound physical or students with severe disability receive segregated education. Children with one type of impairment will be grouped together and given education along with boarding and lodging.

The exceptional children who are segregated are given education by resource teacher. A resource teacher is a highly trained professional who is capable of diagnosing the child, planning and implementing the programme, providing continuous evaluation of the child etc. The role of the resource teacher includes direct services to individuals and small groups of children and assessment and delivery of individualized programmes.

4.2.1 Merits of Segregation

- It prevents the dependency on others.
- Children are independent of themselves either to get education or to solve their problem related to education.
- It helps to develop good study habits.
- It helps to develop study skills from seniors or other peers.
- It helps to develop friendly and competent attitude towards learning.
- Children feel secure and understand the there are many others who have similar problem.
- After proper education and training exceptional children will lead an independent life.

4.2.2 Demerits of Segregation

- Scope is limited because only one type of children with common disabilities has to be taught.
- Children will be deprived of love and affection and interaction of parents and society.
- This approach is very expensive to maintain.
- In this system the children are inhibited to mix with other members of society. Since they are always under the invigilation of a supervisor it does not provide freedom for the inmates of the school.
- This approach is very difficult to organize due to lack of good and efficient teachers.

4.2.3 Role of Resource Teacher/Special Education Teacher

— Identify the student's strengths and weakness.

— Determine the special services needed by students.

— Develop special programmes.

— Gather information to determine the educational needs of each student.

— Evaluate each student's present level of functioning.

— Determine goals for each student that are appropriate, realistic and measurable.

— Design a variety of alternative teaching strategies.

— Develop plans for using human and material resources.

— Develop Individual Education Programme (IEP)

— Develop a flexible time schedule that provides for learning as well as the physical and social needs of each student.

Sometimes we provide segregated and integrated education to the same child. An exceptional child may benefit from both types of education. For example, a visually impaired child may be educated in a normal class and he can be segregated for some period and can be taught in resource room (using Braille, use of equipments, orientation and mobility, social skills, sensory training) and can be again integrated for co-curricular activities. Mild and moderate hearing impaired children can be integrated with normal children for some classes and they can be segregated for teaching sign language, lip reading etc. But children who have severe disability are placed in special schools.

4.3 Inclusive Education

Researches in Psychology and Education have made great strides in developing educational provisions that effectively adapt to students' differences and help in providing education for all. Although there are certain factors like students' aptitude, instructions and environment that have been identified as influential in learning, helping schools to create effective and practical learning environments that meet students' needs has been a continuing challenge in the history of school improvement efforts and quality education. One premise of this approach is that students learn in different ways and at varying speed, but a major task of the schools is to provide educational experiences that include and accommodate these differences in order to optimize each student's education irrespective of his/her social or economic status.

To say that there are benefits and advantages associated with strong efforts to serve all students seems to be a statement of the obvious; yet it is important to remember why the concept is so pertinent for today's schools. The following list attempts to detail some of the general advantages commonly associated with a learning-for-all mission. Emphasis on serving all students will:

- Teach students that all people are equally valued members of the school and society.
- Create an atmosphere of trust and respect as students learn that differences enrich learning and that all have valuable contributions to make

- Empower students who have previously had unsuccessful school experiences or experienced school failure.
- Broaden students' views of others, helping them to be more accepting
- Help students to work in varied settings with many types of people.
- Ensure that all students have the opportunity to become contributing members of society.
- Empower educators to expand their skills and techniques beyond that which is routine or comfortable.
- Encourage parents and the community to become partners with the school in establishing and reinforcing the mission.

4.3.1 Concept of Inclusive Education

Inclusive Education means welcoming all children, without discrimination, into regular or ordinary schools. It refers to the process of educating all children in their neighborhood school, regardless of the nature of their disabilities. Students participating in an inclusion program follow the same schedule as their classmates and participate in age appropriate academic classes. They don't receive Special Education services in separated or isolated places. Students with disabilities are not required to be "ready" and don't have to "earn" their way into regular classrooms based upon their academic skills. A well-run inclusion program provides an appropriate inclusion program for all students. It does not ignore children's individual needs or parents' concerns. It doesn't sacrifice the education of students with special needs or that of the general run of students.

Social inclusion provides a myriad of opportunities for students with and without disabilities to interact in a mainstream environment. Students with disabilities use the school library, playground and participate alongside with their non-disabled peers in extra-curricular activities such as art, music, gym, fieldtrips etc. Inclusion teaches all children to understand and accept human differences and provides all students enhanced opportunities to learn each other's contribution; friendship between students with and without disabilities becomes a possibility in a school that accepts inclusion students.

Inclusion provides the appropriate support for everyone involved in the inclusion process. A full inclusion program will not "dump" students with disabilities into regular classes without preparation or support. Teachers are provided with time, training, teamwork, resources, and strategies. No unreasonable demands are placed upon the teachers. They are not expected to teach students with disabilities without the support that they need to teach the children effectively.

Indeed, there are some children with severe disabilities for whom it would be extremely difficult to create a truly inclusive educational environment; it would neither benefit the child nor others in the setting. However, this does not mean that the child should be segregated and isolated from all life in the community. There should be a range of inclusive settings whereby the child can feel included and be best served. Such settings could be arranged within the school premises, family circles, at community gatherings, at sports events, religious services and other recreation centers which are likely to ensure the opportunities for social interaction (Evans I.L., 1999).

4.3.2 Rationale for Inclusion

In an Indian perspective, all life is viewed as precious and of value. Each individual contributes his or her unique part to the world, whether great or small. Perfection of the world lies in the development of each and every individual to his/her maximum potential. We don't all possess the same talent or the same degree of talents. We are not intended to duplicate what everyone does. Each of us has his/her own task to complete his/her potential to be realized. Only by working together as teams, assisting everyone to maximize their abilities, do we bring completion to the world. All children are capable of receiving education according to their capabilities.

4.3.3 Challenges of Inclusive Education

The real challenge of Inclusive Education is to meet the special needs of all children with and without disabilities (Kajubi, 1999). Inclusion is not a soft process. It requires a lot of struggle and commitment to overcome all types of barriers mainly attitudinal and social. Inclusive Education can only flourish in a system, which generates inclusive ideology. People have to change their established beliefs, practices and modes of working.

Indeed, practical problems could be encountered while including children with diverse educational needs. But often, the practical difficulties have more to do with bringing attitudinal change and the organization of learning environments and school activities, with the reallocation of money and resources than with the needs of children.

Many determinant factors affect and regulate the development of inclusion. Limited understandings of the concept of disability, negative attitude towards persons with disabilities and a hardened resistance to change are the major barriers impeding Inclusive Education (IDDC, 1998). Of particular concern is the fact that teachers' attitudes are seen as the decisive factors for successful inclusion. Inclusion has been based on the assumption that teachers are willing to admit students with disability into regular classes and be responsible for meeting their needs. However, regular classroom teachers don't perceive themselves as having the appropriate training and skills to meet the instructional needs of students with disabilities. Unfortunately, evaluation studies indicate that teachers don't always have the support they need to make inclusion successful.

In some schools, regular teachers are asked to teach special needs students without receiving any formal training as well as administrative assistance. Without support, teachers who do not have sufficient background knowledge in Special Education are at a loss. Inclusive Education demands the class teacher to be innovative, flexible, creative, ready to learn from the learners and capable of imitating active learning. The development of an inclusive educational policy, curriculum and teacher training programs are frontiers of challenges encountered in course of implementing inclusive education. Generally, the challenge towards inclusive education could emanate from different directions such as attitudinal factors, rigid school system, and resistance to change, lack of clear educational guideline, and fear of losing one's job on the part of special school/teachers.

4.3.4 Advantages of Inclusion

From a humanitarian viewpoint, we believe that all children share equal value and status. Exclusion, therefore, is devaluating and is discriminating. Continued segregation of children with disabilities only helps to foster stereotypes and teaches children to be fearful, ignorant, and prejudiced. Inclusion has the potential to:

— Reduce fear and to build friendship, understanding, and respect. It reduces or eliminates the stigma associated with disabilities as familiarity and tolerance increase.

— The child without disabilities learns to value the contributions of all children, despite any disabling conditions.

— It helps the mainstream child to be tolerant of his weaknesses and appreciate his own strengths.

— Involvement with children with special needs can build positive character traits, such as patience, empathy, and acceptance.

— Full inclusion prepares all children for the roles they will play in mainstream society after finishing their schooling.

4.3.5 Components of Successful Inclusion

In order to meet those challenges inclusive programs may take considerable effort and resources. The following important factors can be taken into account for successful inclusion practices and programmes.

a) Establish a Philosophy that Supports Appropriate Inclusionary Practices

The philosophy will serve as both the foundation for and a stepping stone to achieving inclusion. A philosophy supporting and affirming the learning of all students needs to be established from top to bottom level through discussion and agreement of major stakeholders. The responsibility for educating 'Special Education Need (SEN) children and for deciding how and where these children will be educated exists at all levels, A clearly articulated philosophy provides decision makers with a framework within which to weigh educational choices and alternatives. It also gives them the authority to commit resources to support the decisions that are made.

b) Plan Effectively for Inclusion

Planning needs to include all those who will be involved in and affected by whatever inclusion is planned. If large-scale inclusion is anticipated, meaning if the government is interested to educate children's with disabilities in general educational environments, then system-wise planning and capacity building must take place. If the inclusionary effort is limited to one school, then planning and preparation needs to occur at that site. Teamwork and collaboration in the school are essential to addressing the many questions that come with inclusion generally and the specific issues associated with the inclusion of each student. It is vital that there may be someone clearly in charge of the inclusion effort. Among other things, this individual would have responsibility for calling meetings, coordinating and overseeing IEP development and implementation, ensuring that staff (including paraprofessionals) receive ongoing training; ensuring that needed resources are made available; and monitoring the overall inclusion effort. Going slowly and thoughtfully and planning thoroughly maximize the probability of success for all those involved: teachers, parents, and all students, particularly those with disabilities.

c) Involve the Top Administrator as a Change Agent

The presence of a proactive, visible and committed administrator is crucial to successful inclusion. If that person is not already involved in the inclusion movement, then his/her support must be enlisted. Through the administrator's leadership, a model of accepting and welcoming students with disabilities can be established, collaborative learning encouraged, planning time for inclusion sanctioned, resources made available, parents involved, and progress made.

d) Involve Parents

Parents have in-depth knowledge of their child's personality, strengths, and needs and can make substantial contributions to the inclusion effort. Parents should be included through out the entire planning and implementation process. Professional members of the team planning for inclusion can promote involvement of parent team members by appreciating and valuing the type of knowledge that parents bring to the planning table, by communicating openly and honestly with parents, by respecting the family's cultural patterns and beliefs, and by listening carefully to the suggestions and concerns that parents have.

e) Gain outside Support

Gaining the support of the outside community including businesses, social service agencies, and policymakers is crucial to the effort. Partnerships will enhance the school's service network and make serving all students a community mission. Keep in mind, however, that if outside support systems are shaky, start small (Williamson, 1994; Golomb & Hammeken, 1996). Some suggestions for partnerships are:

- Work with local businesses to involve community members in the school and its mission, and to put students in touch with their community resources
- Work with local social and health agencies to provide services and educate students and their families about pertinent issues
- Keep an "open door" policy in the school that invites community members and policymakers to become involved in the school and its mission.

f) Develop the Disability Awareness among Staff and Students:

Teachers, classroom aides, typical students in the classroom and their parents need to have an understanding of disabilities and the special needs that having a disability can create. Teachers and aides need in-depth knowledge to understand and meet the student's needs. This will also help teachers establish an atmosphere of acceptance and to plan activities that foster inclusion.

g) General students also need information

A discussion of disability – what it means to have a disability, what it does not mean – can help students understand and interact with their peers with disabilities. Depending on the nature of the student's disability, classmates may also need information about classroom routines that might be used by the student, safety issues, and any additional individuals who may be in the class assisting the student. Disability awareness of staff and students is an ongoing activity. Staff leave and new personnel are hired; student's leave and new ones arrive. Disability awareness training and activities should be provided on a continual process. Provide training to general education teachers: It is unrealistic and unfair to expect general education teachers to creatively and productively educate and include students with disabilities in their classrooms in the absence of adequate training. General educators must be provided with the training they need in order to meet the special learning and behavioral needs of students. This training can come in many forms: seminars/ workshops at local universities; in-service sessions provided by special educators; and materials specific to the nature of students' disabilities. Ensure that there is adequate support in the classroom: The Individuals with Disabilities Education Act (IDEA) states that when children with disabilities are educated in regular classes, accommodations and supports must be provided as appropriate to each child's special needs. Supplementary aids and services that educators have used successfully include modifications to the regular class curriculum, assistance of an itinerant teacher with Special Education training, Special Education training for the regular teacher, use of computer-assisted devices, provision of note takers, and use of a resource room. The supports to be provided should be listed explicitly in the student's IEP.

h) Initiating Extra-curricular Activities and Out of School Inclusive Programme

Extra-curricular activities for all children are essential. This may include organizing fieldtrips and visits and formations of clubs like for example, music, art, photography, debate, natural science, research, drama and other recreational programs. This is an important parameter not only for promoting inclusion outside the classroom among students but also for unfolding of the diverse potentials and talents of both children with and without disabilities. Such a habit needs to be nurtured right at primary school level so that children will be used to wisely spending their out of school time.

i) Provide Structure and Support for Collaboration

Collaboration needs to occur during the initial planning stages, during implementation, between home and school, between all members of the student's individual planning team, between general and special educators during the course of the school day, between teachers and administrators, and between students. It is especially important that time be built into teachers' schedules to allow for collaboration. The administrators can be of great assistance in making this possible.

j) Make Adaptations

One of the challenges of inclusion is adapting the general education curriculum (and environment) to meet the needs of students with disabilities. Adaptations are any adjustments or modifications in the environment, instruction or materials used for learning that enhances the person's performance or allows at least partial participation in an activity. For many students with cognitive disabilities, the mainstream curriculum may be too demanding or fast-paced. For students with physical disabilities, many academic tasks pose unrealistic physical demands. To allow their participation, adaptations must be made because a student should not be excluded from an activity due to the fact that he/she can perform only a portion of the required skills. These modifications may mean adapting skill sequences, providing personal assistance, adapting rules, and adapting the physical environments.

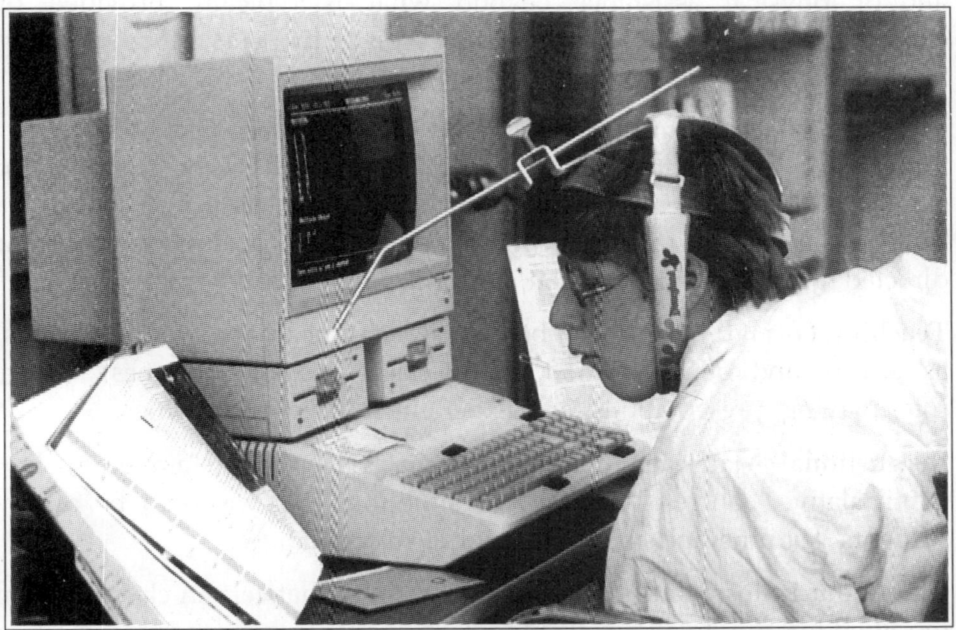

Fig.-4.1: Gregory's mastery of a headstick compensates for the impaired muscular control of his hands and arms

There are many times when an individual learner or group of learners can benefit from slight to detailed adaptations or modifications to the everyday learning structure. Many times, teachers make these changes without even realizing it. Sometimes, the changes require the intricate cooperation of a team of teachers, administrators, specialists, and parents. There also will be times when certain adaptations are not feasible for particular situations. In such cases, schools must do what is possible and reasonable, including the exploration of alternatives, to serve student needs. The following list details different instructional variables that can be manipulated to suit individual learner needs.

- **Learning Objective:** Certain students may be helped by having personalized learning objectives that differ slightly from the whole-class learning objectives. For example, a specific lesson objective for the whole class may be mastery of an entire list of vocabulary words, but for certain students the lesson objective might be to master the same list with a little extra time.
- **Learning Environment:** Classroom lighting, noise level, and visual stimulation can all be modified to suit learner needs. Portions of the classroom can be designed to afford students more or less of any of these variables as determined by student needs.
- **Learning assistance***:* Students may require varying levels of instructional and/or physical assistance beyond what is typically provided by the classroom teacher. Such assistance can be given by peers, other school staff, or volunteers.
- **Instructional grouping arrangement:** Teachers can take advantage of a number of different grouping arrangements and tailor them to specific situations. Ideas for arrangements include: whole-class instruction, teacher-directed small group instruction, cooperative learning groups, student-directed small group instruction, and independent seatwork.
- **Teaching Format:** Lessons can be delivered using a variety of techniques, such as lecture and demonstration, whole-class discussion, games, simulations, role- playing, presentations, and experiential-learning activities.
- **Instructional Materials:** Instructional materials can be altered to be more manipulative, concrete, tangible, or simplified. They should be matched to students' learning and comprehension levels.
- **Classroom Rules:** Some situations may require that certain classroom rules be modified in order to allow all students to successfully participate in a lesson or activity. For example, a rule might state that no talking is permitted during test taking, but a language-minority student might need an interpreter to successfully complete the test.

Regardless of what adaptations may be used and what brought them about, a team approach and shared responsibility are crucial. Team members can include the special and regular education teacher, the principal, parents, tutors, school psychologists, and other parties who are relevant to a child's education.

Assessment Approaches in Special Education

5.1 Assessment for Decision Making

Assessment is part and parcel of each phase of Special Education process. The decisions that are made using assessment information are listed below (Yesseldyke and Algozzine 1998).

— Screening is the process of collecting data to decide whether more intensive assessment is necessary.

— Decision to provide special help or enrichment. Special help may be remedial designed to correct a deficit or difficulty, compensatory designed to make up for a disability, enriching designed to enhance classroom activities.

— Referral to an Intervention Assistance Team.

— Decision to provide Intervention Assistance, Peripheral Intervention, Multidisciplinary, Interdisciplinary, or transdiciplinary interventions.

— Exceptionality Decision: To categorize an M.R, L.D, gifted sensory disabled etc.

— Decision about special learning need. Ex: Braille if blind.

— Decisions about eligibility or entitlement: what type of Special Education services should be provided if the team has declared that the student is eligible or entitled for Special Education services.

— Instructional Planning decision; deciding what to teach, deciding how to teach, and communicating realistic exceptions.

— Progress evaluation decisions; Measuring progress by giving unit tests, criterion-referenced tests.

— Program Evaluation decision; is the program effective? If yes continue; if not modify or restructure the appropriate suitable program.

— Accountability Decision: The extent to which particular schools, administrators, teachers should be held responsible for student's performance.

5.2 Common Assessment Practices

Several Common Practices of Assessment are usually used. They are:

5.2.1 Curriculum Based Assessment (CBA)

"C B A is a procedure for determining the instructional need of a student based on the student's ongoing performance within existing course content (Gickling & Haver tape 1981). C B A is informal assessment directly related to classroom curriculum (Salvia & Hugha 1990). If the content prepared by experts does not match the content taught, the test is useless for evaluating what a student has learned from school instruction. The 8 steps in Selvia & Hugha curriculum-based assessment model are:

1. Specify reasons for assessment
2. Analyze curriculum
3. Formulate behaviour objectives.
4. Develop appropriate assessment procedure
5. Collect data
6. Summarize data.
7. Display data.
8. Interpret data and make decision.

In the most simplified form CBA might include the following steps.

1. List skills in target material
2. Arrange skills in logical order
3. Develop a written objective for each skill listed.
4. Develop items and prepare materials to test for each objective.
5. Give the test as a pretest before teaching the targeted material.
6. Evaluate pretest results (which skill is mastered and whether the prerequisite skill is required)
7. Initiate instruction based on information obtained in step six.

8. After completion of instruction re-administer the test to determine which students have mastered which skills.

9. Modify instruction as indicated.

5.2.2.1 Uses of Curriculum Based Assessment

C.B.A when conducted properly can be an important tool for teachers and diagnostic specialists in a number of ways.

- Analysis of the learning environment: By careful examination of the learning environment, curriculum based assessment helps to identify pitfalls that may interfere with the students learning. Such assessment can isolate problems with instructional materials, with the ways in which instruction in organized or sequenced, with the manner of presentation and grouping of students in the classroom.
- Analysis of task approach strategies: By focusing on the students task approach strategies C.B.A helps teachers identify basic learning skills that the student may need to develop.
- Examination of students products: Through systematic examination of a student's work samples C.B.A can spot particular error patterns.
- Controlling and arranging students' tasks: By manipulating the ways in which materials are presented and the specific tasks that students are asked to perform, the C.B.A procedure helps teachers determine which approaches are most productive.
- It complies with procedural requirement of public law for assessing students in need of Special Education.
- It is efficient.
- It is a valid, reliable basis for making decisions.
- It can be used to make different kinds of decisions (*e.g.* screening, program effectiveness)
- It increases student's achievement.
- It helps teachers decide what to teach.

5.2.2 Instructional Diagnosis

Another common assessment practice is Instructional diagnosis, which identifies the extent to which a student's poor performance is caused by poor Instruction and indicates possible remedies for the problem. It consists of systematic analysis of the requirement of instruction including the kinds of demands put on the learner. During instructional diagnosis educators look at the skills to complete instructional tasks and compare them to the skills students do and do not have.

Task analysis is one part of Instructional diagnosis. Task analysis is the process of breaking complex tasks into their component skills. For *e.g.* 1. A teacher might break a complex skill like brushing one's teeth into its component skills like moving towards bathroom, taking brush in hand, taking paste and opening its lid, pressing the paste and applying it on brush, taking the brush with paste in hand and taking near mouth, etc.

Ex: 2. Alphabetizing the following words each of which has been placed on separate card. Task analysis helps teachers identify:

- What steps are necessary to accomplish the task.
- Where students have difficulty with a task from where the problem begins.
- What should be taught next
- What adaptations may assist students with task accomplishment. (Bigge 1991)
- What component skills have been missed out (Verbal chaining, Motor chaining)

5.2.3 Academic Time Analysis

Academic Time Analysis is the study of how time is allocated in school. Contemporary educators have developed new tools to engage in formal and systematic analysis of how students spend their time in school. Greenwood and Carta (1993) have developed a computer program called EBASS (Eco Behavioral Assessment System for Students) that educators can use to gather data on the exact amounts or proportion of time students spend engaged in academic work, inappropriate behavior, and so forth. They use this approach to report academic engaged time for individual pupils. The phrase 'eco behavior assessment' is often used to describe the assessment of the relationship between contextual factors and student behavior.

5.2.4 Assessment of Instructional Environment

The "bottom line" in assessment is improved instruction and instructional outcomes for students. As educators attempt to develop appropriate instructional intervention they increasingly measure the extent to which the factors that lead to improved outcomes are occurring for individual students. When educators assess students' needs in the context of classroom and home environments and when they systematically appraise the presence or absence of components of effectiveness, they are engaged in assessment of instructional environments. (Ysseldyke and Christenson, 1993)

5.2.5 Assessing Outcomes

Using an outcome-based approach the National Center on Educational Outcomes (NCEO) at the University of Minnesota developed a conceptual model for students with disabilities. The center concerned involving many groups of stakeholders like teaches, parents, school administrators, policy makers, legislators etc came to an agreement on major desired outcomes of education for students with disabilities.

The outcomes in the figure below do not include all the possible outcomes of schooling; rather they are the outcomes the stakeholders valued most. E.g.

— Students completed schooling

— Competent in communication (either verbal or sign language in whichever they are able)

— Able to cope effectively with personal challenges, frustration and stress.

— Physically fit

— Aware of voting and procedures necessary for voting.

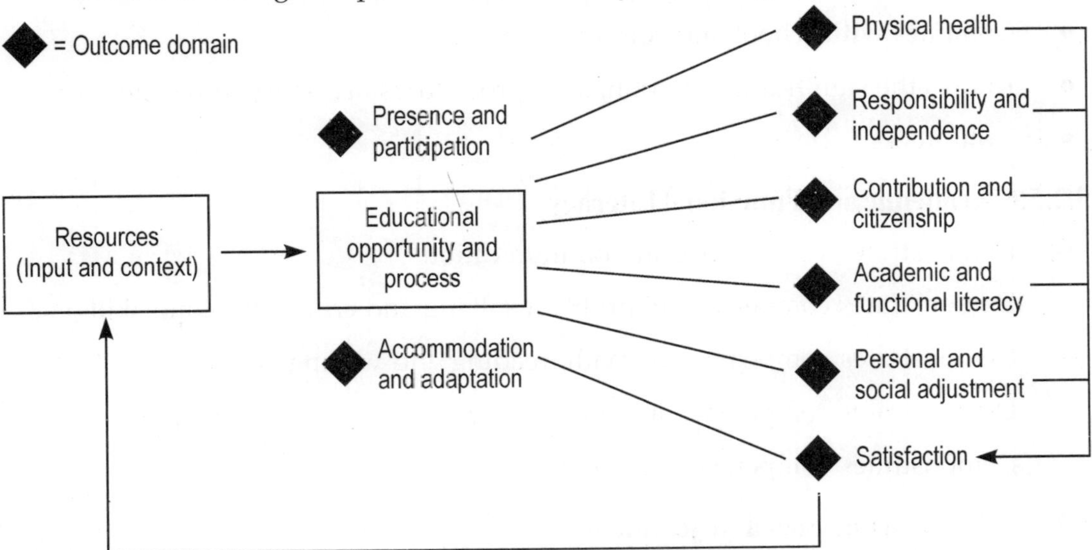

Fig.-5.1: Conceptual Model of Outcome Domain

Source:: Ysseldyke James E. et al., Educational outcomes and indicators for students completing school.

5.2.5.1 Presence and Participation

- Is present in school
- Participates
- Completes school

5.2.5.2 Accommodation and Adaptation

- Makes adaptation, accommodations, or compensations necessary to achieve outcomes in each of major domains.
- Demonstrates family support and coping skills

5.2.5.3 Physical Health

- Makes healthy lifestyle choices.
- Is aware of basic safety, fitness and healthcare needs.
- Is physically fit.

5.2.5.4 Responsibility and Independence

- Gets about in the environment
- Is responsible for self.

5.2.5.5 Contribution and Citizenship

- Compiles with school and community rules.
- Knows the significance of voting and procedures necessary to register vote.
- Volunteers.

5.2.5.6 Academic and Functional Literacy

— Demonstrates competence in communication

— Demonstrates competence in problem solving and critical thinking skills.

— Demonstrates competence in math, reading and writing skills.

— Demonstrates competence in other non-academic and academic, skills.

— Demonstrates competence in using technology.

5.2.5.7 Personal and Social Adjustment

- Copes effectively with personal challenges, frustrations and stressors.
- Has good self-image.

- Respects cultural and individual differences.
- Gets along with other people, tolerance.

5.2.5.8 Satisfaction

- Student satisfaction with high school experience.
- Parent/guardian satisfaction with the education that student received
- Community satisfaction with the education that student received

5.2.6 Performance Assessment

Performance assessment involves gathering data on pupils' performance directly by having them work singly or in groups to perform tasks. Data are gathered on the quality with which tasks are competed, as well as on how students work together to perform tasks.

5.3 Collecting Assessment Data

5.3.1 Methods for Collecting Data

We use four processes to gather information about students who are exceptional.

1. **Testing:** It is the process of administering a set of items to obtain a score. A test is a collection of items designed to measure knowledge in a content area.
2. **Observation:** It is the process of watching an individual perform a set of behaviors to obtain information about the rate or duration of those behaviors. An observation is a record of performance.
3. **Interviewing:** It is the process of asking questions to obtain information about an individual's background, current levels of performance, and plans. Interview is a set of questions designed to provide information about a content area of interest.
4. **Work sample assessment:** It involves collecting the products of an individual's work. Because these products can be put into portfolios, (proforma) this method is also called portfolio assessment.

There is no strict rule for deciding which assessment method to use. Teachers and other professionals use tests, observations, interviews etc to make decisions whichever gives best information for decision making.

5.3.2 Tests

- **Formal tests** have standardized administration procedures, have norms, are produced by psychological companies for use with large groups of people, but primarily for individuals.
- **Informal tests** are developed by teachers to measure knowledge in a content area recently taught.

Another way of describing tests is by administration.

- **Group tests** are tests administered for large groups, or class to obtain data of an entire class in a short time.
- **Individual tests** are tests administered to a single individual, so that close observation can be done while testing. Case study procedures use individual tests.
  - Verbal tests
  - Performance tests.

5.3.2.1 Categories of Use

Tests differ in intended uses.

- **Screening tests** are used to spot pupils who are making little or too much progress compared to others or to objectives of curriculum.
- **Diagnostic tests** are designed to provide more specific information, usually in the form of a description of strengths and weakness in the development of a specific skill.

Tests can be also be categorized as

- **Norm-referenced tests** where interpretations are made by comparing the students performance with the performance of other students. They are standardized and given to large number of students to obtain an index of 'typical' or 'average' performance. By definition, students who earn significantly higher or lower scores than their age mates or grade mates are said to perform "abnormally". Students who perform very poorly on a test relative to others of their age are said to be deficient; those who perform much better than their age mates are said to be exceptionally proficient.
- **Criterion-referenced tests** give teachers a measure of the extent to which individuals or groups have mastered specific curricular content. These tests are also called objective-reference tests or curriculum-referenced tests. These tests are developed by specifying the objectives or criteria to be mastered,

usually in basic skills, areas like reading, maths, then writing the items to assess mastery of those objectives or criteria. The results indicate how much mastery in a particular instructional objective a student has attained. Items in these tests are innumerable arranged in increasing order of complexity. They are elaborate and given in different sessions.

In Special Education tests commonly are used to assess

— Intelligence

— Achievement

— Sensory-Acuity (testing vision and hearing)

— Perceptual-Motor abilities. (Bender visual-Motor gestalt test)

— Adaptive behavior: Self-help skills, communication skills, social skills.

— Language functioning: Speech, word recognition comprehension.

— Psychological functioning: Personality, problem behaviors, adjustment problem.

5.3.3 Observation

- **Active observation** records ongoing behavior like watching him perform a task and recording. (Doing maths, how may times a child is out of seat, raises hands for help)
- **Passive observation** is looking at a product produced last week at test records or information in cumulative folders. Observation can be formal using systematic procedures or informal using spontaneous data collecting procedures.

Observation provides different information than that available from tests and interviews.

5.3.4 Interviews

Interviews are conducted by asking questions to people in group or individually.

- **Formal interview**: predetermined, written down, and administered the same way each time.
- **Informal interview**: Developed as the interview proceeds from initial questions.

- **Structured interview**: We ask the same set of questions in the same way each time we use them.
- **Unstructured interview**: Exact nature of the interview is not known before it is administered.

The Steps in Interviewing are:

— Establish rapport by being sincere and honest and showing interest.

— Present reasons for interview.

— Formulate open-ended questions avoiding yes or no questions.

— Listen in an accepting environment to gain information and insight into the problem

— Terminate the interview with a goal or plan of action.

5.3.5 Work Samples

Teacher makes extensive collection of the products of students work. Besides reviewing individual products to see if students are performing tasks correctly, they review entire portfolios of products to make judgments about the extent to which students are making progress.

PART-II

Education of Children with Special Needs

Gifted, Creative and Talented Children

The term gifted is used to designate people who are intellectually, creatively, academically, or otherwise superior to a comparison group of peers or older age mates. These children are also referred to as genius because their strengths are far beyond even those of their peers who are perceived as smart, bright, and artistic. These are people who can solve problems in traditional and nontraditional ways and demonstrate consistently high performance in areas requiring considerable mental ability. These people are recognized and considered exceptional because of the contributions they make and the performances they demonstrate.

6.1 Giftedness Defined

The term gifted is usually used to refer to people with superior intellectual or cognitive performance, while the term talented is usually used to refer to people who show outstanding performance in a specific area such as the performing or visual arts. Public law of US defines gifted and talented children as the following.

The term "gifted and talented" means children, and wherever applicable, youth who are identified at the preschool, elementary, or secondary level as possessing demonstrated or potential abilities, that give evidence of high performance capability in areas such as intellectual, creative, specific academic, or leadership ability, or in the performing and visual arts and who by reason thereof require services or activities not ordinarily provided by the school (section 902).

- **Joseph Renzulli (1979)** described giftedness as represented by the intersection of three basic clusters of human traits; these clusters being above average general ability, high levels of creativity and high levels of task commitment, children who manifest or are capable of developing an interaction among the three clusters require a wide variety of educational opportunities and services that are not ordinarily provided through regular instructional programs.

- **Robert Sternberg (1985)** argued that giftedness has three aspects. The first is cognitive and internal to the individual. The second is experiential, relating thinking to personal experience to solve problems. Third a gifted individual may be superior in adapting to, shaping, and selecting experiences. For Sternberg giftedness comes in several varieties. "Some gifted individuals may be particularly adept at applying the components of intelligence, but only to academic kinds of situations. They may thus be "test smart" but little more. Other individuals who are gifted may be particularly adept at dealing with novelty, but in a synthetic rather than analytic sense: Their creativity is not matched by analytic power; still other individuals who are gifted may be "Street Smart" in external contexts, but at a loss in academic contexts. Thus giftedness is plural rather than singular in nature."
- **Howard Gardner (1983)** proposed a "multiple intelligences" theory in which all normal individuals are capable of at least seven independent forms of intellectual performance: linguistic, musical, logical mathematical, spatial, bodily kinesthetic, interpersonal and intrapersonal. He believed that each could be developed to high levels and that each should be considered in identification efforts.

In 1972 Sidney Marland offered this definition of children who are gifted and talented: Those identified by professionally qualified persons, who by virtue of outstanding abilities are capable of high performance. These are children who require differentiated educational programs and services beyond those normally provided by the regular program in order to realize their contribution to self and society. Children capable of high performance include those with demonstrated and/or potential ability in any of the following areas:

- General intellectual ability
- Specific academic aptitude
- Creative or productive thinking
- Leadership ability
- Visual and performing arts.

Regardless of the definition being used or the availability of resources for providing services to students who are gifted and talented, every teacher has some students who could profit from a special program because of superior abilities in academic and other areas.

6.2 Characteristics of Gifted and Talented Children

— **Cognitive:** Students who are gifted and talented can quickly understand abstract symbols and manipulate them which is a significant indicator of intellectual giftedness. These children have excellent memory and can learn concepts easily when compared to their peers. Cognitive traits regularly associated with giftedness is creativity. They demonstrate fluency, flexibility, originality and foresight, which are the components of divergent thinking. Those who perform well on convergent thinking exhibit high level of reasoning ability, memory and classification, and show high academic aptitude. Clark (1988) describes characteristics of gifted children across five domains cognitive, affective, physical, intuitive, and societal provided in the table below.

— **Academic:** People who are gifted are often first recognized for superior achievement in one or more school subjects. Their performance in mathematics, language, arts, science, social studies, or other academic content area is generally well above average when compared to their age mates. Learning even complex content comes easier to these students than it does to their peers.

— **Physical:** Physically gifted children do not differ substantially from other children of their age. Gifted children are similar in appearance to other students.

— **Communication:** Students who are gifted and talented typically communicate at a higher level than their chronological age peers. Students who are gifted and talented often enjoy conversation with adults or older peers more than other age mates.

— **Behavioral:** Students who are gifted and talented are socially popular and enjoy relatively high social status, but concomitant problems related to their needs and abilities to succeed do exist.

Table-6.1: Differentiating Characteristics of Gifted

I.	The Cognitive Domain
	• Extraordinary quantity of information; unusual retentiveness
	• Advanced comprehension
	• Unusually varied interests and curiosity
	• High level of language development
	• High level of verbal ability
	• High level of visual and spatial ability.
	• Unusual capacity for processing information
	• Accelerated pace of thought processes
	• Flexible thought processes
	• Comprehensive synthesis

- Early ability to delay closure
- Heightened capacity for seeing unusual and diverse relationship and overall gestures.
- Ability to generate original ideas and solutions
- Early differential patterns for thought processing (e.g., thinking in alternatives and abstract terms, sensing consequences, making generalizations)
- Early ability to use and form conceptual frameworks
- An evaluative approach toward oneself and others
- Persistent goal – directed behavior

II. The Affective Domain

- Large accumulation of information about emotions that have not been brought to awareness
- Unusual sensitivity to the expectations and feelings of others
- Keen sense of humor – may be gentle or hostile
- Heightened self-awareness, accompanied by feelings of being different
- Idealism and a sense of justice that appear at an early age
- Earlier development of an inner locus of control and satisfaction
- Advanced levels of moral judgment.
- High expectations of self and others which often lead to high levels of frustration with self, others, and situations.
- Unusual emotional depth and intensity
- Sensitivity to inconsistency between ideals and behavior

III. The Physical Domain

- Unusual discrepancy between physical and intellectual development
- Low tolerance for the lag between their standards and their physical capacity
- Cartesian split – can include neglect of physical well-being and avoidance of physical activity

IV. The Intuitive Domain

- Early involvement and concern for intuitive knowing psychic and metaphysical ideas and phenomena
- Open to experience in this area, will experiment with psi and metaphysical phenomena
- Creativity apparent in all areas of endeavor
- Acceptance and expression of a high level of intuitive ability especially with the highly gifted.

V. The Societal Domain

- Strongly motivated by self-actualization needs
- Advanced cognitive affective capacity for conceptualizing and solving societal problems.

Source: From *"Growing Up Gifted: Developing the Potential of Children at Home and at school"*.

Table-6.2: Characteristics and Related Problems of Students Who Are Gifted and Talented

Area	Characteristics	Potential Problems
Cognitive	Outstanding memory, Much information at Higher-level, abstract thinking Preference for complex and challenging tasks, Simultaneous thinking, Unusual information processing abilities, Creativity	Boredom with pace of instruction, Impatience, Perceived as showoff by peers and other students, "Too many" questions, Resistance to conventional approaches to instruction
Academic	High performance, Ease in learning even complex content, High content mastery, High Problem Solving	Alienation from peers, Expectations from parents for achievement in all areas, Resistance for repetitive tasks, Classroom disruption when work is complete.
Physical	Discrepancies between physical and mental abilities	Limited development of other than mental abilities
Behavioral	Unusual sensitivity to needs of others, Sharp sense of humor, Unusual intensity Persistent, goal directed orientation	Especially vulnerable to criticism, High need for success, Perfectionism, Intolerance and rejection from peers perceived as stubborn
Communication	Higher level of language development, Excellent listening and speaking vocabularies	Alienation from peers, perceived as showoff

6.3 Identification of Gifted Children

Identification usually involves a combination of procedures including

- Intelligence Scores
- Creativity Measurements
- Achievements Measures
- Teacher Nomination
- Parent Nomination
- Peer Nomination
- Self Nomination

6.4 Educational Programmes for Gifted Children

Generally gifted children, when allowed to attend regular classes, face a lot of problems of their own because an average class and its programmes are planned for children of average ability. Therefore they need special help.

Educational provisions for gifted children can be put under the following categories:

1. Acceleration
2. Segregation
3. Enrichment

6.4.1 Acceleration

The tern 'acceleration' refers to various provisions in a school that help a gifted child move through school at speed according to his ability and thus complete his formal education earlier than would normally be accepted.

Various forms of acceleration are:

- ***Early Admission:*** It means admitting the child into the schools earlier then the fixed age limit. It will accelerate his efficiency in school work and subjects.
- ***Quick Promotion:*** Students are promoted to an advanced grade at the end of the half year than after full term. It helps them to make rapid progress and provides a challenge to their genius.
- ***Non-Graded Class:*** Child is provided with facilities to cover various areas of work, which do not have any class label attached to them.
- ***Extra courses:*** The general class textbooks are not enough for the gifted children; the additional courses might be increased horizontally, by making a gifted child go through varieties of experiences.

6.4.2 Segregation

This system has been introduced for gifted children with special facilities of teachers and equipments.

- ***Special classes:*** Arrangement for separate special classes can be made by segregation in the general schools. The arrangement of a more extensive curriculum, extra curricular activities, laboratory work etc, is made specially selected for them.
- ***Coaching section:*** After identification, segregation is made for giving coaching to appear at various scholarship examinations and competitions.

- *Club section:* Various hobby clubs like science club, Language club, Arts Club, etc: may be introduced.
- *Special schools:* Children are placed in special schools where special curriculum expert teachers and extensive study facilities are provided. The standard of education, competency, and physical resources are much higher in these schools.

6.4.3 Enrichment Programme

The major purpose of enriching a school programme for the gifted is to stimulate and foster optimum development.

- *Individual enrichment:* The extra curriculum should be planned is such a way that any gifted child can complete it individually with self-confidence.
- *Group oriented enrichment:* The children should be given work material to complete in a group so that they can be able to complete it by mass activities.
- *Mentor and apprenticeship programs,* These are important and underutilized ways to motivate, challenge, and effectively educate children who are gifted.
- *Library facilities:* Enrichment programme indicates that school should have well equipped libraries. A child should be allowed to use freely library and resources center facilities.
- *Projects and activity-oriented home assignments:* Gifted individuals may be given projects in different areas in which they are gifted. Education through organization of project becomes satisfying for gifted children.
- *Excursions:* Excursions serve the purpose of satisfying their spirit of adventure.
- *Community* Service also helps gifted children to identify themselves as social leaders.

6.4.4 Other Provisions

- *Heuristic method:* This method is based on the maxim 'learning by doing' which is beneficial for gifted children.
- *Individual instructions:* Two types of individualized instructions can be given to gifted children.
  - Programmed learning
  - Computer-assisted instruction.

- ***Extracurricular activities:*** The following activities may be arranged for gifted children:
  - To give opportunities to take part in seminars, debates, competitions etc.,
  - To motivate creative activities.
  - To arrange workshops or plans for the creation of models, charts, painting, etc.,
  - To teach dance, music, group discussion, method for the development of social extra skills.
  - To motivate them to take part in games and sports.

6.5 Educational Provisions for Creative Children

Following are some of the important educational provisions for creative children.

— ***Elaboration***: Here an individual is provided with skeleton outline of the problem and by the use of his imagination he completes the problem. It helps in developing reasoning, thinking and problem-solving abilities.

— ***Brainstorming***: It emphasizes on divergent thinking. It involves generating the ideas in response to some problems in a group. It has two types of mental activities; creative and judicial. The function of creative mind is to invent, the function of judicial mind is to critically examine the ideas which emerge from creative mind.

— ***Heuristic method***: Here the teacher should provide a problematic situation and the individual should investigate in this way to solve the problem. It helps in the development of thinking and reasoning abilities.

— ***Project method***: Students are given learning material in the form of projects. It helps in developing divergent thinking. Here the individual moves in his own way and at his pace to complete the project and thinks in his own ways, when projects is given individually.

— ***Computer Assisted Instructions (CAI)***: The aim of CAI is to meet the special needs of learner. A computer can store vast amount of information suiting to different needs of creative children.

— ***Programmed instruction***: Programming is the process of arranging the material to be learnt by the student into a series of steps arranged in logical sequence and moving from concrete to abstract. It provides a learning environment that encourages the creative child to be motivated intrinsically.

— *Teaching machines*: Teaching machines require an answer and the pupil usually writes or speaks into the machine. This provides a means whereby the child may respond to the programme and the child will get immediate information of some kind concerning his response that can act as a psychological reinforce.

— *Enrichment programme*: Enrichment means providing educational programme to creative children who have special needs providing good library and laboratory facilities for challenging works which involve critical and divergent thinking, imagination etc. Facilities for arts like painting, drawing, models preparation, music, and dance may be provided.

— *Extracurricular activities*: Arrangement of some extra-curricular activities are very beneficial. They are:

  - Seminars, debates, workshops, educational tours, exhibitions etc.,
  - Giving responsible works, activity oriented home assignments.
  - Providing intellectual games for mental development.
  - Self-motivated learning and its evaluation should be emphasized in an unburdened manner.

6.5.1 Tips for Teaching Gifted Students

- Have students work with you in selecting a diversity of learning materials that challenge and motivate their interest and academic abilities.
- Provide curriculum that challenges gifted students to understand learning in real-life applications. Once they've shown evidence of mastery, keep the learning proactive and productive.
- Use technology, fieldtrips, interviews, science fairs and student portfolios to provide additional learning resources between the classroom curriculum and the global classroom.
- Use high leverage teaching to promote high leverage learning for gifted students.
- Make sure that curriculum provides relevancy, rigor and real-life application for students eager to process the world around them and explore learning applications of that world in their own lives.
- Have students keep an organized checklist of accomplished assignments during the week.

- Students should be provided with exciting curriculum that promotes multiple learning strategies and applications to learning outcomes.
- Allow gifted students processing time in order to reflect on their learning experiences.
- Present learning activities outside the box for gifted students who are self-motivated to challenge and evaluate their own learning. Make sure your grade book maintains their individual assessments and current scores.
- Keep a library of interesting reading materials in the classroom.
- Create individual and group projects that promote both a social engagement and academic challenge for gifted students and their peers.
- Celebrate the academic and behavioral accomplishments of gifted students in mainstream classrooms.

6.5.2 Tips for Teachers of Students who are Gifted and Talented

- Provide alternative instructional activities addressing students' interests and preferences, celebrate diversity.
- Provide guest speakers, fieldtrips, practical demonstrations, and other enrichment activities.
- Model higher level thinking skills and creative problem- solving approaches.
- Develop instructional activities that generate problems requiring different types of thinking and solutions.
- Allow students to move though the curriculum at their own pace.
- Identify advanced content and assign independent reading, projects, worksheets, reports, and other enrichment activities.
- Provide opportunities and an environment for sharing novel ideas and solutions to practical problems.
- Allow students who are gifted to have input in deciding how classroom time is allocated.
- Provide and encourage independent learning opportunities.
- Eliminate material from the curriculum that students have mastered.

The tips could go on and on, not just for gifted students, but for all students needing challenge and rigor in the learning process. The educational journey for gifted students may start in the classroom and end in the application of learning skills in every aspect of their life. Challenging gifted students shouldn't be extra work for the teacher or the other students. Gifted students can be a true gift to any classroom. Provide some instructional tips and you will create eager learners ready to share their exceptional skills and make learning fun for all students.

6.6 Gifted Underachiever

There is perhaps no situation more frustrating for parents or teachers than living or working with children who do not perform as well academically as their potential indicates they can. These children are labeled as underachievers. At what point does underachievement end and achievement begin? Is a gifted student who is failing in mathematics while doing superior work in reading an underachiever? Does underachievement occur suddenly, or is it better defined as a series of poor performances over an extended period of time? Certainly the phenomenon of underachievement is as complex and multifaceted as the children to whom this label has been applied.

Creative scientists, innovative planners, intuitive technocrats and intelligent politicians are the human potential for any country and the gifted can contribute much to this human potential. But this human resource is reducing. This does not mean that now we are not having enough number of gifted children, rather the fact is that the ability of the gifted children is not becoming the resource for this nation. In particular we can say that the gifted children are not achieving up to their ability.

Concerning this of the teacher and parents of the gifted children can play a major role in making the gifted child a natural resource for the nation. For this the teacher should know about the gifted underachievers, their identification, their problems and educational programmes that he can be provided for them.

6.6.1 Meaning of Gifted Underachievers

The phrase gifted underachiever contains two terms gifted and underachiever.

Gifted refers to individual who have

- High ability (including high intelligence)
- High creativity.
- High task commitment.

Underachiever refers to the individual who fails to achieve at a level consistent with the ability.

Thus gifted underachievers are those who fail in their studies or achieve results quite below their ability and standard expected of them.

6.6.1.1 Definition of Gifted Underachiever

- Dehaan and Havighurst (1975) defined those as gifted underachievers who rank in the upper length or upper quarters in their standards in terms of ability but whose course grades are average or below.
- Dowd (1962) called those students as gifted underachievers who exceed 90 percent of their classmates for scholastics aptitude but fail to exceed 50 percent academically.
- Gallagher (1979) defined underachieving gifted students as those who exhibit a gap between achievement test scores and intelligence test scores.

6.6.1.2 Types of Gifted Underachievers

Gifted underachievers are of two types

1. Depressive type gifted underachievers.
2. Aggressive type gifted underachievers

1. **Depressive type gifted underachievers:** This type of gifted underachievers are those who are more withdrawn, passive individuals who never reach their potential.

   They suffer from negative self-concept and lack of motivation. They are very shy and timid.

2. **Aggressive type of gifted underachievers:** This type of gifted underachievers are those who are hyperactive and aggressive, who disrupt classes and annoy their teachers. They suffer from antagonistic attitude towards authority. They are very vocal and critical about school.

6.6.2 Characteristics of Gifted Underachievers

The gifted underachievers will be a kind of intellectual delinquent who withdraw from goals and activities and active social participation generally. Their characteristics are discussed below.

6.6.2.1 Educational Characteristics

Gifted underachievers tend to be

- Far below their ability in academic achievement
- Poor study habits
- Lack of clear vision and definiteness of academic and occupational choice.
- Poor use of time and money.

- Show hostility towards teachers (authoritarian)
- They lack proper interaction with the teachers or new learning experience.
- Has little interest in academic, untried activities; dislikes schools.
- Unable to have realistic goals.
- Lower aspirations.
- They avoid learning from books.
- They have narrower interests.

6.6.2.2 Social and Emotional Characteristics

- Disinterest in other people.
- They are often changeable or unstable or they may have an inferiority complex.
- Weak ego control, unable to cope with anxiety.
- Withdrawal
- Lack of maturity and responsibility.
- Lack of dominance and leadership status.
- Lack of positive self-concept.
- Feeling of worthlessness.
- Unable to maintain positive relationship with their peers.
- Has conflict over independence-dependence decisions.
- Pessimistic
- Lack of self-confidence.

6.6.3 Identification of Gifted Underachievers

Gifted children show their rays of excellence in one way or the other and the gifted underachievers differ from gifted achievers in certain non-intellectual variables. This knowledge helps the teacher to identify the gifted underachievers. The teacher may use the following techniques to identify the gifted underachievers.

Testing by the teacher: The teacher assesses the scholastic aptitude of the children by conducting intelligence test, aptitude test etc., and measures the scholastic achievement as measured by school grades. Then the students who show marked difference between scholarship aptitude and scholastic achievement are identified as gifted underachievers.

Observation: The systematic observation intended at finding the abilities and behavioral characteristics of the student will also help in identifying gifted underachievers.

Interviews: Interviewing the parents regarding the activities of the child at home, interviewing the peer group, taking the opinion of teachers and authority regarding work method, ability of learning, classroom behaviour will all help the teacher to identify the gifted underachiever.

6.6.4 Causes for Gifted Underachievement

Gifted children may become underachievers for many reasons but the general causes are listed below.

6.6.4.1 Motivation

Lack of motivation is the major cause for gifted underachievement. According to the formula given by R.S. Wood Wroth

$$\text{Ability} \times \text{Motivation} = \text{Achievement},$$

the achievement will be zero for the zero motivation however high the ability may be.

The factors such as narrow and non-challenging curriculum, boredom, lack of variety in school tasks etc will cause lack of motivation for learning. Due to these factors gifted children become lazy, lack persistence when faced with a dull routine or hard task and prefer pleasure to work. Also when a gifted child experiences failures frequently, he develops negative accomplishment motivation. Lack of motivation in school tasks severely affects their level of achievement.

On the other hand a serious or protest underachievement will occur for excessive motivation which may be due to too much pressure of parents, extrinsic drive or aggressive achievement motivation.

6.6.4.2 Emotional Problem

The motivational factors such as inferiority feelings, lack of interest in studies, hostile towards teachers and school will affect the achievements of the student. These emotional factors may arise in a child due to

- Considerable strife and strain at home.
- Sibling rivalry
- Decrease in affection of parents

- Authoritative and annoying behaviour of parents and teachers when children do not immediately behave appropriately and successfully.
- Too much protection of parents towards the child

6.6.4.3 Fear

Fear is another cause for underachievement. The child may fear punishment, criticism, ridicule, disapproval, no acceptance, failure, and of losing status in the eyes of teachers/ parents, other adults, by being considered stupid, inferior etc.,

When the children fear they lose their flexibility, freeze at the switch and lose their distinctiveness, confidence, and their intellectual function is disturbed which leads to underachievement.

6.6.4.4 Insufficient Grasp of Fundamentals

Until a gifted child learns the fundamentals of a subject thoroughly, he remains a handicap in it. As time goes on he begins to feel as not good in as those subjects. The gifted child may also neglect the slow and accurate procedures to solve the problems. This is due to lack of opportunity to serve improper problems. This results in underachievement.

Besides this, due to lack of opportunity, improper training lack of encouragement, the child may not develop some fundamental skills such as reading writing, study skills etc., Lack of these fundamental skills affects the performance of the child in various subject area.

6.6.4.5 Miscellaneous

Other than the above mentioned factors the following factors may lead to underachievement.

- Poor physical health.
- Physical handicaps
- Frequent absents.
- Poor social adjustment.

6.6.5 Educational Programmes for Gifted Underachiever

Educational programme of gifted underachiever should aim at the elimination of causes of underachievement, rehabilitating him up to his ability and fostering giftedness. In this regard the following strategies should be considered.

6.6.5.1 Supportive Strategies

- Classroom techniques and designs that allow students to feel' they are part of a "family versus a "factory."
- Include methods such as holding class meetings to discuss student concerns.
- Designing curriculum activities based on the needs and interests of the children and allowing students to bypass assignment on subjects in which they have previously shown competency.

6.6.5.2 Intrinsic Strategies

- These strategies incorporate the idea that students self-concept as learners is tied closely to their design to achieve academically (purvey and Novak. 1984).
- A classroom that invites positive attitudes is likely to encourage achievements.
- Teachers encourage attempts not just successes; they value student input in creating classroom rules and responsibilities and they allow students to evaluate their own work before receiving a grade from the teacher.

6.6.5.3 Remedial Strategies

- Teachers who are effective in reversing underachieving behaviors recognize that students are not perfect; that each child has specific strength and weakness as well as social emotional and intellectual needs.
- With remedial strategies students are given chances to excel in their areas of strength and interest while opportunities are provided in specific areas of learning deficiencies.
- This remediation is done in a safe environment in which mistakes are considered a part of learning for everyone including the teacher.

The key to eventual success lies in the willingness of parents and teachers to encourage students whenever their performances or attitude shifts (even slightly) in a positive direction.

6.6.5.4 Participation in Gifted Programs

Students who underachieve in some aspect of school performance but whose talents exceed the bounds of what is generally covered in the standard curriculum have a right to an education that matches their potential. To be sure, a program for gifted students may need to alter its structure or content to meet these students' specific learning needs, but this is preferable to denying gifted children access to educational services that are the most accommodating to their abilities.

6.6.6 Role of the Family

6.6.6.1 Supportive Strategies

- Gifted children thrive in a mutually respectful non-authoritarian, flexible questioning atmosphere.
- They need reasonable rules and guidelines, strong support and encouragement.
- Consistently positive feedback and help to accept some limitations, their own, as well as those of others. Although these principles are appropriate for all children, parents of gifted children, believing that advanced intellectual ability also means advanced social and emotional skills, may allow their children excessive decision-making power before they have the wisdom and experience to handle such responsibility
- Gifted youngsters need adults who are willing to listen to their questions without comment. Some questions merely preface their opinions, and quick answers prevent them from using adults as a sounding board.
- When problem solving is appropriate, offer a solution and encourage students to come up with their own answers and criteria for choosing the best solution.
- Listen carefully, show genuine enthusiasm about students observations, interests, activities and goals.
- Be sensitive to problems but avoid transmitting unrealistic or conflicting expectations and solving problems a student is capable of managing.
- Provides students with a wide variety of opportunities for success; a sense of accomplishment and acceptance of human limitations.
- Guide them toward activities and goals that reflect their values, interests and needs.
- Reserve some time to have fun to be silly to share daily activities.
- Like all youngsters gifted children need to feel connected to people who are consistently supportive.

6.6.6.2 Intrinsic Strategies

- Weather or not a gifted youngster uses exceptional ability in constructive ways depends in part on self-acceptance and self-concept.
- An intellectually gifted child will not be happy and complete until he is using intellectual ability at a level approaching full capacity. It is important that

parents and teachers see intellectual development as a requirement for these children and not merely as an interest, flair or a phase they will outgrow.

- Providing an early and appropriate educational environment can stimulate an early love for learning. A young curious student may easily become "turned off" if the educational environment is not stimulating, class placement and teaching approaches are inappropriate, the child experiences ineffective teachers or assignment consistently too different or too easy.
- The gifted youngster's ability to define and solve problems in many ways may not be compatible with traditional gifted education programs or specific classroom requirements.
- Older students can participate in pressure-free non-competitive summer activities that provide a wide variety of educational opportunities including indepth exploration, hands on learning and mentor relationships (Berger 1989).
- Some Students are more interested in learning than in working for grades. Such students might spend hours in a project that is unrelated to academic classes and fail to turn in required work. They should be strongly encouraged to purse their interests particularly since those interests may led to career decisions and lifelong passions
- Early career guidance emphasizing creative problem solving, decision making and setting short and long-term goals often helps them to complete required assignments, pass high school courses and plan for college (Berger 1989).
- Providing real world experiences in an area of potential career interest may also provide inspiration and motivation toward academic achievement.

6.6.6.3 Praise versus Encouragement

Overemphasis on achievement or outcomes rather than a child's efforts, involvement and desire to learn about topics of interests is a common parental pitfall. The line between pressure and encouragement is subtle but important. Pressure to perform emphasizes outcomes such as winning awards and getting 'A's for which the student is highly praised. Encouragement emphasizes effort, the process used to achieve, steps taken toward accomplishing a goal and improvement. It leaves appraisal and valuation to the youngster. Underachieving gifted students may be thought of as discouraged individuals who need encouragement but tend to reject praise as artificial or inauthentic (Kaufmann 1987). Listen carefully to yourself. Tell your children when you are proud of their efforts.

6.6.6.4 Remedial Strategies

Dinkmeyer and Losoncy (1980) caution to avoid discouraging their children by domination, insensitivity, salience or intimidation. Discouraging comments such as "If you're so gifted why did you get a D in maths ?" or "I've given you everything why are you so bad?" are never effective. Constant competition may also lead to underachievement especially when a child consistently feels like earlier a winner or a loser. Avoid comparing children with others. Show children how to function in competition and how to recover after losses.

Study-skills courses, time management classes or special tutoring may be ineffective if a student is a long-term underachiever. This approach will work only if the student is willing and eager, if the teacher is chosen carefully, and the course is supplemented by additional strategies designed to help the student. On the other hand special tutoring may help the concerned student who is experiencing short-term academic difficulty. In general special tutoring for a gifted student is most helpful when the tutor is carefully chosen to match the interests and learning style of the student.

Mental Retardation

Mental retardation is perceived differently by different people, ranging from 'burdens to the family' to 'productive member of the society'. Though mental retardation is a condition such as visual, hearing or orthopaedic disabilities, it is less 'understood or misunderstood 'because of its, inconspicuous nature. While the other disabilities are obvious when we look at the person affected, a mentally retarded person most often looks normal without physical deformities and therefore people have difficulty in understanding why he acts differently from others.

A mentally retarded person is slow, or lacking in the development of mental functioning when compared to those of his age level. Therefore, for instance a 10 year old mentally retarded child may exhibit behavior like that of a 3 or 4 year old child depending on his level of retardation. This apparently is not expected of his age and so he is perceived as different from others.

7.1 Definition of Mental Retardation

There are a number of definitions for mental retardation. The one that is most commonly used by the educators is the one by American Association of Mental Deficiency (AAMD) which is now known as American Association of Mental Retardation (AAMR). This definition underwent a few revisions and the one currently in use is as follows:

"Mental retardation refers to significantly sub average general intellectual functioning resulting in or associated with concurrent impairment in adaptive behaviour, manifested during the developmental period".

As it is seen, the definition includes essentially three components to call a person as mentally retarded

1. Significantly subaverage general intellectual functioning
2. Deficits/impairment in adaptive behaviour
3. Manifested during developmental period.

7.1.1 Subaverage General Intellectual Functioning

Average general intellectual functioning is considered to be an Intelligent Quotient (IQ) between 90 and 110 on a standardized intelligence test. The two commonly used standardized tests in India to measure the IQ are the Indian adaptation of Stanford Binet and Wechsler Intelligence Scale for children. As per the definition two standard deviations below the average is considered significantly sub-average. As can be seen in figure below depending on the IQ scores of a person, the level of retardation is determined, and is classified accordingly as borderline, mild, moderate, severe or profound

7.1.2 Deficits in Adaptive Behaviour

The second component of the definition points to deficits in adaptive behaviour. Adaptive behaviour is defined as the effectiveness with which a person meets the standards of personal independence and social responsibility expected of his age and cultural group. These reflect in the development of sensory motor skills, communication, skills, self-help skills, and socialization in early childhood; application of reasoning and judgment in mastery of environment, social skills in childhood, adolescence; and vocational and social responsibilities in adult life.

Any deficiency in these aspects will be considered as a deficit in adaptive behaviour. For instance if a 3 year old child with no physical defects does not walk or a 10 year old child does not have toilet control or an 18 year old boy does not identify a five rupee note or 50p. coin, it is considered to be deficit/impairment in their adaptive behaviour.

7.1.3 Manifested during Developmental Period

The third component of the definition focuses on the onset of the condition - the developmental period, which is considered to be below the age of 18 years.

In short, a person to be diagnosed as mentally retarded should essentially have his intellectual functioning significantly below average, which results in or is associated with impairments in adaptive behaviour and should have acquired the condition before the age of 18 years.

7.2 Classification of Mental Retardation

Though the widely used classification system is that of AAMR as mentioned earlier there are other terminologies used, as seen in table below.

Table-7.1: Selected Symptom Severity Classifications

Source	Measured Intelligence* 90	80	70	60	50	40	30	20	10
Terman (1916)	Border line-IQ 70 to 79		Moron IQ 50 to 69		Imbecile-IQ 25 to 49		Idiot-IQ 24 or below		
Wechaler (1958)	Border line-IQ 70 to 79		Moron 50 to 69		Imbecile-IQ 30 to 49		Idiot-IQ 29 or below		
American Association on Mental Deficiency (1961)	Borderline Intelligence-1 SD IQ 68 to 83		Mildly Mentally Retarded-2 SD IQ 52 to 67		Moderately Mentally Retarded-3 SD IQ 36 to 51		Severely Mentally Retarded-4 SD IQ 20 to 35		Profoundly Mentally Retarded-5 SD IQ 19 or below.
American Association on Mental Deficiency (1973, 1977) +			Mildly Mentally Retarded-2 SD IQ 52 to 67		Moderately Mentally Retarded-3 SD IQ 36 to 51		Severely Mentally Retarded-4 SD IQ 20 to 35		Profoundly Mentally Retarded-5 SD IQ 19 or below.
American Psychiatric Association (1980)			Mildly Mentally Retarded IQ 50 to 70		Moderately Mentally Retarded IQ 35 to 49		Severely Mentally Retarded IQ 20 to 34		Profoundly Mentally Retarded IQ below 20

* IQ ranges from Stanford-Binet standard deviations (S.D.)

\+ The 1983 AAMD classification (released at the time this volume was being prepared for press) placed a narrow band of IQ scores at each end of each level but are essentially the same as those in the table.

The educators use the terms slow learners, educable, trainable and custodial mentally retarded synonymously with borderline, mild, moderate, severe/ profound respectively. The educational classification is made based on the level of functioning of the mentally retarded persons. For instance, those who need to be totally taken care of for all their needs are called custodial because they are under custody; those who can be trained in certain semiskilled or unskilled jobs are called trainable (TMR); those who can be educated in the basic functional literacy are called educable (EMR), and those who can be educated like other normal children but are slow in learning are called slow learners, or dull normal.

However, there has been a movement by the professionals and parents regarding the issue of classifying and labeling the mentally retarded persons. It is considered to be stigmatizing them with a label and would also restrict the teacher to concentrating on specific abilities only. For example, a child who is labelled trainable may get a school programme in training in various skills and the teacher may not try to teach him any reading or writing as the name suggests training only. Thus currently there is a trend towards delabelling (not referring to them by their level of retardation).

Ideally classification and label should be used only for administrative purposes such as availing of social benefits like travel concessions, maintenance allowance, job reservation and so on.

For an educator the focus should be on the current level of functioning of the child which would help the educator to further develop programme for training the child towards social competence to be as independent as possible in the society.

7.3 Characteristics of Persons with Mental Retardation

Describing the characteristics of a person with mental retardation is difficult because all the retarded individuals do not have the same characteristics and no single child has all the characteristics also. However, it is important that a teacher is aware of the various characteristics so that she can plan her educational programming accordingly.

7.3.1 Physical Characteristics

— Generally they have a marked delay in their developmental milestones when compared to normal children, such as, their sitting, standing, walking, talking and so on. Mildly retarded children usually have their physical characteristics close to their normal peers. Some of the moderately retarded and severely retarded ones might have clumsy gait and poor motor coordination. The profoundly retarded individuals usually have associated physical handicaps and many a time, they are non-ambulatory.

— The physical characteristics also depend on the causes and the clinical features of the individual. For instance, the one with microcephaly has a very small head with receding chin and forehead, while the one with hydrocephalus has a very large head. A child with Down syndrome has very distinct features such as slanting eyes, flat nose bridge, flabby skin, little finger turned inwards, wide gap between big toe and the next toe and fissured tongue. Those with mental retardation with cerebral palsy will have spasticity or stiffness of the limb or limbs and may have drooling of saliva.

Table-7.2: Characteristics of Persons with Various Degrees of Mental Retardation

Severity level Description	*Mild M.R*	*Moderate M.R*	*Severe M.R*	*Profound M.R*
Preschool 0–5 yrs	Can develop social and communication skills, minimal retardation in sensory motor areas, often not distinguished from normal until late age.	Can talk or learn to communicate; poor social awareness; fair motor development, profits from training in self help; can be managed with moderate supervision.	Poor motor development, speech minimal; generally unable to profit from training in self-help; little or no communication skills.	Gross retardation; minimal capacity for functioning in sensory motor areas; needs nursing care.
School age 6–20 yrs Training and Education	Can learn academic skills upto approximately 6th grade level by late teens; can be guided toward social confirmity.	Can profit from training in social and occupational skills; unlikely to progress beyond 2nd grade level in academic subjects; may learn to travel alone in familiar places.	Can talk or learn to communicate; can be trained in elemental health habits; profits from systematic habit training.	Some motor development present; may respond to minimal or limited training in self help.
Adult 21 and over Social and vocational adequacy	Can usually achieve social and vocational skills adequate to minimum self support but may need guidance and assistance when under unusual social or economic stress.	May achieve self maintenance in unskilled or semi-skilled work under sheltered conditions; needs supervision and guidance when under mild social or economic stress.	May contribute partially to self maintenance under complete super-vision; can develop self protection skills to a minimal useful level in controlled environment.	Some motor and speech development; may achieve very limited self-care; needs nursing care

Adapted from Mental Retardation Activities of U S Department of Health and Education

— The mentally retarded persons have problems in language and communication, which are found more with severely/profoundly retarded and less with mildly retarded persons.

— A small number of mentally retarded persons have dual or multiple handicaps such as impairment in visual, hearing or motor abilities.

Table-7.3: Down Syndrome (Trisomy 21)

Down syndrome is a chromosomal disorder which causes physical and intellectual delays in development and occurs when there are 3 chromosome 21's, resulting in 47 total chromosomes instead of the normal 46. The most common clinical features are short neck and flat face, upward slanting eyes, low muscle tone and a single crease across the palm of the hand. Congenital heart defects accompany Down syndrome in about 40% of the cases. Vision and hearing problems are also common.

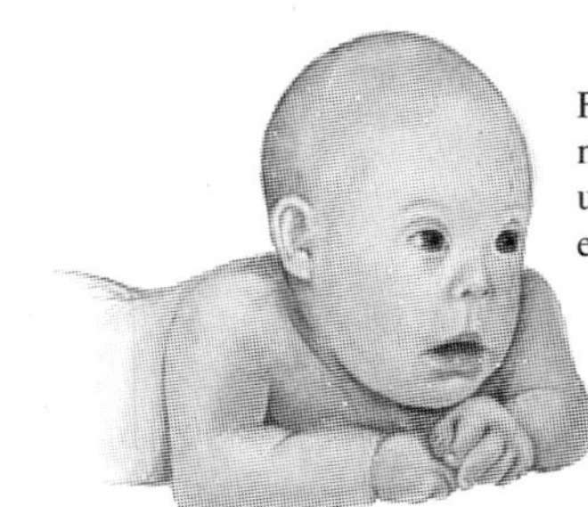

Flattened nose and face, upward slanting eyes,

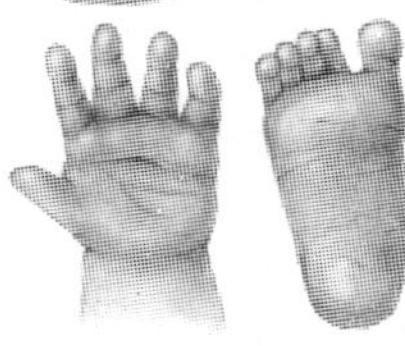

Single palmer crease, short fifth finger that curves inward

Widely separated first and second toes and increased skin creases

7.3.2 Social Characteristics

The social characteristics stand out in a retarded child because of the discrepancy between his abilities and the expectation of the society from him.

— One commonly found characteristic is short attention, and lack of concentration among many retarded children. They will switch from one activity to another without completing any of them.

— There are also those retarded persons who are lethargic, do not get motivated to do any task or continue to do the same task or have difficulty in changing from one activity to another.

— Some of them exhibit problematic behaviours which are either self-injurious or harmful to others. Self-injurious behaviours include hand biting, pulling own hair, nail biting, eye poking, beating on the face, banging head on wall or floor and so on. Those that harm others or destructive are the ones who beat and pinch others, throwing things, tearing clothes, and breaking articles. Other problematic behaviours include running away from home, stealing and so on. Most of such behaviour can be controlled by systematic intervention.

— There are some retarded persons who are indifferent to their surroundings and not responding when communicated with, though they may not have hearing problems. Irrelevant laughing or talking is also found with some retarded persons.

— While the mild and some of the moderately retarded ones can perform regular jobs they are trained in, their problem-solving ability will be poor and are found incompetent in taking decisions independently. Even if their work skills are good, many tend to lose their jobs due to poor social competence.

Table-7.4: Representative Characteristics and Concomitant Problems of Students with Mental Retardation

Area	**Characteristics**	**Potential problems**
Cognitive	Limited memory Limited general knowledge and information Concrete rather than abstract thinking Slower learning rate	Inattention Inefficient learning style Difficulty communicating Prone to failure Standard teaching practices ineffective
Academic	Difficulty learning most academic content Limited performance in most content areas Limited problem solving ability Limited content mastery	Limited attention, organizational skills, questioning behaviors, direction following monitoring of time and other school coping skills
Physical	Some discrepancies between physical and mental abilities	Performance often less than expected, based on physical appearance
Behavioral	Limited social and personal competence Limited coping skills Limited personal life skills and competence	Tardiness, complaints of illness, classroom disruptiveness, social isolation, inappropriate activity
Communication	Lower levels of language development, limited listening and speaking vocabularies	Trouble following directions, making requests, interacting, or communicating

It is essential for the teachers to keep in mind the characteristics of every child she teaches as she is required to plan teaching programme based on the child's alround profile. To quote an example, there may be a child in her class with epileptic fits 'who would exhibit certain behaviour just before or after an attack of the fit. Only if the teacher is aware of it, would she be able to take appropriate action in the right time. She should work in close coordination with medical personnel and the other therapists to help the child in total.

7.4 Prevalence of Mental Retardation

Approximately 2% of the population is considered to be mentally retarded. There has not been a prevalence study in the country except for a few sample surveys. It is difficult to estimate the number of mentally retarded persons as they are not readily recognizable. This holds true especially with those who are mildly retarded in whom mostly the difference is seen in academic performance rather that the general social competence. In rural India where many do not go to school, such retarded persons do not get identified at all, as they are not perceived to be different by the immediate society. The family generally would recognize his shortcomings and would train him in the society without any stigma. This is one of the reasons for the sample surveys done in a country having a wide range of data prevalence. Among the mentally retarded population majority are mildly retarded.

7.5 Causes and Prevention

There are various factors that lead to mental retardation. While a teacher is more concerned with the present level of functioning of the child to plan training programme, it is important that she has adequate knowledge about causes of mental retardation and the preventive measures, so that she would be in a position to guide the parents and families who approach her. Causes for mental retardation can be **preconceptional, prenatal, natal, and post-natal factors.**

7.5.1 Preconceptional Factors

This Includes factors before a woman conceives: Some of the preconceptional factors are history of mental retardation in the family of either the husband or the wife, maternal age at conception and history of infertility or repeated abortions in the mother.

7.5.2 Prenatal Factors

Factors affecting during pregnancy are called prenatal factors. This includes

- Infection in the mother such as jaundice, chickenpox and measles especially in the first three months of pregnancy.

- Injury to the abdomen of the mother due to accidents,
- X-ray exposure of the abdomen especially in the early months.
- Drug intake without medical advice.
- Attempted abortion,
- Mother getting fits during pregnancy and Rh blood incompatibility and so on.
- Rh blood incompatibility is a result of maternal and fetal blood being different from each other.
- Consuming alcohol and tobacco is harmful to the growing child during pregnancy.
- Chromosomal aberrations also cause mental retardation, when at conception an extra chromosome may be formed resulting in Down's syndrome.
- Maternal malnutrition is reported to be one of the causes for the birth of a retarded child.

7.5.3 Natal Causes

Natal causes are those factors that affect the child during birth. This would include

- Premature delivery.
- Prolonged labour when the oxygen supply to the child's brain may be insufficient thus damaging the brain.
- Abnormal presentation of the baby at delivery, too small sized pelvis of the mother to allow easy birth of the baby.
- Inappropriate use of forceps or improperly attended delivery by untrained persons and
- Delayed birth cry of the baby.

7.5.4 Post-Natal Causes

The post-natal causes or the factors affecting after the birth of the child leading to mental retardation include

- Low birth weight,
- Metabolic disorders
- Brain fever or meningitis.
- Encephalitis, epileptic fits, measles, chickenpox.

- Head injury
- Poor nutrition and jaundice in infancy and childhood.

AAMR has categorized the causes of MR into the following seven groups.

i) Infections and intoxications (e.g., rubella, syphilis, encephalitis, meningitis, exposure to drugs or poisons, blood group incompatibility).

ii) Trauma and physical agents (e.g. accidents before, during and after birth; anoxia).

iii) Metabolic and nutritional factors (e.g. Phenylketonuria (PKU)).

iv) Gross post-natal brain diseases (such as tumors)

v) Other post-natal influences (e.g hydrocephalus, microcephalus).

vi) Chromosomal abnormalities (Down's syndrome, Turner's syndrome).

vii) Gestational disorders (e.g. prematurity, low birth weight).

7.5.5 Prevention

The primary steps towards prevention of mental retardation is to have regular medical checkup during pregnancy, intake of healthy and nutritious food, being careful to avoid contact with people who have infections such as measles and chickenpox and avoiding physical trauma or accidents such as carrying heavy weights or reaching for objects which are at a height. If the parents choose to have an abortion it should be conducted by medical personnel. If the elder child is retarded, it is better to get medical advice before having another child. It is advisable to restrict the maternal age of conception between 20 and 30 years.

The delivery should be attended by trained persons and ideally, conducted in the hospitals where facilities are available in case of emergency. The mother should make It a point to have the delivery in a hospital especially if her other baby is already mentally retarded due to birth trauma.

After the birth of the child, he should be duly immunized against tuberculosis, poliomyelitis, diphtheria, whooping cough and tetanus. Care must be taken to see that he does not develop high fever leading to loss of consciousness. Prompt medical attention should be given to keep the temperature reduced. Epileptic fits should be attended by doctors immediately and the medicines prescribed should be given regularly. If there is a delay in the development of the child such as sitting, standing, walking or talking, immediate professional attention should be sought.

It is important that the teachers are aware of the basic facts about causes and prevention, as it would help her to guide and refer the parents who need.

7.6 Identification of Mentally Retarded Children

7.6.1 Measuring Intellectual Functioning

Use of standardized intelligence test such as WISC–R or Stanford-Binet intelligence scale indicates the IQ range of the MR child. According to AAMR definition a child could be labeled MR on the basis of IQ score of two standard deviations below the mean, which is 68 or 70 on the two tests.

7.6.2 Measuring Adaptive Behavior

AAMR defines the areas where deficits in adaptive behavior can be found with different age groups – during infancy and early childhood.

- Sensory-motor skills
- Communication skills (speech and language)
- Self-help skills (eating, grooming, bathing, toilet use, personal hygiene, clothing).
- Socialization skills (interacting and getting along with others.

During childhood and early adolescence:

- Application of basic academic skills in daily life activities.
- Application of appropriate reasoning and judgement in mastery of the environment.
- Social skills (participation in group activities and interpersonal relationships)

During late adolescence and adulthood:

- Vocational and social responsibility and performance.

The most frequently used instruments in assessing adaptive behavior are the

- AAMR Adaptive Behavior Scale (ABS)
- Vineland Social Maturity Scale (VSMC)
- Assessment of Social Competence (ASC)

Table-7.5: Adaptive Skill Areas Evaluated in Diagnosing Mental Retardation

Area	Description
Communication	Communication includes the ability to comprehend and express information through spoken words, written words, graphics symbols, sign language, and manually coded English, non symbolic behaviours such as facial expressions, body movements and gestures.
Self-Care	Self Care involves skills such as eating dressing grooming toileting and personal hygiene.
Home Living	Home living refers to daily functioning related to areas such as housekeeping, clothing care, property maintenance, food preparation. Planning and budgeting for shopping and home safety.
Social Skills	Social Skills include appropriate (for example, making friends, showing appreciation smiling) and inappropriate (for example, tantrums, jealousy public sexual behaviour) Social behaviors.
Community Use	Community use refers to appropriate use of resources in the community including transportation, shopping, obtaining services, worship and using public facilities.
Self-direction	Self-direction refers to making choices related to learning and following a schedule initiating appropriate activities consistent with personal interests, completing tasks seeking assistance when needed and resolving problems productively.
Health and Safety	Health and safety refers to maintaining one's well being including having as appropriative diet, identifying treating and preventing illness, knowing basic first aid, and following rules and laws.
Functional academics	Functional academics include cognitive abilities and skills related to learning in school (for example, Practical reading writing math science geography, and social studies
Leisure	Leisure refers to recreational interest and skills related to them such as choosing and initiating activities taking turns and using home and community activities alone and with others.
Work	Work relates to holding a job (part or full time) or participating in volunteer activities.

Source: Mental retardation, definition classification and systems of support work book, Pp. 7-8. Copyright 1992 American Association on Mental Retardation.

7.7 Functional Programming for the Mentally Retarded Persons

Special Education for mentally retarded children has grown rapidly in the last two decades. Special classes do not serve as a mere respite for parents any more, but specific individualized educational programmes are tailored for each of the children based on the current level of performance of the child and carried out. The progress is monitored periodically and fresh programmes are developed. Techniques have been evolved to quantify progress and precisely measure improvement or problems in the child. Objectivity has been the key factor in programming for mentally retarded children.

The recent development in Special Education has been the development of functional, age appropriate and community referenced goals and objectives for mentally retarded children. This would help a retarded person to acquire those skills that are necessary for independent living in the community. In other words, training should be given in skills that are necessary in school, home, vocational and community environment. Such a functional curriculum is different from the regular education curriculum as the latter is more examination-oriented while the former comprises daily living skills.

7.7.1 Functional Activities

The emphasis in a functional programming is that the activity learnt is directly applicable by the individual in the daily living situation. For instance, in many special schools it is often seen that the children are trained to put nuts and bolts together, or build a tower of wooden blocks or match shapes. But in our daily life how many times do we put a nut and a bolt together or build a tower of blocks? It is true that the general belief had been, training in such skills would improve performance in other tasks requiring such coordination. But in experience it is found that the child does not always apply the skill acquired through these activities in a generalized situation. Instead of anticipating a generalization to occur, the child could be directly trained on a particular activity that he needs to perform more frequently, such as for instance putting the nuts and bolts together in the carpentry unit with appropriate materials to be held together between the nut and bolt. Similarly, to train in self-feeding skill for a child who does not hold food item with fingers; the training should be directly with food items rather than fine motor skills with thread and beads or peg mosaic. The food Items with which the training is given should vary starting from simple ones and proceeding to complex ones such as biscuits, pieces of chapattis, dosas, idlis, small balls of rice, and dal, big pieces of vegetables and finally loose rice food like curd rice. Thus the training for holding with fingers and directing to mouth is given directly with food items and not with other fine motor activities. Such activity training is more functional and easily generalizable.

7.7.2 Age Appropriate Activities

Another important aspect of functional programming is the age appropriateness. An adolescent of 13 years with a mental age of four should be taught skills that are expected of an adolescent, rather than a preschooler. It is not proper to teach him nursery rhymes just because his mental age is four. On the other hand, depending on his physical ability, interest and other details, age appropriate skills such as gardening, packing or sorting may be taught. Through direct teaching, observation of others and the influence of television, retarded people, like everyone else learn that at certain age one should engage in a repertoire of age appropriate behaviour in addition to obvious age role behaviour; there should be a wide variety of tasks whose performance is enhanced through sheer repetition and over-learning.

Taking into account, the need for the skill, age appropriateness, generalizability and ability to maintain, if we take a look at the activities that are carried out for the mentally retarded persons in a classroom, such as putting shapes in form boards, buttoning on button frames or nesting baskets, it is seen that they are inappropriate. If these are replaced by activities directly useful for the child such as buttoning on his own self, stacking in kitchen bricks or wooden blocks in factories or workshops, sorting vegetables, foodgrains, stationery items and packing and sorting them, that will be more useful, generalizable and would lead to domestic *or* vocational skill training. Similarly, shopping skills and restaurant skills should be given in a shop or restaurant situation respectively so that it is learnt in the right place and is generalizable.

A functional programming, in short should aim at leading a child toward reduced dependence on others and provide maximum personal, social and occupational competency.

7.8 Principles of Teaching the Mentally Retarded Children

Though each mentally retarded child is different from the other and hence requires individualized instruction, there are certain fundamental principles that have to be borne in mind while imparting any skill to the child.

The Teaching must always proceed from

1. **Simple to complex:** Always start with a step in which the child is bound to meet with success. This would motivate the child to learn further. Goals which are too high for the child should be avoided. As the child learns the simpler steps, gradually introduce the complex or different steps. For instance, while teaching brushing teeth, one should start with front teeth and slowly proceed to the teeth on either side, then the inside of the teeth.

2. **Known to unknown:** The child's current level of functioning must be the starting point for teaching the skill. Consider what he knows in a skill as the

beginning for teaching the rest of the skill. Thus, if a child needs to be taught reading the word 'dog', one has to start with the identification of picture of the 'dog' which is known to the child, match the word 'dog' to the picture and let him identify the written word 'dog' in two-choice and multi-choice situation.

3. **Concrete to abstract:** Mentally retarded children have difficulty in following abstract concepts. Every teaching must have concrete examples associated with it. For instance, to give the child the concept of 'Sunday' which is abstract, associate it with activities of Sunday such as Daddy won't go to office', "The child will not have to go to school', 'There will be Hindi movie on TV in the evening' and so on.

4. **Whole to part:** Any concept taught must be introduced as a whole. Before teaching about the various parts of the body, introduce the whole self. 'This is a man.' 'This is his head.' "These are his eyes' and so on. Similarly, words must be introduced as a whole before the letters that make up the word are taught.

The above four basic principles must be remembered while teaching any task to the child. While deciding on the teaching procedure, one must stop to think, if the above four principles are followed. If not, necessary alterations need to be made in the teaching steps, for the programme to be effective.

7.9 Stages of Teaching

There are three important stages that have to be followed in teaching a task. The three stages are acquisition, maintenance and generalization.

7.9.1 Acquisition

This is the stage when a child learns a task. To be successful, one has to be very careful in structuring the teaching/learning situation during this time. There is an absolute need for consistency in teaching. The task should be carefully analysed and imparted. For instance, if a child is being taught toileting skill, during the acquisition stage, the toilet used should be the same, the cue word should be the same and initially the associated activity, such as waking up from bed, or drinking milk before toileting should be the same. This helps in conditioning the child. Variations in these will not help the child to get the cue and thus learning will be unsuccessful or delayed.

7.9.2 Maintenance

When the child is found to perform the task consistently in the correct manner in eight out of ten situations, we call this as the maintenance of the skill. Thus the child who is being toilet trained indicates and uses a particular toilet correctly on waking up from sleep or right after drinking milk, or takes hint from a particular cue word used eight times out of ten chances, he is said to be maintaining the skill.

As Horner, Williams and Knobbe (1987) note, maintenance of a skill may be influenced by the rate of opportunities for performing a skill after the training is completed They studied the maintenance of learnt skills in severely retarded children. In each student, they identified and trained in one high and one low opportunity behaviour. After training when the subjects were probed, it was found that 12 of the 17 high opportunity skills were successfully performed while only 4 of the 17 low opportunity' behaviours were successfully performed. Low opportunity rates have been hypothesized as one reason for the poor maintenance of skills by children. Therefore after the child acquires the skill, regular opportunities should be given to perform them.

7.9.3 Generalization

This is the stage when the child is able to apply the learnt skill appropriately in any given situation, that is, the ability to transfer from one situation what is acquired and maintained to other similar situations. If we take the same example of toilet training, when the child is able to use a particular toilet appropriately most of the times, he requires training in using other toilets whenever a need arises. For example, a western toilet, toilet in bus stand or train or public places, understanding other words used for toilet and using whenever he feels the need to use one. If he successfully does so, we may say that the skill has been generalised.

If a child has learnt to add 2+3 = 5 in a classroom correctly, for instance, he should be able to say that Daddy spent Rs.5, if he is told that Daddy has bought bread for Rs.2 and fruits for Rs.3. Often, one of the observations that the teachers make is that the child is very good with arithmetic in classroom, he does even 2 digit addition, but cannot say how many people are there, if there are 3 men and 4 women in a room. Why does this happen? Simply because, the addition taught on paper is not function -oriented and the child has not learnt meaningful counting that can be generalized. The teacher, while teaching addition, should take into consideration, the functional requirement of it in everyday living and let the child experience it.

The important point to remember here is that training in every task must follow these stages in sequence, failing which the child may not learn to use a skill functionally.

7.9.4 Reinforcements

Another most important aspect in training in any skill is rewarding the child appropriately for each attempt he makes. Such rewards may range from a simple smile or pat, to expensive presents to the child, depending upon the situation. A child, who is asked to get up and close the door, may be told 'good' or smiled at for obeying the instruction. Another child who has completed making a glass of juice independently as per the training given may be given the juice as a reward. Another mentally retarded person who completes packing 25 cartons of pencil boxes may be given money as a reward at the rate of 50ps./carton and so on. Behaviour is likely to repeat in a person if rewarded for the behaviour. Therefore one has to always remember to reward/reinforce the child for every desirable behaviour shown by him or the desired task performed by him. One has to be cautious not to make the rewards like bribes to the child. As he learns a task and gains competence, the reinforcement also should be altered, made intermittent and finally, but systematically faded.

7.10 Methods of Teaching

The various methods commonly used for teaching are:

- Prompting,
- Modeling,
- Shaping
- Chaining.

Though the terms seem technical they are used by all of us in the day-to-day living while teaching.

7.10.1 Shaping

Shaping means rewarding a child for a behaviour that is a step towards the desired behaviour. Thus if a child whose target behaviour is to ask verbally for water, he will be rewarded for attempting to say 'Wa initially. Gradually the reward will be given when the progress is made in reaching the target, perhaps 'wat' followed by 'water' finally. This is generally called as reinforcing successive approximations.

7.10.2 Prompting

Prompting is simply assisting a child in various degrees depending on his current level of functioning. For instance, a physical prompt is one where one physically assists the child by holding him. Helping a child by holding his hand to pick up food and direct it to his mouth is a physical prompt. On the other hand, telling him to pick up food, and telling him to direct to his mouth is a verbal prompt.

7.10.3 Modelling

Modelling is a visual prompt. When the child is watching, performing the desired task for him to follow is modelling. Brushing one's own teeth when the child is watching and making him do is an example of modelling. This is a very powerful mode of teaching. Children learn very fast if the model looks like themselves. Therefore, use peer models wherever possible for teaching a skill.

7.10.4 Chaining

Every task that is to be taught is broken down into smaller steps. This is called task analysis. Linking each subtask of the task is called chaining. Teaching the tasks from the beginning to the end is called forward chaining. In contrast teaching from the last step and moving towards the first step is called backward chaining. To quote an example, bathing skill has the following subtasks in brief: pouring water till clean, wiping dry with towel.

Linking each of these steps is chaining. If one teaches from pouring water, down to the last step, it is forward chaining. If he is taught from wiping dry with towel, it is backward chaining. Depending on the skill selected, each of the subtasks and the child's ability, forward or backward chaining can be used. All the methods used for teaching are to be reduced gradually letting the child perform independently. This is called fading.

7.11 Grouping and Programming for Education

It is difficult to achieve total homogenity in the grouping of mentally retarded children. However, groups can be formed based on the skill and ability of the child and their mental age. There can be five groups namely

- Pre-Primary,
- Primary,
- Secondary and
- Pre-vocational levels with two groups in preprimary level.

7.11.1 Pre-primary Level

The pre-primary level is one where the curriculum Includes skills required below the mental age of 5 years. Therefore, moderately and mildly retarded children below the mental age of 5 years can form one group as chronologically they may not be very old while compared to a severely retarded child with the same mental age. A 14 or 15 year old severely retarded with a mental age of 3 or 4 years will need to be separated, as physically he will be big for this group. Though the skills required to be trained will be almost the same, minor alterations based on physical needs and age appropriate activities, such as menstrual hygiene, shaving skills and so on, should be made. Therefore, preprimary level should have 2 groups with separate sections for the severely retarded ones. Skills imparted at this level are motor, self-help, language, social skills and pre-academics. A checklist developed with skills required at this level will aid in initial and continuous assessment.

7.11.2 Primary Level

This is an extension of preprimary level. Those children who achieve 80% of the skills at preprimary level will be eligible for this level. The curriculum at this level will include personal adequacy skills, functional academics and social competence. Children with a mental age of 5–7 years generally fit in this group. A checklist of skills to be trained in this level should be developed based on the local needs of the city or village, that the programme is tailored to suit the specific needs. The checklist must have provision for the continuous assessment.

7.11.3 Secondary Level

In this level, the skills developed at primary level are further strengthened and emphasis is on functional academics, vocational skills and social competence necessary for daily living such as time and money concept, reading sign boards and survival words and signing and independent travel skills, which will form important components of the curriculum. Children with a mental age of 7 to 9 years fit in this group.

7.11.4 Pre-vocational Level

Here the emphasis should be on work skills and social competence. Vocational aptitude and capability of the child should be kept in mind while planning for this level. Work routine discipline, good manners and personal skills such as appropriate grooming, shaving and menstrual hygiene and recreation skill will be strengthened at this stage.

The curricular areas given above for various groups are broad guidelines. Specific details have to be worked out based on the local needs.

7.12 Education of Mentally Retarded Children

7.12.1 Education of Mildly Mental Retarded Individual

Special Education classes at the primary level (6–8 days) provide experiences in oral language and speech development, sensory-motor development, self-awareness, group membership and social adjustment, self-care, safety, manipulation of materials, work habits, direction following, and reading readiness. Academic tasks are not generally emphasized except for beginning instruction in counting and recognition of letters or words. By the elementary level (8–13 years) mildly mentally retarded have begun to learn tool skill subjects such as reading, writing spelling, and math.

The secondary program provides increasing emphasis on preparation for work and home living, civic responsibilities, news media, use of leisure time, family life education, consumer education, finances, practical law, social roles, travel and vocational choices.

Special Education for Mildly M.R. Children should focus on

— Developing basic academic skills

— Social competence

— Personal adjustment

— Occupational adequacy.

7.12.2 Education of Severely Mentally Retarded Individuals

Emphasis should generally be on

— Language development

— Self-help skills

— Socialization

— Preparation for living and working in sheltered environments

School activities include practice in listening, following directions, communicating with others, reading and recognizing common signs and labels, counting and telling time. Self-help activities include lessons in dressing, grooming, eating, care of personal belongings, toileting, and safety. They may also engage in arts and crafts, motor and recreational activities, some vocational experiences and practice in home living.

7.12.3 Education of Profoundly Mentally Retarded Individuals

Care of profoundly mentally retarded involves treatment and education, medical prevention, and family management, which often require efforts of several professionals. These children have to be placed in residential facilities and provide as much as possible, with the right decision making, and privileges allowed for normal citizens, along with interdisciplinary care, treatment, or other lifelong extended services.

Table-7.6: Classification by Educational Expectation

Terminology	Approximate IQ Range*	Educational Expectation
Dull Normal	IQ 75 or 80 to 90	Capable of competing in school in most areas, except in the strictly academic areas in which performance is below average Social adjustment that is not noticeably different from the larger population, although in the lower segment of adequate adjustment. Occupational performance satisfactory in non technical areas, with total self support highly probable.
Educable	IQ 50 or 75 to 90	Second to fifth grade achievement in school academic areas. Social adjustment that will permit some degree of independence in the community. Occupational Sufficiency that will permit partial or total self support.
Trainable	IQ 20 to 49	Learning primarily in the areas of self help skills, very limited achievement in areas considered academic. Social adjustment usually limited to home and closely surrounding area. Occupational performance primarily in sheltered workshop or an institutional setting.
Custodial	IQ below 20	Usually unable to achieve even sufficient skills to care for basic needs. Will usually require nearly total care and supervision for duration of lifetime.

* IQ ranges represent approximate ranges, which vary to some degree, depending on the source of data.

7.12.4 Tips for Teachers of Students with Mental Retardation

— Provide alternative instructional presentations using varied examples and focus on functional skills.

— Provide opportunities for students to demonstrate understanding actively before moving to independent practice.

— Provide more opportunities for practice than appropriate if necessary for classmates.

— Use concrete examples when teaching new skills.

— Provide supportive and corrective feedback more often than necessary for classmates.

— Modify tests and evaluation measures to compensate for learning problems.

— Evaluate students' performance and regress more frequently than appropriate or necessary for classmates.

— Adapt instruction to the environments where what is being learned will be used.

— Break lessons into smaller parts when teaching complex skills.

— Be prepared to repeat teaching more frequently than necessary for peers.

7.13 Slow Learners

It is a universal truth that no two individual are identical in their behaviour and abilities. Even the identical twins differ to some extent that we call as individual difference. This difference may be physical/mental/emotional/psychological. So depending on the intellectual abilities the children are classified into; Slow Learner, Gifted Children and Mentally Retarded Children.

7.13.1 Slow Learner Defined

Slow learner is one who is unable to learn what the average child learns in the normal classroom. Slow learners are also called as "Backward Children". Their IQ ranges from 70 to 90. They are normal in their behaviour and appearance also. Their academic achievement is low when compared with that of normal children especially reading, writing and arithmetic.

According to Burt: "A slow learner is one who in his middle school career would be unable to do the work of class next below that which is normal for their age."

According to Schonnel: "Slow learner is one who compared with other pupil of same chorological age shows marked educational deficiency."

7.13.2 Characteristics of Slow Learners

On the basis of the research studies conducted in the recent years certain general characteristics of the slow learners are listed below.

7.13.2.1 Physical Characters

- **Slow Sensory motor development:** When compared with that of normal child slow learners show slow sensory motor development. They take time to make progress such as in walking, self-feeding as well as in language development.
- **More Reaction Time:** The other character of slow learners is that they take more time to respond properly to the stimulus. The stimulus may be visual or auditory or both.
- **Defect in Vision Hearing and Speech:** Slow learners find it difficult to discriminate between colour and size. They focus their eyes on the blackboard in a peculiar manner. They also find it difficult to respond when a question is asked to them.

7.13.2.2 Mental/Intellectual Characters

- **Low Memory:** One of pertinent characteristic of slow learners is poor memory; it occurs due to
  - Lack of concentration
  - Poor attention span
  - Fail to retain what they have learned
  - Poor ability in the formation of concept and general ideas.
  - Unable to plan and work on their own.
  - Poor in creativity and critical thinking.
- **Low Intelligent Quotient:** They have low IQ when compared to the normal children; they have the IQ between 70 to 90. They fail to cope with situations and to react or reason abstractly.
- **Lack of Reasoning Ability:** Inability to express his ideas through language is another important characteristic of slow learner. They also lack imagination and foresight. He has the tendency to accept suggestions of others without considering failure and past thinking.

- **Lack of Abstract Thinking:** They always prefer concrete learning than abstract learning. The important feature of slow learner is the lack of abstract thinking and ideas. They lack the ability to think in abstract ways. They have poor ability of abstract concepts.

7.13.2.3 Educational Characters

A slow learner has limited cognitive capacities. Slow learners are unable to learn what the average child can learn in the normal classroom. Due to intellectual deficiency they show slowness in one or more subject or in all subjects.

- Poor language ability – reading writing and spelling ability.
- Have negative attitude toward learning.
- They have low academic achievement.

7.13.2.4 Psychological Characters

Though educational backwardness is primarily an intellectual or scholastic deficiency it is a psychological characteristic that arises from child's personality.

- Lack of imagination
- Lack of generalization
- Lack of discrimination
- Difficulty in detection of logical statement
- Nail biting

7.13.2.5 Social and Moral Characters

When compared to that of normal children of their age, social development in slow learner is low.

- Lack of stamina to sit in class for a long time
- Fail to make friends and not at all sociable.
- Afraid and self-conscious.
- Daydream
- Make good adjustment in non-academic pursuit.

7.13.3 Identification Methods

No doubt that every classroom has some slow learners. They have mild handicappers, who come to school regularly but they are likely to become dropouts if their need are not met. To identify them psychologists and experts use various tools and techniques. They are:

7.13.3.1 Observation Method

In this method the observation of child's behaviour can be made by the (researcher) teacher, experts, which help in identifying slow learners. It is of two types 1) control 2) uncontrolled method. An observer should have the capacity to analyse and interpret the information that he gets from his observations.

7.13.3.2 Case Study Method

By this technique the total history of the child -his family, his early life and home environment are revealed. Through this method the psychologists will try to study the learning difficulties, and behavioral problems of the slow learner. By finding the causes psychologists will suggest the best remedial measures.

7.13.3.3 Intelligence Test

By the use of any standard intelligence test the intellectual level of the child can be assessed. Both verbal and nonverbal intelligence tests are used for this purpose. But mostly individual verbal tests are used so that an expert can get an idea about the mental capacities of the particular child.

7.13.3.4 Medical Examination

Before labeling the child as slow learner a thorough medical examination is essential to know the physical and physiological conditions made by a qualified medical expert.

7.13.3.5 Scholastic Tests

Evaluation in school achievement can be possible through scholastic tests. These tests can throw light on areas like arithmetic, reading, spelling, writing, languages and comprehension, so that area of problem can be known and causes of anomalies can be evaluated properly.

7.13.4 Causes

It is difficult to list out the general causes for slow learning. The causes may be hereditary as well as environmental. Some of the important causes are as follows.

- **Intelligence of Family Members:** The level of intelligence of parents as well as family members has indirect effect on the language of family members which has indirect effect on the language of the child. It is true that educated and intelligent parents can provide education, experience and material to their children according to their own intellectual level. But if the parents are not intelligent enough they may not be able to take positive steps towards the education of the child.

- **Economic Condition:** The economic status of the family also plays a major role in child's learning. The family which is economically fit will provide better opportunities for their children than that of a poor family. Children from low income families often lack sufficient sensory stimulation, perceptual experiences, adequate adult language models and a variety of other experiences, necessary for cognitive growth and development.
- **Emotional Factors:** Emotional factors contribute a lot to the slow learning of children. Through the research analysis, psychologists have confirmed that when a child comes to school he/she brings his emotional world with him. Tensions and conflicts, broken homes, relationship with parents and other family members, have an effect on the emotions of children.
- **Personal Factors:** Beside all these factors there are some personal factors which are more/less responsible for slow learning such as long illness, absence from school, lack of self-confidence etc.,
- **Environmental Causes:** Children who lack sufficient environmental stimulation usually fail to develop at normal rate.
- **Condition of School:** Poor school conditions may also lead to slowness in learning among the children.
    - Ineffective method of teaching
    - Lack of efficient and qualified teachers.
    - Bad examination and evaluation system.
    - Improper curriculum.
    - Improper classroom climate etc.

7.13.5 Education for Slow Learners

Most of the slow learners are not properly identified till they attend school. So schoolteacher, parents, social workers. counselors and psychologists should contribute to the diagnosis and treatment of slowness.

Therefore psychologists recommended the following remedial measures which are useful in guiding the slow learners.

7.13.5.1 Flexible Curriculum

Curriculum should be flexible and suit to the needs and requirements of the individual students. Slow learners are generally interested in concrete experiences. So more emphasis is given to visual and concrete aspects, which include mental work, woodwork, leatherwork, cane work, tailoring and other subjects of household work.

7.13.5.2 Remedial Instruction

Researches have shown that remedial instruction proved profitable in case of specific slowness in a specific subject/area. First deficiencies are determined and confirmed by the experts and some diagnostic tests are given

7.13.5.3 Motivation

Motivation means "arousal of interest" toward learners. Usually slow learners are unable to solve the problem because of the fear of failure. Therefore the teacher must use suitable motivational technique in classroom, develop self-confidence and remove fear from the child's mind.

7.13.5.4 Special Methods of Teaching

Educationalists as well as psychologists have conducted many experiments to suggest special methods of teaching for slow learners.

- Short and simple method of instruction based on concrete experience.
- Verbal instruction should be minimized.
- Repetitive practice/Drill work should be emphasized.
- Encouraging memorization.
- Allowing learning in his own language by doing.
- Project method should be employed in imparting education to slow learners.
- Educational excursions to the place of historical geographical scientific and cultural interest are conducted, to give real life experience.
- Use of audiovisual aids such as pictures, models, charts, films to make language more understandable to the slow learner.

7.13.5.5 Healthy Environment

One of the remedial measures for slow learner is to provide rich environment for learning both at home and at school. The school atmosphere should be healthy and reasonably free and democratic which help to stimulate/ interest towards learning.

7.13.5.6 Nonpromotion

Some of the educationalists are of the opinion of non-promotion of slow learners. But many of the educationalists opposed this view. Due to detention in the same class, child perceives himself as incapable which brings negative attitude towards learning. Therefore instead of no promotion, remedial teaching should be thought of as a better alternative.

7.13.5.7 Periodical Medical Checkup

Physical abnormalities are one of the important factors for slow learning. So school authorities and management should arrange for free medical checkup in the schools so that particular abnormality could be detected early and appropriate treatment given in time.

7.13.5.8 Individual Attention

Slow learners should be given individual attention. Teachers should emphasize on recognition of individual difference among students. They should respect the individuality of the child, and should be very kind and sympathetic towards them. Students should be allowed to proceed at their own pace of learning, under teacher guidance; Complete freedom should be given to slow learners but under teachers supervision.

7.13.5.9 Home Visit by the Teacher

In order to make family environment healthy and happy the teacher should visit learners homes and should advise the parents, and suggest some remedial steps to parents of slow learner to modify the environment at home.

7.13.6 Strategies for Educating Slow Learners

Here are some strategies that might be used to help slow learners succeed academically.

— Slow learners need to be academically challenged like everybody else.

— Each student's strengths and weaknesses need to be identified and specifically addressed.

— Slow learners need to be provided with an enriched environment through numerous experiences and opportunities for learning. Especially in case of a maturational lag, development is stimulated through multiple opportunities for learning.

— Teachers may design creative activities that will improve memory, attention, problem-solving skills, comprehension, language development, etc.

— Slow learners may be paired up with peer tutors who will provide study guides, lecture notes, copies of overheads, etc.

— If needed, slow learners may be provided with extra time or assigned less work.

— Longer assignments may be broken down into shorter ones. A 30-minute long assignment may be broken down into six five-minute assignments.

— The slow learner may be allowed more time to understand and think through the instructional materials.

— Teachers may need to use simple concrete language when teaching and giving directions to slow learners. A series of directions need to be broken down and given one at a time.

— Slow learners may be asked to repeat directions to ensure understanding.

— Slow learners may need advance organizers in order to understand important points that are going to be covered during instructional time.

— Teaching may focus on a single concept and gradually move to more abstract ideas. When the student experiences problems in understanding the concept, the teacher may check if the student has prerequisite skills needed to relate to the concept.

— In teaching new concepts to slow learners, teachers may use manipulatives or demonstrations.

— Teachers may use a variety of activities to teach and reinforce the concepts taught.

— Teachers should repeat information especially with those learners who experience maturational lags.

— Information should be presented in bite-sizes to slow learners. Too much of information at one time will confuse the slow learner.

— Teachers need to present information through visual and auditory channels, and kinesthetically. Eiszler (1983) claims that varying teaching strategies to address all channels promote learning no matter what students' preferences of cognitive styles are. Dunn (1979) showed that all learners tend to increase their academic success when varied multi-sensory methods were used as a form of instruction.

— Computers and other technology applications help the slow learner in all academic areas. Today's different kinds of software help with tutoring, drill, simulation,, and practice activities. Technology is very useful because it is self-pacing and individualized, and increases time on task. With its sound and color effects, it is very motivating to the slow learner (Smith, Polloway, Patton & Dowdy, 2007).

These are just a handful of techniques that may help slow learners achieve academic success. What is important in the education of slow learners is that teachers evaluate and understand the individual needs of each student, and use appropriate teaching strategies that will maximize the educational outcomes of this population of students.

Learning Disabilities

8.1 Background

The new born infant is an active organism who is genetically endowed at birth with biological intelligence, capable of adaptively interacting with the environment. The maturation of structural and functional changes within the body systems together with the effects of cumulative experience, facilitates developmental progress. In the process of development, learning also takes place. Learning can take place in a formal situation or in an informal situation. Learning in formal situation takes place in the teaching-learning process where the child is given utmost importance.

Learning is knowledge got by study, by experience, or by teaching. When children fail to learn, they impair the capacity to profit from new experiences. They are not able to learn because something prevents them from doing something, may be internal or external causes. This is termed as LEARNING DISABILITY (LD).

It is very difficult to recognise the child with learning disability when it is too young. Once the child starts going to school, is participating in the teaching-learning process, and other co-curricular activities, these learning disabilities show up and are recognised.

The phrase "Learning Disability" was coined in 1963 by SAMUEL KIRK while he was addressing a group of parents at the conference on exploration into the problems of the perceptually handicapped children. He used the phrase learning disability to refer to children who were hyperactive and who had reading difficulty or disorders of language. This was an attempt to diagnose children simply and behaviorally. It was also the beginning of the learning disability movement which was to bring about considerable social, educational, economic and legislative changes.

Five movements have significantly influenced the field of LD; perceptual, neurological, multisensory, psycholinguistics and precise teaching. Prior to understanding the definition of LD, it may help us to put it in perspective if we briefly know about these movements.

Some professionals attributed this type of inability in reading and academic subjects to perceptual problems. Due to deficits in visual or motor perception such children fail to read.

There are several researchers who maintained that 'LD is result of neurologic disorders. Mykle Bust conducted considerable research in this area.

Multisensory disorder specialists believe that several sensory channels should be used to instruct some youngsters. Samuel Orton, a neuropathologist, was one of the most influential advocates of this view.

Several researchers have taken the position that learning to receive and express information is a prerequisite to reading, writing and spelling. The curriculum can then be arranged accordingly. Kirk was the main advocate of this view. This idea of psycholinguistics is probably his best contribution to understanding the area of learning disability.

Many in the field of LD adopted precision teaching approach. This group of specialists are not greatly interested in neurology but believe in directing attention to behaviours such as speaking, writing and walking.

These five movements give us an idea of how varied approaches on learning disability emerged over a period of time.

The child thus can be considered as learning disabled if

a) He has considerable difficulty in understanding or using spoken language, reading, writing, spelling and/or arithmetic during the developmental period (before 16 years of age).

b) He is free from visual, hearing or motor disability, mental retardation, severe emotional problems,

c) He has adequate facilities, interest and motivation to learn.

d) He has atleast 2 years of instructions/ training or is backward by atleast 2 years in the school in spite of regular attendance.

8.2 Learning Disability Defined

Historically the concept of a learning disability was narrowly defined but in recent years physicians, psychologists and educators have been increasingly likely to describe any academic difficulty as a learning disability. When the teacher observes that a pupil is consistently unable to keep up with classroom assignments she refers to difficulty such as "Unable to progress in arithmetic even though his work in all other areas is average" or "does average work in reading and other subjects but consistently fails in spelling," where he cannot differentiate such words as lake and like. The problem often centres around a marked lack of attainment in a particular area in the face of average achievement in other areas to indications of atleast average intellectual ability. This lack of attainment in a particular area is termed as learning disability.

8.2.1 Definition of Learning Disability

- Samuel Kirk first defined a learning disability as a disorder or a retardation of development affecting specific academic area, such as reading, spelling, arithmetic, and writing as well as delays in language in general.
- Bateman (1964) later offered a definition that advanced a quantitative basis for defining the concept of learning disabilities. A child was considered learning disabled when he or she exhibited "An educationally significant discrepancy between their estimated intellectual potential and the actual level of performance related to basic disorders in the learning process". Bateman's definition added a method of discriminating learning disabled from normal children.
- CLEMENTS (1966): The level of the intellectual potential that must be present in order that the underachievement be labeled as a learning disability – near average, average, or above average general intelligence with certain learning or behavioural disabilities ranging from mild to severe.

Many school systems have adopted the Bateman and Clements criteria for selecting children for Special Education classes in learning disability. The IQ scores of the learning disabled children are two years or 2 grade levels below the expected level based on IQ.

Since the 1980s the broad definition of LD formulated by the US National Joint Committee on LD (NJCLD, 1981/1988) with representation from all concerned disciplines has been widely used. It reads as follows:

> LD is a general term that refers to a heterogeneous group of disorders manifested by significant difficulties in the acquisition and use of listening, speaking, reading, writing, reasoning or mathematical abilities. These disorders are intrinsic to the individual, presumed to be due to central nervous system dysfunction and may occur across the life

> span. Problems in self-regulatory behaviors, social perception and social interaction may exist with learning disabilities but do not by themselves constitute a learning disability. Although learning disabilities may occur concomitantly with other handicapping conditions (for example sensory impairment, mental retardation, serious emotional disturbance) or with extrinsic influences such as cultural differences, insufficient or inappropriate instruction, they are not the result of these conditions or influences (Wong, 1996).

This broad definition reflects a gradual shift from the traditional categorical approach which broadly characterised children with learning disability into those with 'specific reading retardation' and those with 'general reading backwardness' to a newer (1990s) dimensional approach of individual differences in reading achievement. This latter approach has been increasingly adopted by most researchers but has yet to be adopted by practitioners.

The Federal Government of the USA has defined learning disability in Public Law 94-142 (Education for All Handicapped Children Act) as follows:

> Specific learning disability means a disorder in one or more of basic psychological processes involved in understanding or in using language, spoken or written, which may manifest itself as an imperfect ability to listen, think, speak, read, write, spell or to do mathematical calculations. The term includes such conditions as perceptual handicap, brain injury, minimal brain dysfunction, dyslexia and developmental aphasia. The phrase does not include children who have learning problems which are primarily the result of visual, hearing or motor handicaps, of mental retardation, of emotional disturbances or of environmental, cultural or economic disadvantages (Education for All Handicapped Children Act, 1975).

Nevertheless, there is no universally accepted definition of learning disability, because the criteria for diagnosis of individual disorders varied from time to time.

8.3 Characteristics Dysfunction of Learning Disability

8.3.1 Visual Spatial Orientation

From birth infants begin to understand spatial relations by moving their bodies. By employing sensory cues they construct a world of objects and bodies. This stage according to Piaget has been called as sensory motor stage.

Perception is a process whereby the central nervous system organizes sensory data. Visual perception enables the ability to recognise or discriminate patterns and relationships in space. It plays a central role in learning, particularly in earliest grades. The child's perception of spatial relationships entails the appreciation of the properties , relative position, size etc.

The ability to differentiate visually between symbols or letters is a critical prerequisite for reading and ultimately for writing.

Another accompanying factor of visual perception is visual motor coordination. There, are many tasks in which a child must obtain data through vision and then utilize this information to plan and execute a motor movement. (a process called praxis) Ex: Catching a ball, tying shoe laces, buttoning shirt.

8.3.1.1 Visual Spatial Dysfunction

Children with delays in development of visual-perceptual or visual perceptual motor function may be difficult to identify. Initial manifestations may include difficulty, learning how to tie shoe laces, problems with learning discrimination between left and right, confusion and anxiety over recognition of letters, trouble in catching a ball or riding a bicycle, or delay in acquiring skills in drawing or copying. Ultimately a child with visual spatial disorganisation may encounter problems in learning to read. This might first involve confusion between similar letters such as 'b' & 'd' or p and q. There might be difficulty in recognizing certain words despite repeated exposures like – "left and felt" or in developing stable associations between sounds and visual symbols. Visual spatial disorganisation may in time interfere with writing and can effect arithmetic process

8.3.2 Temporal Sequential Organization and Memory

Just as children acquire a schema for vision and space, a schema for time and sequence emerges during development. Much of the child's information gathering and daily activity depend upon sequence, i.e. routine order of meals, days of the week, months of the year, and understand concepts such as before and after, today and tomorrow and next week. etc. Sequential organization is closely related to memory. The retention of sequential information is essential for following instructions in school and at home. There are visual sequences *e.g.* objects or symbols, musical notes.

Memory is fundamental to learning. 3 basic stages of memory have been described.

1. Reception of information
2. Data storage
3. Retrieval – (recall to mind)

For learning children must be able to use appropriate stimuli to file these data for later use, and when an appropriate occasion arises, to retrieve what has been stored without undue effort or delay.

8.3.2.1 Dysfunction

Children with deficits in sequential organizations may show serious problems with short term and intermediate memory. Parents and teachers complain that children with this disability seldom follow instructions, seem unable to retain what has just been said or get overloaded or bewildered when a series of directions is presented. Such children may show maladaptive classroom behaviours and may be labelled lazy or may show signs of frustrations.

This disorder can interfere with spelling and arithmetic. An ability to grasp the concept of numbers or a predicable order within a word may result. Children with deficits of visual memory may retain only vague impressions of the configuration of words. Other problems can interfere with memory. It is difficult to separate problems of attention from those of retention.

8.3.3 Auditory Processing

Capacity to decode words and sentences dramatically facilitates children's understanding and assimilation of their surroundings, their perception of themselves etc. In addition children acquire "syntax" (arrangement of words in sentences showing their connections and relation) or a sense of rules of grammar by which words are linked together to give them meaning.

8.3.3.1 Auditory Dysfunction

Auditory perceptual difficulties can include problems with auditory discrimination and with the decoding of complex syntactical structures. The child may not be able to discriminates the short vowel sound in 'PIN' and 'PEN'. They may be slow to associate meanings with words. Affected children may be restless and inattentive in noisy environments.

8.3.4 Expressive Language

Useful language depends on the capacity to call up relevant words, arrangements of these words in phrases or sentences. Development of ideas in a meaningful sequence and planning and execution of the highly complex motor act of speech. During school years written spoken language comes to occupy the stage in education.

8.3.4.1 Language Disabilities

Receptive Language Disability

Receptive language function is the interpretation of auditory stimuli in extraction of meaning from words and sentences. The first step involves selective attention to human speech sounds. This is followed by auditory discrimination. With lack of good language reception, children with language disabilities may have trouble analyzing words phonetically. Significant delays in reading, spelling, and written can result from relative subtle receptive weaknesses in the language area.

Expressive Language Disability

Disorder of expressive language includes:

1. *Deficits of resonance:* Abnormal oral-nasal sound balances, most commonly heard as hypernasality or hyponasality.
2. *Voice disorders:* Deviations in quality pitch or loudness, which may have psychologic or physiologic bases.
3. *Fluency disorders:* Disruption in the natural flow of connected speech, most commonly as stuttering.
4. *Articulation disorder:* A major group of problems in which the production of speech sounds is imprecise.
5. *Language disorders:* Problems in comprehension and manipulation of the symbol system of the language community.

During the course of normal language development all children show some evidence of non-fluent speech or descriptions in the natural flow of language. It may consists of repetitions of sounds. It should not be mistaken for a disorder.

Stuttering is a disorder in which the flow of speech is interrupted abnormally by repetition or prolongation of sound. Mild hesitation is normally present in the speech of most individuals. But when the hesitations increase in frequency and severity and calls attention to itself, it is labelled stuttering.

Disorders of articulation are the most common encountered speech problems in children, and involve three types of errors.

1. *Substitution:* Replacement of one sound with another (i.e. weight for light)
2. *Omissions:* Failure to produce certain speech sounds (i.e. boo for book).
3. *Distortions:* Inappropriate sounds replacing the correct one. Often children with this disability are shy, they rely on gesturers and on communication

through single words or phrases; at times they appear to speak in telegraphic style, deleting words. Another type of disability is that the child cant say what he wants. This is word finding problem called "Dysnomia".

8.3.5 Motor Disabilities

Inefficiencies of fine motor performance may directly affect the ability to write, to copy from a blackboard and to draw. Grasp of the pencil may be awkward or ineffective, catching a ball may not be possible. Tying shoe laces, balancing the body on one foot, drawing vertical lines connecting horizontal lines may not be possible. This disability is due to the lack of planning and execution of sequential motor acts, and the coordination and integration of muscles activity with sensory feedback and memory.

8.3.6 Selective Attention

Attention is a continuing and self-reinforcing process of selection. At any given instant a host of internal and external stimuli compete for attention. They include –immediate auditory or visual sensations, data stored in long or short-term memory, impulses originating in viscera, muscles, joints or fantasies feeling, and associations. With the process of selection one or a few of these inputs take priority, while the others are relegated to the background or pushed beyond conscious awareness.

The process of selective attention allows children to focus purposefully and for appropriate lengths of time on incoming data that will lead them toward productive activities or learning. There is adequate resistance to distraction.

Children with effective selectivity for activity may be exploratory, purposeful, efficient and goal – directed much of the time, the level and quality of their activity adjusting to changing demands and expectation. The concept of selectivity of attention and activity is an outgrowth of study of hyperactivity syndromes, and of increasing concern with quality rather than the amount of activity.

8.3.6.1 Attention Deficit Hyperactivity Disorder

The effective controls of activity and attention may or may not be associated with learning handicaps, but chronic inattention and poorly controlled activity are frequent concomitants of academic and social failure in school-aged children. These children show excessive impulsivity, or an exaggerated inability to plan, to reflect, or to delay gratification. They may become quite disruptive and difficult to manage. They are most commonly described as hyperkinetic or overactive. Their activity may be purposeless and inappropriate, within a given situation. They have free flight of ideas, impersistance at tasks, extreme insatiability (a continual state of want), easy fatigability, chronic sleep problem, poor self-monitoring and relative resistance to effects of rewards or punishment.

8.4 Areas of Performance

8.4.1 Reading Disability (Dyslexia)

Reading Disability is the most frequently reported subtype of learning disability. Incidence of reading problems ranges as high as 2/3 of all learning disabled children. Hinshelwood used the phrase "Word blindness" to refer to inability to read visible words. He observed that a word blind patient could write fluently to dictation, although he could not read what he himself has written. Later Hinshelwood distinguished between complete word blindness – Alexia, which is the absolute inability to interpret written words or printed language and partial word blindness dyslexia, in which there may be great difficulty but not inability to read.

Table-8.1: Common Types of Learning Disabilities

Dyslexia	Difficulty processing language	Problems reading, writing, spelling, speaking
Dyscalculia	Difficulty with math	Problems doing math problems, understanding time, using money
Dysgraphia	Difficulty with writing	Problems with handwriting, spelling, organizing ideas
Dyspraxia (Sensory Integration Disorder)	Difficulty with fine motor skills	Problems with hand–eye coordination, balance, manual dexterity
Auditory Processing Disorder	Difficulty hearing differences between sounds	Problems with reading, comprehension, language
Visual Processing Disorder	Difficulty interpreting visual information	Problems with reading, math, maps, charts, symbols, pictures

8.4.1.1 Characteristic Factors of Dyslexia

Benton lists the critical errors that are most often made by dyslexics.

- Defective visual discrimination of graphemes. (printed letters)
- Faulty oral reading of vowels and consonants; vowels are more often mislead than consonants.
- Reversals in the reading of letters such as n for u, p for q, d for b and also monosyllabic word reversals such as no for on, was for saw.

- Omissions and additions of words in oral sentence reading. Excessive slowness in reading.
- Poor retention of material that has been read
- Difficulty with spontaneous writing and writing to dictation.

It is helpful to know the factors that have been hypothesized to underline these errors. They include psychological factors that have been found to correlate with reading difficulty to have been regarded as the fundamental cognitive and performance deficits underlying dyslexia. Four of these deficits are frequently described as characteristics of dyslexics. These are deficits in

- Visual perception, cross model sensory integration, temporal sequencing and verbal language development. Other characteristics are right and left orientation, neurologic dysfunction, figure localization, intellectual functioning, unresolved conflict and familial genetic factors.

8.4.2 Writing Disabilities (Dysgraphia)

A variety of dysfunctions may underlie disorders of writing. Some children have multiple deficits, others have isolated or discrete problems; the common disturbances are

- Weakness of fine motor control; difficulty with eye hand coordination, defective or insufficient pencil grasp, or problems in executing the motor patterns needed to form letters, numbers or words.
- Disorders of visual-motor integration; children may have problems perceiving visual configuration and converting them into a blueprint (revisualization) from which written words or sentences can be drawn. Such children may be able to spell, narrate and read with fluency, but still encounter obstacles in writing. This condition has been called "DYSGRAPHIA".
- Spatial organization; children with visual spatial disorganization may have difficulty arranging words, letters or sentences in an orderly manner on page.

8.4.3 Mathematics Disability (Dyscalculia)

Children with visual processing problems may have impaired visual recognition of numbers; those with visual spatial problems encounter obstacles in arranging numbers or columns of numbers systematically on a page or many have difficulties with the geometric aspects of mathematics.

Children with sequencing problems have particular difficulty learning the multiplication tables and integrating basic number problems. Children with fine motor problems have difficulty aligning numbers for addition, subtraction, and multiplication.

Higher order conceptualization is critical in arithmetic. Children with arithmetic disorders may have difficulty conceptualizing the notion of conservation of quantity. Ex: (1 Rupee – 100 Ps).

8.4.4 Social Interaction Disability

Children with gross motor delays may have difficulty establishing gratifying social interaction. Impulsive and inattentive children are often rejected by their peers and may experience isolation as early as preschool years. Children with receptive and expressive language difficulties may have problems in the verbal aspects of relationship building as may those with stuttering, stammering and other articulation problems.

Some children may lack the capacity or sensitivity to read facial expressions of approval or disapproval, to perceive and respond to the needs of others.

8.5 Causes of Learning Disability

Heinicke has described four widely accepted hypotheses about learning disorders. The four hypotheses are that learning disability results from

1. Maturation lag.
2. Minimal brain dysfunction,
3. Inherited neurologic disorder (constitutional organicity,)
4. Psychological conflict

8.5.1 Maturation Lag

According to this hypothesis the affected child demonstrates a slower rate of acquisition of reading ability, motor co-ordination and right-left orientation. The rate at which children learn is considered while assessing maturation. If the child performs less considerably when compared to normal developmental test then it is said there is a maturation lag – lag in the maturation of structural and functional changes within the central nervous system together with the effects of cumulative experience.

8.5.2 Minimal Brain Dysfunctions

This hypothesis says that learning disability is caused by a type of brain dysfunction that it is so minimal that it is difficult to detect except through behaviour observation. Subtle aberrations in the brain may have developed during perinatal period of the nervous system. Any damage to the brain during delivery by using forceps may also cause minimal brain dysfunction. High BP, low oxygen supply to brain, foetal distress during delivery may cause death of cell in the brain which leads to minimal brain dysfunction.

8.5.3 Constitutional Organicity

This hypothesis focusses on central nervous system deficit and the cause is innate neurologic organisation. It may be due to faulty genetic constitution. Learning disability may also run in families.

8.5.4 Psychological Conflict

The fourth hypothesis is advanced by psycho-dynamically oriented theorists. They say that learning disorder may be caused by inadequate resolution of conflicts that are either intra psychic or environmental. Blan Chard found both internal or intrapsychic conflict (such as overuse of neurotic defenses) and external or environmental conflicts (such as disturbed family interaction) in learning disabled children.

8.6 Identification of Learning Disabled Children

The following inclusion criteria are used in identification of L.D. Children.

- Normal intelligence: performance or verbal IQ equal or greater than normal range.
- Normal sensory functioning (after correction).
- Retardation in learning areas such as reading, writing and arithmetic. Minimum of 2 years of retardation when compared to relative chronological age.
- Average or above average in socio-economic status.
- Not suffering from serious emotional disturbance.
- Adequate educational opportunity.
- At or above 8 years of age.
- Exhibits symptoms of perceptual deficits.

8.7 Assessment of Learning Disabilities

The phrase 'learning disabilities' arose from the need to identify and help children who were scholastically backward in school and yet eluded the categories of exceptionality. A number of terms and definitions emerged from the multidisciplinary base adopted for helping children with learning disabilities. Many attempts were made to describe and define this phrase. All these definitions refer to the discrepancies between the child's potential for learning and his actual achievement. From this point of view, an assessment of mental abilities becomes imperative.

The Wechsler Intelligence Scale for Children (WISQ (Wechsler, 1949) is the most commonly used test with learning disabled children. It comprises 12 subtests both verbal and nonverbal; the subtest patterns have been of interest to many investigators. Wide differences between verbal and nonverbal abilities have frequently been reported. Variability may occur on both dimensions; the verbal score may be significantly higher than the nonverbal score or vice versa. Brown (1986) noted that children with reading disabilities scored lower on verbal IQ compared to performance IQ. Heinicke (1972) observed that children with markedly low verbal IQ exhibited speech, hearing or reading disabilities.

For the purpose of identifying children with learning disabilities, Bannatyne (1968) proposed the recategorising of WISC Scale scores into spatial, conceptual and sequential categories. The spatial score was derived from three performance subtest scale scores –object assembly, block design and picture compilation, which usually involve the ability to manipulate objects perceptually either concretely or symbolically. Comprehension, similarities and vocabulary comprised the conceptual score. This category represents the child's ability to respond verbally. Digit span coding and picture arrangement comprised the sequential category. The subtests tap the child's ability to process short-term memory items and storage of auditory and visual stimuli. Bannatyne's sample of dyslexic children scored highest on spatial, lowest on sequential and their scores on conceptual were in the middle.

Professional diagnosis is the first step towards appropriate teaching and progress for the dyslexic. Besides intelligence tests, a range of tests is administered to determine the various strengths and deficits of the child in academic skills. These tests include reading, writing, comprehension and spelling.

8.7.1 Reading

Reading is one of the most important skills a child learns at school. The fact, however, is that hundreds of children face difficulties in reading and are poor readers. Harris and Sipay (1980) observed that 10 to 15 percent of children have reading disabilities. Reading requires the child to recognise the word and decode the printed letters to match letters and words with sounds and comprehend the meaning of what is read.

According to Wallace and Larsen (1978), detailed information about a particular child's reading skills can be obtained by administering either a formal individual reading test or an informal teacher constructed test. Formal tests such as Diagnostic Reading Scales (Spache, 1981), Durrell Analysis of Reading Difficulty (Durrell & Catterson, 1980), Stanford Diagnostic Reading Test (Karlsen, Madden, & Gardner, 1977) and Woodcock Reading Mastery Tests (Woodcock, 1973) provide detailed information about a child's abilities in word recognition, word analysis, comprehension and related components of general reading skills. These tests, however, have been developed and standardised on samples in western countries and their utility and applicability with Indian children is suspect. As India has cultural diversity, teachers can effectively develop their own informal reading inventories; such informal methods are inexpensive, flexible and easily administered. An informal reading inventory can be prepared by carefully selecting graded reading passages appropriate for reading levels from primer through Grade 8. Such an inventory can be used to determine the grade level of the child and to determine the types of errors made by the child. Hammill and Bartel (1982) provided a list of directions for designing an informal inventory.

8.7.1.1 Selection of a Standard Basal Series

Any series that goes from primer to the eighth grade level may be used.

a) Materials that the child has not previously used should be included.

8.7.1.2 Selection of Passages

a) Choose a selection that makes a complete story.

b) Choose about 50 words at the primary level, 100 words at the first and second level and about 150 words at the upper level.

8.7.1.3 Construction of Questions

a) Build five questions for each passage.

b) Avoid yes and no questions.

c) Construct three kinds of questions at each level; factual 40%, inferential 40% and vocabulary 20% (Mercer & Mercer, 1985).

Independent reading levels, that is, reading with understanding and ease without assistance determine the reading level of the child. Specific reading errors as well as the actual number of errors can be determined by using a scoring sheet with commonly found errors, such as

i) Word by word reading.

ii) Incorrect phrasing.

iii) Poor pronunciation.

iv) Omissions.

v) Repetitions.

vi) Inversion or reversals.

vii) Insertions.

viii) Substitutions.

ix) Basic sight words not known.

x) Sight vocabulary not up to grade level.

xi) Guesses at words.

xii) Consonant sounds not known.

xiii) Vowel sounds not known.

xiv) Vowel pairs and/or consonant clusters not known (digraphs, diphthongs, blends).

xv) Lacks structural analysis (morphology).

xvi) Unable to use context clues.

xvii) Others/specify (Ekwall, 1985).

Another method commonly used for reading assessment is the Cloze procedure. In this procedure every nth word in a reading passage, beginning with the second sentence, is replaced with a blank line. Children are expected to read the passage and fill in the blanks with correct words. This method can be meaningfully used only with older children who have developed sufficient reading and comprehension skills.

8.7.2 Writing

Writing is a tool for communication. It is both a skill as well as a means of self-expression. The complex process of writing integrates visual, motor and conceptual abilities, and is a major medium through which children demonstrate their knowledge in academic subjects. Classroom instruction in handwriting usually begins at the kindergarten level. Until approximately Grade 3, instruction is given on the formation of letters, numbers and words. After Grade 3 greater emphasis is placed on writing as a form of meaningful self-expression.

Mercer and Mercer (1985) listed common errors observed among children with writing disabilities. These are slowness, incorrect directionality of letters and numbers, too much or too little slant, spacing difficulty, messiness, and inability to write on a horizontal line, illegible letters, too much or too little pencil pressure and mirror writing.

Assessment of writing is divided into two broad categories. First is assessing the child's ability to copy written passages which are appropriate to his age. A checklist can be used for error analysis.

8.7.2.1 Checklist for Writing Assessment

i) No space between words

ii) Substitute letters.

iii) Reverses letters/words.

iv) Omits letters.

v) Adds letters.

vi) Poor punctuation.

vii) No or wrong capital letters.

viii) Poor letter formations.

ix) Others:

  a) Poor slanting.

  b) Messy, too many cancellations.

  c) Line quality.

  d) Holding of pen.

  e) Placement of paper.

Many children with poor writing skills also have poor co-ordination and visual perceptual skills. Visual perception is the ability to give meaning to what is seen. Visual perceptual skills include visual discrimination, visual memory, visual spatial relationships, visual form constancy, visual sequential memory, visual figure ground and visual closure.

Another aspect of writing involves written expression. To assess expressive writing skills, Myklebust (1965) proposed that the child may be asked to write a story following the presentation of a picture and the written material scored for productivity, correctness and meaning. The number of words, sentences and words per sentence are computed for productivity. Capitals, words usage, word endings and punctuation are judged for correctness, and the story content is appraised for meaning. In informal assessment, subjective judgement is used to assess the age levels in writing expressions.

8.7.3 Spelling

Spelling refers to the formation of words through a traditional arrangement of letters. In general, spelling instruction is introduced at the beginning of Grade 2 or at the end of Grade 1. The ability to spell is essential because it allows the child to read correctly what is written. Carpenter and Miller (1982) observed that children who had trouble recognising words in reading had poor spelling skills. They also noted that sometimes children were able to read but were unable to reproduce words in spelling. Reading is a decoding process in which the child receives clues for word recognition. Spelling is an encoding process in which the child responds without being shown the visual stimulus.

According to Ekwall (1985), in order to spell a child should be able to read the word, possess knowledge and skill in certain relationships of phonics and structural analysis, apply phonic generalisations, visualise the word and possess motor ability to write the word. He added that spelling difficulties may be due to problems in visual memory, auditory memory, auditory and visual discrimination and motor skills.

In informal assessment, the teacher selects a sample of 15 to 20 words from each basal reader textbook. Words from each list are dictated to students, until six consecutive words are missed. A student's achievement level is assessed by determining the highest level at which a score of 90 to 100 percent is obtained. The teaching can start at a level at which the child obtains a score of 75 to 80 percent. Lack of specific spelling skills can be identified by analysing various spelling errors.

A checklist may be successfully used to analyse the child's performance for specific error pattern in spelling.

A. Spelling errors primarily due to auditory channel deficits: Substitutes t for d, f for v, sh for ch (auditory discrimination) Does not hear subtle differences in or discriminate between sounds and often leaves vowels out of two syllable words – for example spells pises for polish (auditory accuracy or discrimination).

Discerns the beginning or ending of a word but not the middle of the word, which may be missing or spelt wrong -for example spells Rd for Rand (auditory acuity and/or discrimination).

Confuses vowels —for example, spells bit as bet (auditory discrimination).

Omits the second letter in blends, spelling fled as fed (auditory acuity and/or discrimination.)

Uses a synonym, such as house for home (auditory visual association).

Omits word endings such as ed, s and ing (cultural or auditory discrimination).

Takes wild guesses with little or no relationship between the letters or words (auditory visual channel deficits).

The misspellings are typically nonphonetic because the students often lack phonetic skills.

B. Spelling errors primarily due to visual channel deficits: Visualizes the beginning or the ending of words but omits the middle of the word -for example, spells hapy for happy (visual memory).

- Gives the correct letters but in the wrong sequence. The word 'the' may be written as teh or hte (visual memory sequence).
- Reverses letters or words for example b for d, or no for on.
- Inverts letters or writing u for n, m for w (usually visual memory but also could be either visual discrimination or spatial).
- Mixes up capitals and small letters cAt (poor transitional teaching or visual memory).

Spelling words phonetically that are nonphonetic in configuration – for example tuff for tough (visual memory). The misspellings are typically phonetic and therefore often intelligible, although incorrect (Mann, Suiter, & McClung, 1985).

8.7.4 Developmental Screening

Developmental screening has two major goals. The first goal is to identify high risk children and design intervention procedures. The second goal is to minimise the risk of exposing children to academic failures when they enter formal academics.

Checklists used for developmental screening help teachers to observe children and record their performance in various areas and identify the difficulties faced by them. These tests have productive validity and assess skills needed by children to succeed in school. Several such checklists are available for classroom teachers. When a child of 6 years of age or below, initiated into the formal academic learning of reading and writing, faces problems in learning, a developmental screening is advisable. Developmental screening assesses the child's readiness skills for academic learning.

What constitutes an effective assessment? There is consensus among researchers and clinicians about certain factors that need to be assessed. Any assessment procedure for learning disabilities requires informal observation, diagnostic case history and formal testing. The diagnostic case history includes pre- and postnatal history, birth history, developmental milestones, academic history, family history and social and emotional stresses.

Formal testing assesses areas like attention, auditory and visual memory, fine motor skills, oral language, number skills, cognition, reading, writing, comprehension and spelling.

Torgesen (1985) emphasised the importance of dynamic interactive strategies based assessment. Such methods examine the process by which children arrive at solutions. This allows the teacher to train children in new strategies to master the task. In addition to comprehensive developmental history, formal evaluation of information processing and psychological assessment, the school context must also be taken into consideration. It is equally important that the examiner is aware of the curriculum demands on and expectations from the child.

In most cases the goal of assessment is to identify the student's strengths and weaknesses. By describing the assessment data in detail, it is possible to present a highly individualised profile of the child's cognitive as well as personality style and make specific recommendations as to the way in which the child learns best.

8.8 Remediation of Learning Disabilities

8.8.1 Remediation of Reading Disabilities

Once an assessment has been done and conclusions drawn, the student should participate in a well organised remedial programme. Based on the student's level of reading, it is ideal to begin at the independent reading level. Ideally, the teacher should begin with word recognition skills. Five major skills are necessary for the development of independence in word recognition:

a) recognising whole words by sight,

b) using context clues,

c) analysing words phonetically,

d) using structural analysis of words, and

e) using the dictionary.

8.8.1.1 Word Recognition

According to DeBoer and Dallman (1967), it is easier for a student to recognise larger visual shapes first and examine details only when the larger configuration cannot be readily identified. Thus, it is easier for a student to recognise the word 'cat' as a unit than to discover the phonetic values of the three letters and to combine them. This method is known as the sight method. Several strategies are used to teach reading through the sight method. Multisensory approaches are also used.

8.8.1.2 Phonic Approach

Instruction in phonic analysis should be systematic. The student first learns the sounds of the English letters with differences in vowels and consonants. He is subsequently taught to blend the sounds together to make meaningful words. As many phonetic rules as applicable to the student's experience are taught. The sequence is as follows:

1. The basic sounds of speech or phonemes.
2. Digraphs or symbols made up of two letters representing one phoneme sound.
3. Diphthongs or two vowels blended together to produce almost a single phoneme sound.
4. Consonant blends or a combination of two or three consonants blended in such a way that the identity of each letter remains intact.

Once the student has mastered these, he is taught to syllabicate so that he can blend the phonemes to make meaningful words.

8.8.1.3 Use of Context Clues

For a visual learner, the teacher may use pictures and sketches to provide relevant clues to the student. The teacher may also provide verbal clues for auditory learners. However, the teacher should bear in mind that an adequate background is necessary for using verbal and visual clues.

8.8.1.4 Structural Analysis

In structural analysis, the student is taught to recognise the word presented by identifying the root word therein. In effect, he breaks the word into smaller words. This method of recognising words may be used when the reader has reached a certain level of reading ability.

8.8.1.5 Developing Comprehension

Once the student has attained some degree of mastery over word recognition he has to be instructed in reading with comprehension. The student is taught to break the sentences given into simple phrases, to stress the correct syllables with the correct intonation. These help the learner to select the main idea of the matter that he has read. The next step is to read to select significant details. This is followed by learning to read to answer questions. Developing comprehension is summed up in the following:

- Reading to get the main idea.
- Reading to select significant ideas.
- Reading to answer questions.
- Reading to summarise and organise.
- Reading to follow directions.
- Reading to predict outcomes.
- Reading to evaluate.

8.8.2 Remediation of Mathematic Disabilities

Low achievement in mathematics is less common than low achievement in reading. Yet for many students with learning disabilities, computation and analytical reasoning are the major areas of learning difficulties. The following activities have been used to help students with learning disabilities in mathematics.

- **To reduce distractions and improve accuracy:** Provide cues and organizers to focus attention. For example, mark student worksheets with vertical and horizontal lines and place math problems in the squares created by them. This helps students with learning disabilities keep track of their progress and find their place a little easily. Some teachers also use answer blocks and other cues to help these students complete math problems.

[1]	[ ][ ]	[ ]	[ ]
2 3	5 4 7	6 2	9 2 3
+ 3 9	+ 2 9 3	– 4 7	– 7 8 1
[6][2]	[ ][ ][ ]	[ ][ ]	[ ][ ][ ]

- **To focus attention and reduce distraction:** Modify assignments. Reduce the number of problems presented on a page if students are reluctant to complete a worksheet. Have them complete a longer sheet by finishing several smaller assignments with in-between breaks. For example, if a student has 20 math problems to complete, four or five mini-assignments of 4 or 5 problems each are more likely to be finished than one with all 20 problems on it.

- **To improve accuracy:** Provide multiple opportunities for success. Define mastery in a new way (such as 100 percent correct after being told a previous attempt has errors in it). Have students try to achieve mastery with less than three retries.
- **To improve knowledge of basic facts:** Use manipulatives. Beans, blocks, game chips, stickers, paper clips, and other small objects are useful in helping students learn relationships between numbers and what they mean.
- **To make math meaningful:** Use real-life problems and applications. Set up a class checking account and use it to help students with learning disabilities learn about money and math related to it (for example, adding and subtracting credits and debits). Have students write checks to be used in a classroom store.
- **To improve problem solving:** Teach basic concepts and have students practice using them. For instance, teach students with learning disabilities to look for clues in word problems. Words such as altogether, sum, and plus usually mean the problem requires addition. Spent, remains, left, and lost are used frequently in subtraction problems.
- **To improve performance:** Simplify structure and content of assignments. Make complex work easier exchanging words. Solving word problems can be difficult when the vocabulary and writing style being used are above students' reading levels. Reducing the number of words in a sentence from 15 or 20 to 5 or 6 can have a positive influence on the performance of students with learning disabilities. Reducing the reading level by changing words like remainder to how many left can also help these students.
- **To improve interest and motivation:** Use activities that make math fun. Students with learning disabilities at all grade levels often report "hating" math. Effective teachers use "tricks" to keep these students interested in math calculations and their applications.

Left to Right Addition (a "tricky" way to add)	
53	Start with the first number at the top of the left-
17	hand column and call it by its "tens name" (50).
24	Add each number in the left-hand column to each
+ 19	preceding number using the "tens names" and
113	continue down the ones column.
(50 + 10 = 60 + 20 = 80 + 10 = 90 + 3 = 93 + 7 = 100 + 4 = 104 + 9 = 113)	

8.8.3 Remediation of Writing Disabilities

Along with listening, speaking, and reading, written language is an important part of any language arts program. Because so many children have problems with reading, many also experience difficulties with writing or written expression in general. Teachers working with students with written language problems have found the following tactics useful.

- **To improve written products:** Focus on quantity before quality in written work. Students with learning disabilities often produce minimal amounts of written work when asked to demonstrate their writing skills, or they produce large numbers of grammatical errors when their written work is evaluated. By encouraging students to write as much as possible without concern for errors, many teachers achieve quantitative improvements that become a source for qualitative changes in their instructions. For example, have students write as many words as they can as a brief, timed exercise. Provide an option that the words can be related, but don't require it. Provide an option that the words can be in sentence form, but don't require it. At the end of the work period, count the number of written words and record the performance on a chart or graph. Repeat the activity on the subsequent days and encourage students to improve their writing by producing more words, by writing more correctly spelled words, by writing more complete sentences, or by writing about a topic.
- **To improve written products: Use checklists to guide students** before they write. Simple features differentiate well-prepared written work from writing that causes negative impressions. Many students with learning disabilities do not know what these features are, and many others simply fail to attend to the mechanics of writing. Preparing a simple checklist for students to use to evaluate a report or writing assignment can improve the overall quality of their work, decide which features are important. For example, some teachers

are concerned about form as well as content. They want written products to reflect appropriate use of headings, references, and style. Others are more concerned about the visual appearance of written work, such as absence of unnecessary marks, clean erasures, and word or page limits. Whatever your pleasure, letting students know about it and helping them evaluate their work before turning it in will greatly improve their performance.

- **To improve written products: Teach specific skills and have** students monitor their written work. Composition skills are teachable, and written products are improved by using them. Targeted composition skills (for example, use of action words, action helpers, or describing words) should be taught using teacher guided practice lessons. Students should then be asked to monitor their own written products {"Did I use action words?" "Can I use more describing words?" "Did I tell how the action was done?").
- **To improve spelling:** Use familiar words for practice. Teach students to look for familiar words as they think of correct spellings. Common sight words that have at least five rhyming words and a similar spelling pattern (big: pig, rig, jig, dig, and fig) serve as targeted spelling vocabulary. Have students read the rhyming words and teach them a simple rule to use when spelling them ("When words rhyme, the last parts are often spelled the same"). Give spelling tests using the rhyming words to improve the confidence of students with learning disabilities.
- **To improve written expression:** Use computers and word processing tools. Many teachers report that writing instruction is easier for students with learning disabilities when they use computers as the primary means for producing written products. Many of these students are more receptive to revising their work when they can do it with a word processing program, and the work produced on a computer is easier to proofread and edit for students and teachers. Using computer-assisted grammar checkers or spelling checkers is also appealing to students with academic problems commonly associated with learning disabilities. There are also software tools to help students brainstorm and organize their ideas before writing. Some programs guide students through the entire writing process, from brainstorming through revision. Desktop publishing software, which allows students to create newsletters and other in-class publications, can boost their motivation to produce high-quality final products.

❖ ❖ ❖

Visual Impairments

Students with visual impairments were among the first to receive Special Education services in United States. Of the human senses, seeing and hearing are most important for translating external information to traditional learning, and these two senses are involved in what we broadly call sensory disabilities. More specifically the term visual impairments refers to all degrees of vision loss.

9.1 Visual Impairment Defined

According to federal definition, a vision impairment is a problem in seeing, that, even with correction, adversely affects a child's educational performance. The phrase does not include people with normal or near normal vision, but does include people with low visual functioning (partial sight) as well as those who have only light perception or those who are totally without the sense of vision. People with normal or near normal vision can perform tasks without special assistance. People with low vision may have difficulty with detailed visual tasks or may perform them at reduced levels of speed, endurance, or accuracy, even with assistance; these people are referred to as partially sighted people who are blind or near blind, have unreliable vision and rely primarily or exclusively on other senses.

Definition: Visual impairment is defined in terms of visual acuity, field of vision and visual efficiency. Visual acuity is measured by having people read letters or discriminate objects at a distance of 20 feet. Those who are able to read the letters correctly have normal vision. Visual acuity is expressed as a ratio that tells us how well the individual sees. The expression 20/20 vision describes perfect (normal) vision; it means that the person can see at 20 feet what people with normal vision see at 20 ft. A person with 20/90 vision needs to be 20 feet away to discriminate letters or objects that people with normal vision can read or discriminate at 90 feet.

How poor does visual acuity have to be before a person is considered to have a visual impairment? To address this question, the American Medical Association adopted a definition of blindness is 1934 that is still used today. According to that definition, the criterion for blindness is "Central visual acuity of 20/200 or less in the better eye with corrective glasses or central visual acuity of more than 20/200 if there is a visual field defect in which the peripheral field is contracted to such an extent that the widest diameter of the visual fields subtends an angular distance no greater than 20 degrees in the better eye." (Koestler 1976).

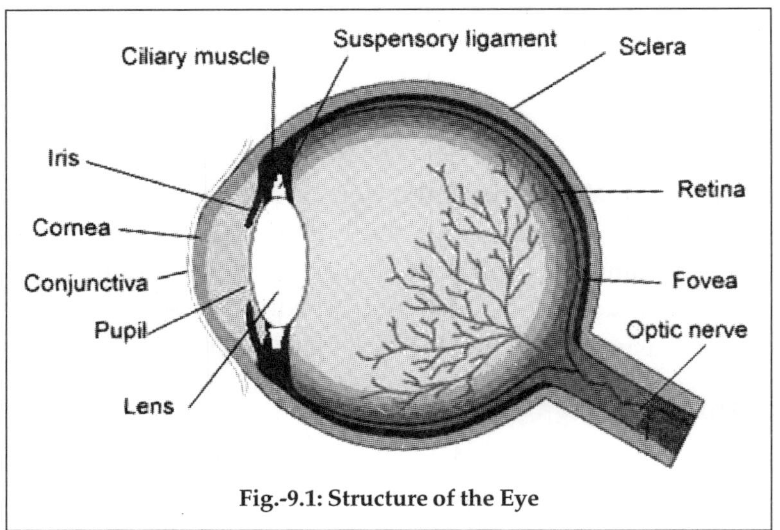

Fig.-9.1: Structure of the Eye

A person who needs to stand at a distance of the 20 feet to see with correction what people with normal vision can see from 200 ft away is considered blind.

People with a severely restricted field of vision are also considered blind. When looking straight ahead, a person with a normal field of vision is able to see objects within a range of appropriately 180 degrees. If a person's field of vision is 10 degrees, then he is able to see only a limited area at any one time, even though her visual acuity in that area is actually quite good.

The phrase visual efficiency and functional vision denote how well a person uses whatever vision he has, Functional vision is the "visual ability sufficient for utilizing visual information in the planning and execution of a task." Functional vision cannot be determined by visual acuity or visual field, nor can it be predicted. Some children with relatively minor visual impairments are unable to function as learners; they may even behave as though they are blind.

9.2 Types and Causes of Visual Impairment

9.2.1 Focusing Problems

9.2.1.1 Near Sightedness or Myopia

Many problems with visual acuity result from difficulties in focusing. Near sightedness or Myopia: In this problem distant objects are blurred although nearer objects remain clear.

9.2.1.2 Far Sightedness or Hyperopia

In this problem the reverse is true. Distant objects are in clear focus but nearer ones are blurred.

9.2.1.3 Astigmatism

This condition stems from irregular curvature in the eye's refractive surfaces, with the result that objects at any distance may be blurred or distorted.

Since the above three conditions can be corrected before or during school years they do not affect school performance and are not generally considered visual impairments requiring Special Education services.

9.2.2 Problems of Eye Movement

There are several other significant ways one's vision may be impaired.

9.2.2.1 Ocular Motility

The eyes ability to move may be impaired. This impairment can cause problems in binocular vision, which is the ability of the two eyes to focus on one object and fuse two images into a single clear image. Binocular vision is actually a complicated process, requiring good vision in each eye, normal eye muscles, and smooth functioning of the co-ordinating centers of the brain. Ocular motility problems affect the eyes ability to move smoothly and focus properly; several conditions make it difficult or impossible for a child to use his eyes together effectively. Strabismus describes an inability to focus on the same object with both eyes, because of an inward or outward deviation of one or both eyes. If left untreated, strabismus and other disorders of ocular motility can lead to a permanent loss of vision. When the two eyes cannot focus simultaneously, the brain avoids a double image by suppressing the visual input from one eye. Thus the weaker eye -usually the one that turns inward or outward can actually lose its ability to see.

9.2.2.2 Amblyopia

Refers to the reduction in or loss of vision in the weaker eye from lack of use, even though no disease is present.

9.2.2.3 Nystagmus

Which produces rapid, involuntary movement of the eye that interferes with focusing objects.

9.2.2.4 Photophobia

It is a condition where the eyes are unusually sensitive to light. Colour vision can also be impaired, but it is usually not considered an educationally significant visual impairment.

9.2.3 Other Types / Causes of Visual Impairment

9.2.3.1 Cataract

Cataract is the condition in the lens of the eye that blocks the light necessary for seeing clearly, vision may be blurred, distorted or incomplete; cataracts are common in older people, but may also occur in children.

9.2.3.2 Glaucoma

Galucoma is prevalent disease marked by abnormally high pressure within eye. There are various types of glaucoma all related to disturbances or blockages of the fluids that normally circulate within the eye. Central and peripheral vision are impaired or lost entirely when the increased pressure damages the optic nerve.

9.2.3.3 Diabetic Retinopathy

Damage to the retina -a light sensitive tissue – causes visual impairment and blindness. Children and adults with diabetes frequently have impaired vision as a result of hemorrhages.

9.2.3.4 Retinitis Pigmentosa

This condition most commonly causes gradual degeneration of the retina. The symptoms is usually difficulty in seeing at night followed by loss of peripheral vision.

9.2.3.5 Retinopathy of Prematurity (ROP)

This disease may result from placing low birth weight babies is incubators and administering high levels of oxygen.

9.3 Characteristics of Visually Impaired Children

9.3.1 Cognitive

Students who have visual impairments are not necessarily intellectually retarded, but they may perform poorly on most standard intelligence tests. Many concepts are learned entirely through visual means; students with visual impairments have difficulty learning some concepts.

9.3.2 Academic

With the exception of unique problems of input and possibly a greater demand in processing the fundamental learning procedures of blind children do not differ from those of non-impaired children. The impact of visual impairments on academic performance is very much a function of the severity of the condition and the age at which the students' vision was reduced.

9.3.3 Physical

In terms of size and appearance people with visual impairments are no different from those with normal vision. However low vision and blindness may impact movement and the quality of motor skills. Some children may develop repetitive stereotypic movements commonly referred to as "blindisms" such as rocking, eye packing, head rolling, and hand waving.

9.3.4 Behavioral

There are a few social emotional characteristics specific to visual disabilities. They cannot see nonverbal forms of communication, nonverbal understanding and body language behaviour.

9.3.5 Communication

Visually impaired children experience difficulty to read and understand body language.

9.4 Identification of Visually Impaired Children

- Student frequently experiences watery eyes.
- Student frequently experiences red or inflamed eyes.
- Student's eye movements are jumpy or not synchronized.
- Student experiences difficulty reading small print.
- Student experiences difficulty moving around the classroom.

- Student experiences difficulty identifying small details in pictures or illustrations.
- Student frequently complains of dizziness after reading a passage or completing an assignment involving vision.
- Student tilts head or squints eyes to achieve better focus.
- Student uses one eye more than the other for reading or completing assignments.
- Student frequently complains of headaches or eye infections.
- Reference to ophthalmologist.

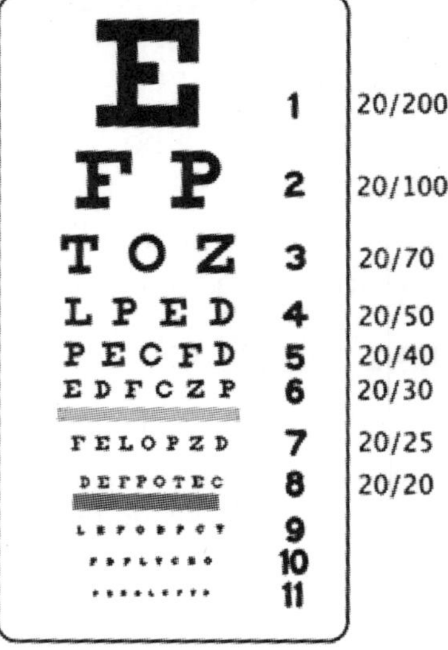

Fig.-9.2: Snelle's Chart

9.5 Educational Provisions for Visually Impaired Children

9.5.1 Visual Functioning

Children with limited visual acuity could be helped to improve visual functioning by increasing visual efficiency which includes skills such as controlling eye movements, adapting to visual environment, paying attention to visual stimuli, and processing visual information rapidly.

9.5.2 Orientation and Mobility Aids

Orientation is a mental map of our environment; mobility is the ability to get around in our environment. Guide dogs, canes, and assistance from a sighted

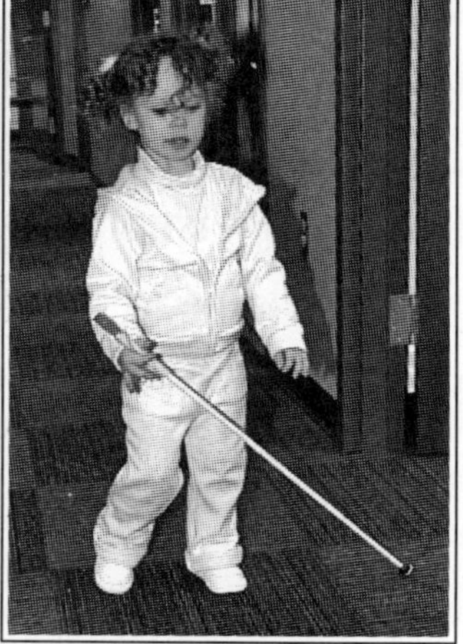
Fig.-9.3: Blind Children using Cane as Mobility Aids

person help people make up for orientation and mobility problems caused by vision impairments. Orientation and mobility instruction is a must for blind or severely visually impaired children.

9.5.3 Listening Skills Training

Many students with vision impairments rely on listening as a primary means of obtaining information. Focusing on a single sound source, analyzing, oral information and focusing on key sound sources are among listening skills taught to people to make up for communication problems caused by vision impairments. Listening involves several need components, including attention, awareness of sound discrimination and assignment of meaning to sound. Good listening skills broaden students' vocabulary and support development of speaking, reading and writing abilities.

9.5.4 Braille

Some students with vision impairments used to learn to read and write using different methods. Braille is a communication system of reading and writing that uses raised dots on paper so that people who are blind or who have low vision can read text by feeling it. Present day technological advances enable computer text files to be converted to Braille on special printers, and paperless Braille devices convert information on computer screens to Braille output. The system was developed around 1830 by Louis Braille a young freshman who was blind. Young children generally learn to write Braille using a brailer, a six keyed device that resembles a type writer; older students are introduced to slate and stylus, in which Braille dots are punched out one at a time by hand, from right to left.

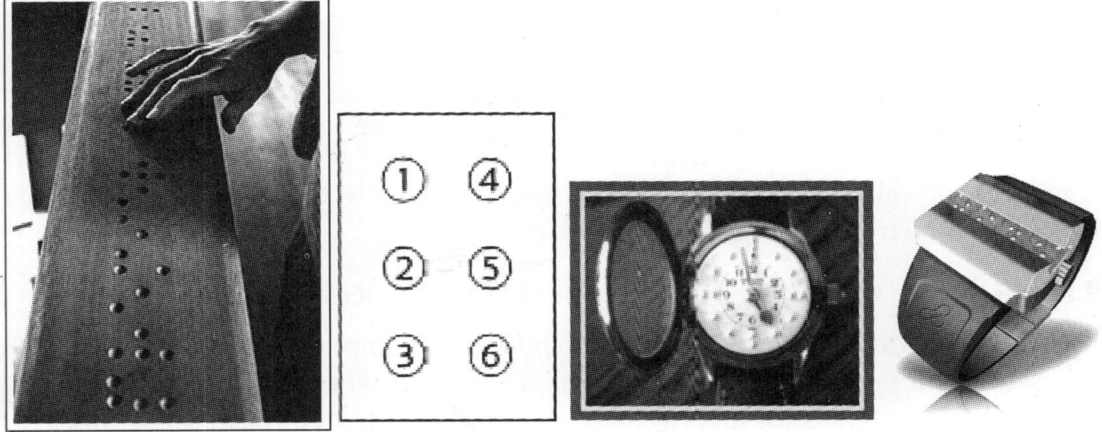

Fig.-9.4: Braille reading

Fig.-9.5: Braille watch

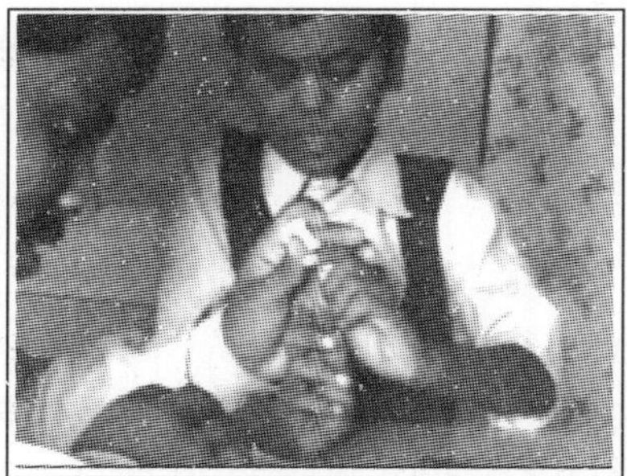

Fig.-9.6: Braille writing

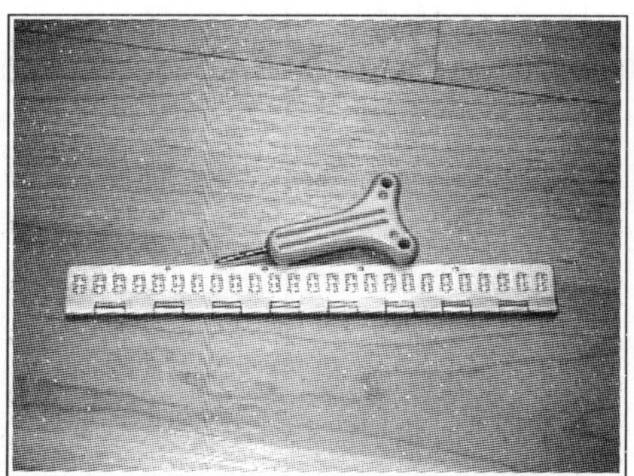

Fig.-9.7: Slate and stylus

9.5.5 Enhanced Image Devices

Many students with vision impairments learn to read using traditional methods with enlarged print. Closed-circuit television systems with a small camera and zoom lens, overhead projectors, micro-computers, telescopic aids and other specialized equipment are used to enlarge text so that it is easier for people with low vision to read.

9.5.6 Audio Aids

People with visual impairments can hear what other people can read. Talking books, talking calculators, and devices that compress speech to speed it up and eliminate natural pauses are audio aids that help people with vision impairments make up for their limited sight.

9.5.7 Optical Character Recognition (OCR) Devices

Some students with vision impairments use a computer-base scanning device (e.g. Kurzweill Personal Reader) that converts printed words into synthetic speech. Recent advances in computer technology have greatly improved these devices. Often they now include small sensors that can be attached to microcomputers to help people who are blind or those with low vision learn printed text.

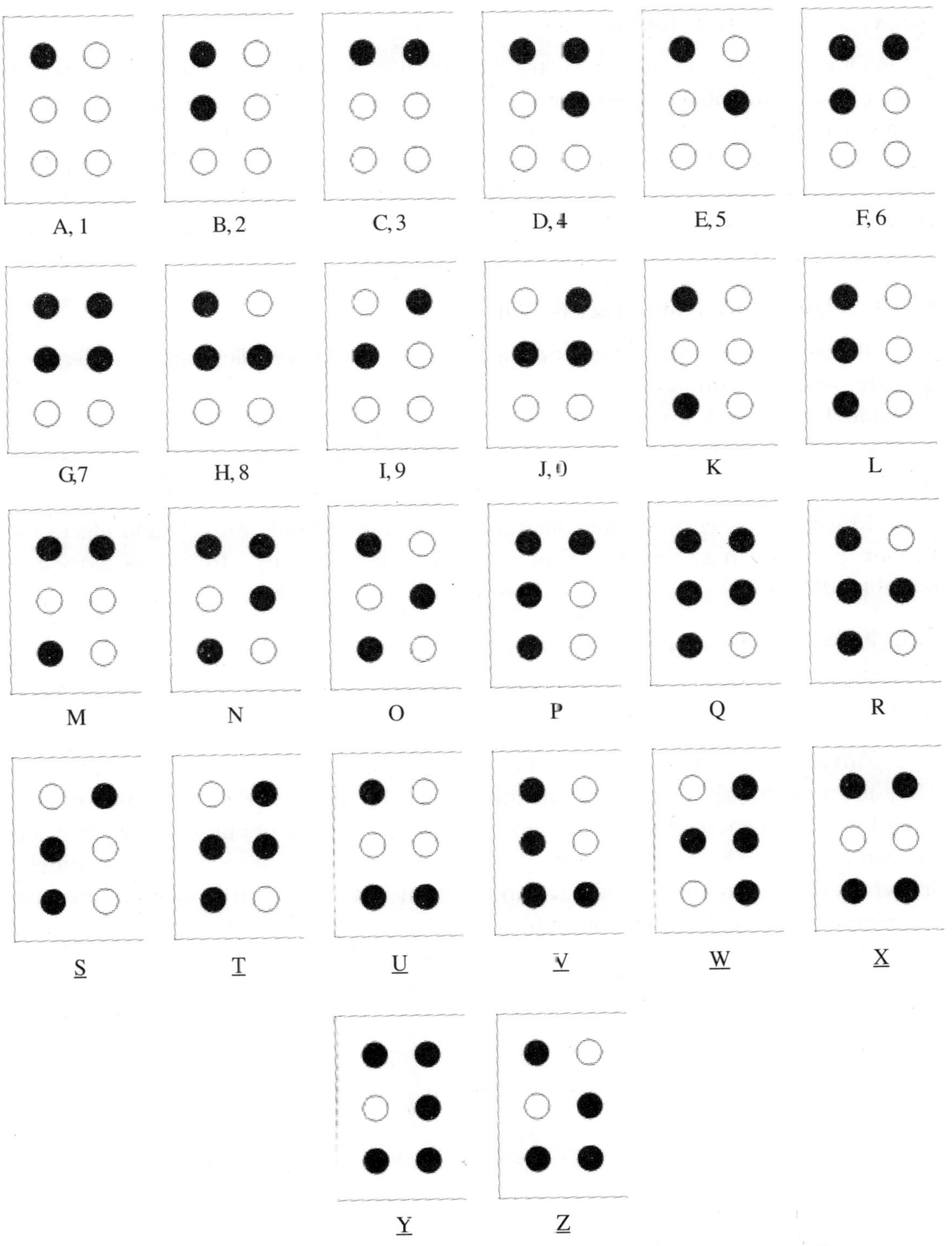

Fig.-9.8: Letters and numbers in braille

9.5.8 Written Communication

One system is known as versa Braille. It is a portable laptop computer on which blind students can take notes and tests is class and prepare assignments at home. The keyboard has six keys that correspond to the dots in a Braille cell, a numeric keypad and a joystick; students can check their work by reading a dynamic tactile display on the top of the versa Braille consisting of 20 Braille cells. Students store their work on a floppy disc that copies by using a talking word processing program, and produces standard English print copies for teachers to read.

9.5.9 Manipulative and Tactile Aids

Belcastro (1989) has developed a set of rods that enables blind students to quickly identify different values by feeling the lengths and tactile markings associated with each number. Another mathematical aid for blind students is the Cranmer Abacus. The abacus has been adapted to assist blind students in learning number concepts and making calculations.

Embossed relief maps and diagrams, three dimensional models and electronic probes that give an audible signal in response to light are used to learn science and social studies.

9.5.10 Technological Aids

The optacom is a small electronic device that converts regular print into a readable vibrating form for blind people.

Advances in technology are influencing the ways all students are taught. They are particularly relevant in methods used by people who are blind or who have low vision to access information that sighted people obtain visually (Schrier, Leventhal, and Uslan, 1991). Techniques using image enhancing systems, synthetic speech systems, Braille technology, and optical character reorganization systems, separately or in combination, provide access to printed information for people with visual impairments.

CHAPTER 10

Hearing Impairment

Hearing is vital to every aspect of our daily existence. If one is unable to hear he would find it difficult to participate fully in the activities of school, college, job or neighborhood. A person with normal hearing can understand speech in daily life situations without relying on any special device or technique.

10.1 Hearing Impairment Defined

There are two types or hearing impairments; they include people who are deaf and people who are hard of hearing.

Hearing impairment means impairment in hearing, whether permanent or fluctuating that adversely affects a child's educational performance but that is not included under the definition of deafness.

Deafness is a severe disability. People who are deaf have a hearing loss that prevents understanding speech through the ear. They have little functional hearing; even with a little hearing, they do not use hearing as their primary sense for gaining information.

According to Federal definition,

> "Deafness" means a hearing impairment that is so severe that the child is impaired in processing linguistic information through hearing, with or without amplification, that adversely affects a child's educational performance (Individuals with Disabilities Education Act, (IDEA) 1990).

Hard of hearing is a less severe disability. People who are hard of hearing can process information from sounds and usually profit from amplification provided by hearing aids. Both deaf and hard of hearing children are said to be hearing impaired. This term, used mainly in education, indicates a child who needs special services because of hearing loss.

Hearing ability i.e., auditory acuity and hearing loss are measured using two dimensions: intensity and frequency. People hear sounds at certain levels of loudness, or intensity. Loudness is expressed in decibels (dB); the greater the decibels, the louder the sound. A decibel level of 125 or louder is painful to the average person. Decibel levels from 0 to 120 are used to test hearing at different frequencies. Frequencies or pitch is measured in hertz (Hz) or cycles per second. The frequency range for conversational speech is between 500 and 2000 Hz. Both loudness and frequency can be measured with an audiometer.

Hearing losses are most often described by the lowest decibel level that a person can hear. Moores (1987) used decibel levels to define deafness and hard of hearing. "A deaf person is one whose hearing is disabled to an extent (usually 70 dB or greater) that precludes the understanding of speech through the ear alone, without or with the use of a hearing aid".

"A hard of hearing person is one whose hearing is disabled to an extent (usually 35 to 69 dB) that makes difficult but does not preclude, the understanding of speech through the ear alone, without or with a hearing aid."

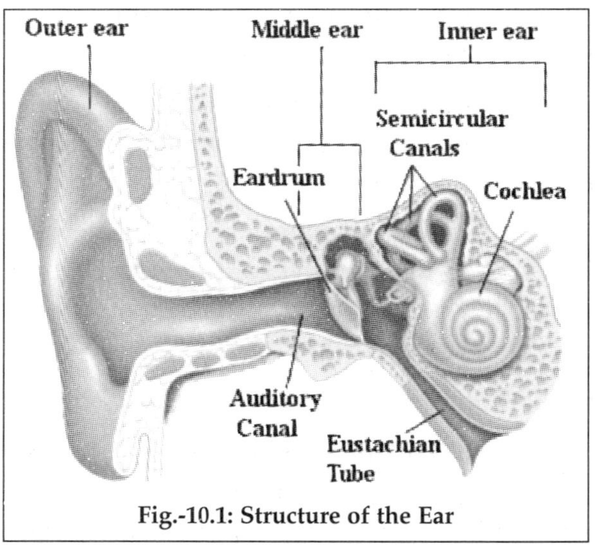

Fig.-10.1: Structure of the Ear

A hearing impairment may also be described in terms of age of outset. It is important to consider whether a hearing loss is congenital (present at birth) or adventitious (acquired later in life). The terms paralinguistic hearing impairment refer to whether or not a hearing loss is sustained before or after the development of spoken language. A child who acquires a hearing impairment after speech and language are well established, usually after age 2, has educational needs very different from the prelinguistically hearing impaired child.

10.2 Types of Hearing Impairment

The two main types of hearing impairment are

1. Conductive
2. Sensory neural

10.2.1 Conductive

A conductive hearing loss results from abnormalities or complications of the outer or middle ear. They are:

- Excessive wax in the auditory canal.
- A disease that leaves fluid or debris.
- If eardrum ossicles do not move properly.

A conducting hearing impairment involves a problem with conducting or transmitting, sound vibrations to inner ear. This can be corrected through surgical or medical treatment. Hearing aids are usually beneficial to persons with conductive hearing.

10.2.2 Sensory Neural

A sensory neural hearing loss refers to damage to the auditory nerve fibers or other sensitive mechanisms in the inner ear. Unfortunately most sensory neural hearing impairments cannot be corrected by surgery or medication.

The combination of both conductive and sensory neural impairments is called mixed hearing loss. Hearing impairments is also described in terms of being unilateral (present in one ear only) or bilateral (present in both ears). Children with unilateral hearing impairments generally learn speech and language without major difficulties, but do have some disadvantages.

10.3 Degrees of Hearing Impairments

An individual hearing impairment is usually described in terms of slight, mild, moderate, severe and profound depending on the average hearing level in decibels. The table below provides effects of hearing loss on understanding language and speech.

Table-10.1: Characteristics of Functional Hearing Losses

Hearing loss	Characteristics
Less than 26dB loss (normal)	No significant difficulty with faint speech
26 – 40 dB loss (slight)	Difficulty only with faint sounds
41 – 55 dB loss (mild)	Understands face to face speech and conversations at 3–5 ft.
56 – 70 dB loss (moderate)	Frequent difficulty with normal conversation and speech
71 – 90 dB loss (severe)	Understands only shouted or amplified speech
91 dB or more loss (profound)	Difficulty even with amplified Speech

10.4 Causes of Hearing Impairment

Causes of hearing impairment are usually classified into exogenous or endogenous. Exogenous causes stem from factors outside the body (such as disease, toxicity or injury) and reduce the auditory systems ability to receive and transmit sounds Endogenous causes are inherited from parent's genes.

According to SC Brown (1986) four prevalent causes of deafness are identified. They are

10.4.1 Maternal Rubella

Also known as German measles rubella causes deafness, visual impairment, heart disorders and a variety of serious disabilities in the developing child when it affects a pregnant woman.

10.4.2 Heredity

Genetic factors are one of the leading causes of deafness. There is strong evidence that congenital hearing impairment runs in some families.

10.4.3 Premature Complications of Pregnancy

Early delivery and lower birth weight have been found to be more common among deaf children. Complication of pregnancy arises from a variety of causes.

10.4.4 Meningitis

It is a bacterial or viral infection that can destroy the sensitive cone apparatus of inner ear.

10.4.5 Otitis Media

It is an infection of inflammation of the middle ear. If untreated, otitis media can result in a buildup of fluid and a ruptured eardrum, causing permanent conductive learning impairment.

10.5 Characteristics of Hearing Impaired Children

10.5.1 Cognitive

Intelligence is developed through hearing and using language. Defenses in the cognitive performance of students who are deaf and of their hearing peers are more due to inadequate development of a conventional language system than to limited intellectual ability.

10.5.2 Academic

The severity of the hearing loss, the age of its onset, the socioeconomic status of the students family, and the hearing status of the parents are related to the academic successes experienced by students with hearing impairments. Even slight hearing impairment however has been shown to have adverse effects on academic achievement.

10.5.3 Physical

Few physical characteristics are specific to those who are deaf or hard of hearing i.e., functional hearing.

10.5.4 Behavioral

People who are deaf prefer to be with others who are deaf; adults who are deaf tend to cluster in groups, socialize and marry and exhibit deaf culture.

10.5.5 Communication

Hearing impaired children are at a great disadvantage in acquiring language skills. Learning to speak is difficult if you can't hear. Communication problems seriously interfere with interpersonal relationships for students with hearing impairments. Interaction is essential to language development. Children, who are deaf are often passive participants in communication; as a result the vocabulary and syntax of children who are deaf grow slowly.

10.6 Identification of Hearing Impaired Children

— Student experiences difficulties following oral presentation and directions.

— Student watches lips of teachers or other speakers very closely.

— Student turns head and leans toward speaker.

— Student use limited vocabulary.

— Student uses speech sounds poorly.

— Student often does not respond when called from behind.

— Student shows delayed language development.

— Student is generally inattentive during oral presentations.

— Student constantly turns volume up on radio or televisions, or has discharge.

— Student complains of earaches, has frequent colds or ear infection, or has ear discharge.

10.6.1 Audiometric Assessment

Hearing is formally assessed by a testing procedure called pure tone audiometry. The examiner uses an audiometer, an electronic device that generates sounds at different levels of intensity and frequency. The test seeks to determine how loud sounds at various frequencies must be before the child is able to hear them. A child with hearing impairment does not begin to detect sounds until a high level of loudness is reached.

An **audiometer** is a machine used for evaluating hearing loss. The invention of this machine is generally credited to Dr. Harvey Fletcher of Brigham Young University. **Audiometers** are standard equipment at ENT clinics and in audiology centers. They usually consist of an embedded hardware unit connected to a pair of headphones and a feedback button, sometimes controlled by a standard PC. Audiometer requirements and the test procedure are specified in IEC 60645, ISO 8253, and ANSI S3.6 standards.

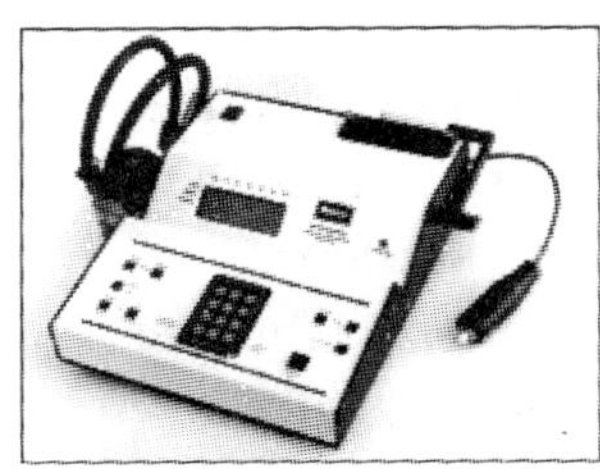

Fig.-10.2: MI-7000 Microproccessor Audiometer

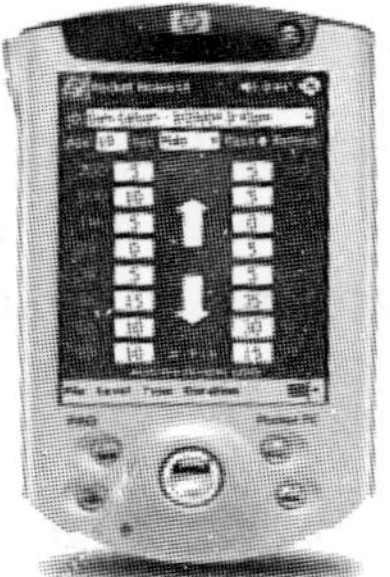

Fig.-10.3: Pocket Hearo Audiometer: Simple, handheld screening audiometer perfect for physicians, clinic, school settings

10.7 Interventions to Assist Students with Hearing Impairments

10.7.1 Oral Communication

An approach in which people with hearing impairments are taught to use speaking and residual hearing as their only means of communicating. Training in producing understanding speech and language is incorporated into all aspects of child's education; auditory, visual and tactile methods are also used.

10.7.2 Sign Language

An approach in which people with hearing impairments are taught to use manual gestures and body movements as their only means of communicating.

10.7.3 Auditory Learning

An approach to teach the child to learn to listen and learn by listening instead of simply learning to hear. Advocates of auditory hearing contend that the first three levels of auditory training – detecting, discriminating and identifying sounds are important but insufficient for developing the student's residual hearing. Auditory learning emphasizes a fourth and highest level of listening skills, the comprehension of meaningful sounds.

10.7.4 Speech Reading

An approach which involves the process of understanding a spoken message by observing the speaker's face. Paying careful attention to a speaker's lips may help a hearing impaired person derive important clues particularly if she is able to gain some information through residual hearing signs, gestures, facial expression, and familiarity with the context or situation.

10.7.5 Cued Speech

An approach in which people with hearing impairments are taught to use visual cues provided by a speaker to decode what is being said. They are in the form of hand signals near the chin to assist the deaf person in identifying sounds that cannot be distinguished through speech reading.

10.7.6 Assistive Listening Devices

Hearing aids, FM transmission and amplification devices, and audio loops are special types of equivalent that help people with hearing impairments make better use of their residual hearing.

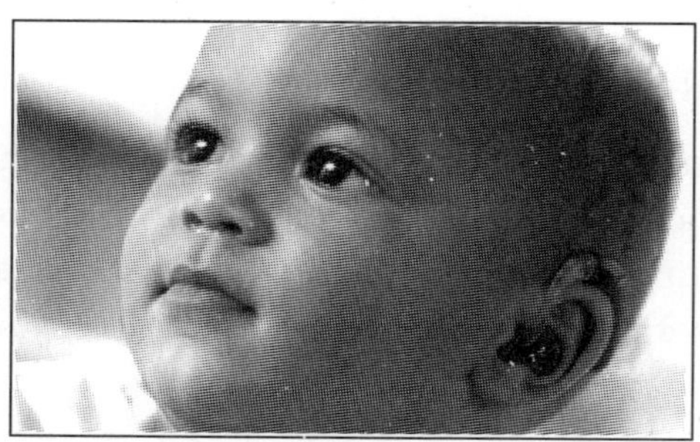

Fig.-10.4: Hearing aid

10.7.7 Telecommunication Devices

Keyboards with screens or printers connected to telephones take advantage of vision to improve communication for people with hearing impairments; computer fax modems and electronic mail are recent developments in this rapidly changing area.

10.7.8 Total Communication

Educational programs with and emphasis on total communication advocate the use of a variety of forms of communication to teach language to hearing impaired students. Practioners of total communication maintain that simultaneous presentation of manual communication by finger spelling and signs and speech through speech reading and residual hearing makes it possible for children to see either one or both types of communication.

10.7.8.1 Sign Language

Sign language uses gestures to represent words ideas and concepts. Some signs use handshapes or motions that look like or appear to initiate or act out the message. Teachers who practice total communication generally speak as they sign and make a special effort to follow the form or structure of spoken English as possible.

10.7.8.2 Finger Spelling

Finger spelling is often used in conjunction with methods of communication Finger spelling or the manual alphabet consists of 26 distinct hand positions – one for each English letter. This approach is the best way to provide a reliable receptive expressive symbol system.

Fig.-10.5: Finger Spelling Alphabets

10.7.8.3 American Sign Language (ASL)

ASL is a visual gestural language with its own rules of syntax, semantics and pragmatics. In ASL the shape, location, and movement pattern of the hands, the intensity of motions and signer's facial expressions all communicate meaning and content ASL has its own vocabulary syntax and grammatical rules.

10.7.8.4 Service Options

The specialized needs of children with severe hearing impairments make special services necessary in all cases. In an integrated school setting special services for hearing impaired include:

- Smaller class size
- Regular speech, language, and auditory training instruction from a specialist.
- Amplification systems
- Services of an interpreters if the child uses manual communication
- Special setting in the classroom to promote speech reading

- Captioned films
- Good acoustics and reduction of background noise
- Special tutoring or review sessions
- Someone to take notes in class so that the hearing impaired student can pay more constant attention
- Instruction for teachers and non handicapped students in sign language or other communication methods used by the hearing impaired student
- Counseling.

10.8 Tips for Teachers of Students with Hearing Impairments

— Reduce distance between student and speaker as much as possible.

— Speak slowly and stress clear articulation rather than loudness when speaking.

— Reduce background noise as much as possible.

— Seat student near center of desk arrangements and away from distracting sounds.

— Use face–to–face contact as much as possible.

— Use complete sentences to provide additional context during conversations or instructional presentations.

— Use visual cues when referring to objects in the classroom and during instructional presentations.

— Have classmates take notes during oral presentations for student to transcribe after the lesson.

— Encourage independent activities and teach social skills.

— Be sure hearing aid is turned on and functioning properly.

Communication Disorder

The category of communication disorders includes people whose problems in producing speech or using language symbols interfere significantly with their ability to communicate. Children who are not able to make themselves understood or who cannot comprehend ideas that are spoken to them by others are children with communication disorder.

11.1 Definition of Communication Disorder

There are two types of communication disorder; those that affect speech and those that affect language called speech and language disorder respectively.

11.1.1 Speech Disorder

Problems with producing speech sounds (articulation), controlling sounds that are produced (voice), and controlling the rate and rhythm of speech (fluency) are generally considered speech disorders. The most widely accepted definition of speech impairment is "speech is abnormal when it deviates so far from the speech of other people that it calls attention to itself, interferes with communication or causes the speaker or his listeners distressed" (Van Ripper & Emerick 1984.)

11.1.2 Language Disorder

Problems with using proper forms of language (phonology, morphology, syntax), using the content of language (semantics), and using the functions of language (pragmatics) are generally considered language disorders. The American Speech Language Hearing Association (ASHA) defines language disorder as "The impairment or deviant development of comprehension and or use of a spoken, written and or other symbol system. The disorder may involve syntactic systems and/or.

1. The form of language (phonologic, morphologic,)
2. The content of language (semantic system)

3. The function of language in communication (pragmatic system) in any combination.

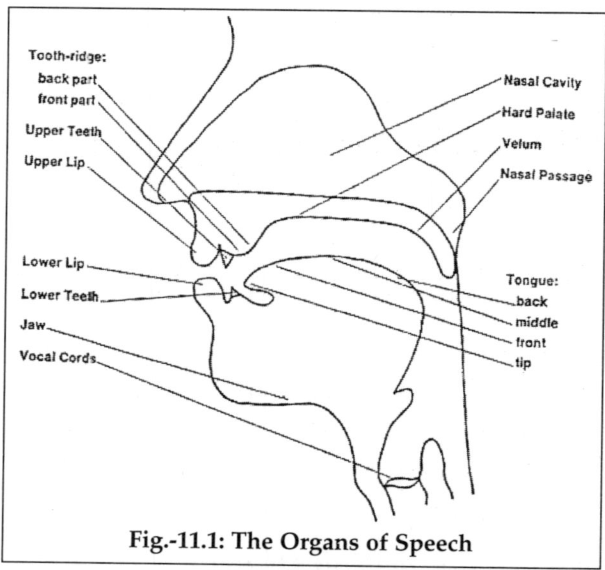

Fig.-11.1: The Organs of Speech

11.2 Types of Speech Disorder

11.2.1 Articulation Disorder

It is defined as the abnormal production of speech sounds. Ex: wabbit for rabbit, poon for spoon. There are four basic kinds of articulation errors; substitution, distortion, omission, addition.

Error type	Definition	Example
Substitution	Replacing one sound with another	Standard: the ball is red Substitution: the ball is wed.
Distortion	Producing a sound in an unfamiliar way	Standard: give the pencil to sally. Distortion: Give the pencil to Sally (the /p/ is nasalized)
Omission	Omiting a sound in a word	Standrd: Play the piano Omission: p_ay the piano
Addition	Inserting an extra sound in a word	Standard: I have a black horse Addition: I have a belack horse

11.2.2 Voice Disorder

It is defined as the absence or abnormal production of vocal quality, pitch, loudness, resonance, and/or duration. Individuals with voice disorders sometimes sound very hoarse, or speak very loudly or in very high of low pitch. The basic types of disorders are phonation and resonance.

1. *Phonation disorder* causes the voice to sound breathy, horse, husky, or strained most of the time. In severe cases there is no voice at all.
2. *Resonance Disorder* causes the voice suffer from either too many sounds coming out through the air passages of the nose or conversely, not enough resonance of the nasal passages. The voice sounds like talking through nose or stuffed nose.

11.2.3 Fluency Disorder

It is defined as the abnormal flow of verbal expression, characterized by impaired rate and rhythm which may be accompanied by struggle disorder. There are two types of fluency disorder.

1. *Cluttering:* a condition in which speech is very rapid with extra sounds or mispronounced sounds. The cluttered speech is garbled to the point of unintelligibility.
2. *Stuttering:* This condition is marked by "rapid free repetitions of consonant or vowel sounds especially at the beginning of words and complete verbal blocks".

   Ex. S –Saying th…, th – the, f – first, S – sound, o – of – a- a. w – word and th – then, S – saying th – the w – word illustrates this problem.

11.3 Language Disorder

Language disorder includes a significance impairment in a child's receptive or expressive language. A receptive language disorder interferes with the understanding of language. An expressive language disorder interferes with production of language. A child may have very limited vocabulary, may use incorrect words and phrases or may not even speak at all, communicating only through gestures. A child may have good receptive, language when an expressive disorder is present or may have both in combination.

The American Speech Language Hearing Association (1982) defines three kinds of language disorders, specifically problems related to form, content, and function.

1. Language form refers to utterance or sentence structure of what is said phonology, morphology and syntax.
2. Language content refers to meanings of words and sentences, including abstract concepts – semantics.
3. Language function refers to the context in which language can be used and the purpose of communication pragmatics.

11.3.1 Receptive Language Disorder

Receptive language involves the reception and understanding of language, involves problems related to hearing, listening to, or receiving language.

11.3.2 Expressive Language Disorder

Expressive language involves the ability to use language to express one's thoughts and communicate with others, problems related to producing or expressing language.

- Phonology is concerned with the smallest units of language (Phonemes or speech sounds)
- Morphology is concerned with the smallest units of meaningful language (morphemes or words and parts of words).
- Syntax is concerned with combining language units into meaningful phrases, clauses, or sentences (grammatically correct language).

Problems with phonology, morphology, and syntax are evident when students are unable to differentiate sounds, words, or grammatically correct sentences or produce appropriate sounds, words, or sentences.

- Semantics is concerned with word and message meanings (vocabulary comprehension, following directions). Problems with semantics are evident when students are unable to identify appropriate pictures when word names are provided, answer simple questions, follow directions, tell how words or messages are similar or different or understand abstract concepts.
- Pragmatic is concerned with the use and function of language in varying settings. Problems with pragmatics are evident when students are unable to use language in social situations, to express feelings, create or understand images, give or request information and /or control actions of listeners.

11.4 Causes of Communication Disorders

11.4.1 Voice Disorders

- Organic Causes
- Cleft Palate
- Paralysis of Speech Muscles
- Absence of teeth, Craniofacial abnormalities
- Enlarged adenoids
- Neurological impairment
- Delayed intellectual Development
- Impaired Hearing
- Cerebral Palsy

11.4.2 Stuttering

Stuttering is caused by

- Pressures placed on child when parents and teachers react to normal hesitations and repetitions
- Labeling him as stutterer and peers teasing him

11.4.3 Language Disorders

- Cognitive limitation or retardation
- Environmental deprivation
- Hearing Impairment
- Emotional deprivation or behaviour disorders
- Structural abnormalities of speech mechanism.

Environmental influences are thought to play an important part in delayed disorders. A child who has little stimulation at home and has few chances to speak, listen, explore and interact with others will probably have little motivation for communication and may well develop disordered patterns of language.

11.5 Characteristics of Children with Communication Disorders

11.5.1 Cognitive

There are two schools of thought which explain cognitive difficulties of these children. According to one the development of cognitive skills which is heavily dependent on language is hampered by their language problems. The other school views that students with communication disorders have normal or average intellectual functioning but appear deficient because of their performance on intelligence test. It may be that difficulties in communicating cause cognitive difficulties, or it may be that cognitive difficulties cause communication difficulties.

11.5.2 Academic

Students who have speech and language problems usually experience difficulties in reading, language arts, social studies, science and other subjects that depend heavily on understanding verbal and written communication skills.

11.5.3 Physical

Individual with certain conditions like cerebral palsy, cleft palate or other kinds of oral facial disorders, and some types of mental retardation may experience speech and language difficulties as well as physical problems. But for most students with speech and language impairments there is no specific correspondence between physical appearance of functioning and speech or language functioning.

11.5.4 Behavioral

Students with communication disorders may withdraw from social situations, be rejected in social situations, and ultimately, they may suffer from a loss of self-confidence.

11.5.5 Communication

Students with speech problems have difficulty in pronouncing words, stuttering, omits words, squeaky or loud voice etc. Students with language disorders have difficulty using language to express themselves or understand others.

11.6 Assessment of Communication Disorders

Assessment of a suspected communication disorder may include some or all of the following components:

— Case history

— Physical examination

— Articulation test
— Hearing test
— Auditory discrimination test
— Language development test
— Overall language test
— Conversation with the child or language sample
— Behavioral observations of child's language competence in social contexts.

11.7 Treatment and Remediation

- The different types of communication disorders call for different approaches to remediation; behavioral approaches are frequently used.
- Articulation disorders may be treated by one of the common models: the discrimination model, the phonological model, the sensorimotor model, or the operant conditioning model.
- Voice disorders can sometimes be treated medically or surgically if there is an organic cause, but the most common remediation is direct vocal rehabilitation.
- Treatment of fluency disorders emphasizes either symptom modification or fluency reinforcement.
- Language disorders are treated by either individual or group approaches.
- Augmentative communication may be necessary in severe situations.
- Most children with speech and language problems attend regular classes. The largest single group of communication disorders specialists is employed in schools.

11.8 Educational Provisions for Speech Defective Children

The following educational provisions can be made for speech impaired children:

11.8.1 Speech Therapy

Speech therapists help children in correcting and removing the disabilities in articulation. But psychotherapists are consulted to treat the cases of stammering.

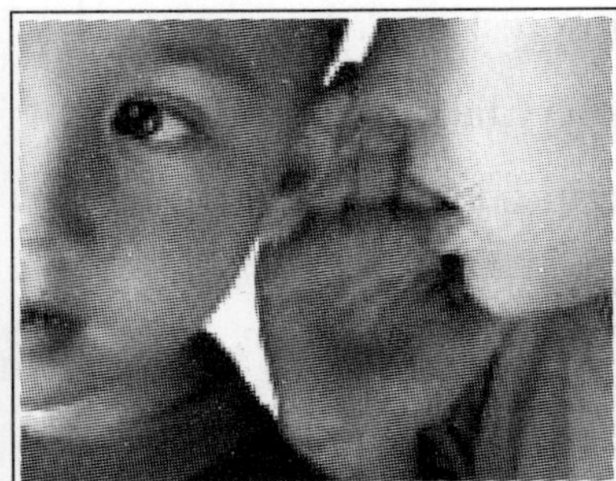

Fig.-11.2: Speech Therapy

11.8.2 Speech Training Activities

Teaching experts can make a more direct contribution by giving the child practice in using correct sound. The activities like rhymes, jingles, and speech games are suggested in speech training activity.

11.8.3 Adequate Motivation

The child should be motivated adequately. He should be made to realize the benefit of speech recovery. The sooner the child learns, the more enthusiastic he will be in practicing and will overcome his defects.

11.8.4 Avoidance of Overemphasis on the Handicap

We should not lay emphasis on level and quantity of handicap. If the child is made to feel that he cannot learn he will be frustrated and confidence will be shattered.

11.8.5 Avoidance of Anxiety

70 or 80% of the speech disorders come under categories of stuttering and stammering. It arises due to factors such as anxiety, shame, guilt, morose thoughts etc. Therefore the teacher should create a joyful, healthy and friendly class atmosphere.

11.8.6 Avoidance of Embarrassment

Teachers should avoid such a situation in class which creates embarrassment or fear.

11.8.7 Extracurricular Activities

These children should be taken to visit places of interest that are historical, social, cultural or geographical places such as museums, factories, workshops. Once their vocabulary is increased they may be encouraged to read books, journals, magazines etc.,

11.8.8 Some Classroom Provisions

- Maintain a relaxed than authoritarian classroom atmosphere.
- Emphasize good listening attitudes among the class members.
- Provide opportunities that will serve to build up the stuttering child's self-esteem.
- Watch for situations in which the stutterer is more likely to be fluent and provide opportunity for those situations.
- Avoid placing the stutterer in situations requiring rapid oral responses such as oral drills.

11.9 Classroom Activities

Classroom activities include the following:

11.9.1 Reducing Speech Problems

- Provide good models of appropriate speech.
- Focus on quantity more than quality of speech.
- Provide opportunities for practice.

11.9.2 Reducing Language Problems

- To improve use of grammar focus on meaning.
- To improve vocabulary focus on meaning and combine gestures with verbal language.
- To improve written expression focus on quantity and quality in written work.
- Teach specific skills and have students monitor their written work.
- Use familiar words as building blocks.
- Use acting games to teach meaning.

11.10 Tips for Teachers of Students with Communication Disorders

— Integrate appropriate language development activities into all curriculum areas.

— Create supportive environment where communication is fostered and valued.

— Provide opportunities during regular instructional day for students to practice skills being learned in therapy.

— Use areas of strength to compensate for weaknesses.

— Value speech and language delivery.

— Arrange activities in which students use language for different purposes -for example, oral book report, mock job interview, speech, surveys with different audiences (for example, another class at same grade level, class at another grade level, parents).

— Provide good speech models.

— Provide opportunities during academic instruction for free exchange of ideas and discussions about what is being taught.

— Organize, classroom space with at lest one area reserved for students to talk to each other.

— Consider development levels before making referral for outside assistance.

Behaviour Disorder

Childhood should be a happy time, a time for playing, growing, learning, and making friends – and for most children it is. But some children's lives seem to be in constant turmoil. They are in conflict, often serious, with others and themselves. Or they are so shy and withdrawn they seem to be in their own world. In either case, playing with others, making friends, and learning all the things a child must learn are extremely difficult for these children. They are children with behavior disorders. These children are referred to by a variety of terms -emotionally disturbed, socially maladjusted, psychologically disordered, emotionally handicapped, or even psychotic if their behavior is extremely abnormal or bizarre.

Behavior disordered children are seldom really liked by anyone – their peers, teachers, siblings, even parents. Sadder still, they often do not even like themselves. The child with behavior disorders is difficult to be around, and attempts to befriend him may lead only to rejection, verbal abuse, or even physical attack. With some emotionally withdrawn children, all overtures seem to fall on deaf ears, and yet these children are not deaf.

Although children with behavior disorders are not physically disabled, their noxious or withdrawn behavior can be as serious a handicap to their development and learning as the mentally retarded child's slowness to learn. Behavior disordered children make up a significant portion of those needing Special Education.

12.1 Defining Behavior Disorders

There is no generally agreed-upon definition of behavior disorders. Like their colleagues in mental retardation and learning disabilities, special educators in the area of behavior disorders have been struggling to reach consensus on definition. The definition of a handicapping condition should provide unambiguous guidance for the reliable identification of students who need Special Education services because of the disability in question. Definitions that appear theoretically sound" or "legally defensible" on paper are often found wanting in practice.

There are numerous reasons for the lack of a clear definition of behavior disorders. First, disordered behavior is a social construct; there is no clear agreement about what constitutes good mental health. Second, different theories of emotional disturbance use concepts and terminology that do little to promote meaning from one definition to another. Third, measuring and interpreting disordered behavior across time and settings is a difficult, exact, and costly endeavor. Cultural influence is another problem; expectations and normality for appropriate behavior are often quite different across ethnic and cultural groups. In addition, frequency and intensity are concerns. All children behave inappropriately at times -how often and with how much intensity must a student engages in a particular behavior before he is considered handicapped because of the behavior? Finally, disordered behavior sometimes occurs in conjunction with other handicapping conditions (most notably mental retardation and learning disabilities), making it difficult to tell whether one condition is the result or the cause of the other.

Although numerous definitions have been proposed, the one first written in 1957 by Eli Bower (I960) has had the most impact on Special Education. Bower's definition, with only a few changes, was adopted by the U.S. Department of Education as the definition of seriously emotionally disturbed children, one of the categories of handicapping conditions covered by Public Law (PL) 94-142.

Seriously emotionally disturbed is defined as follows:

- The term means a condition exhibiting one or more of the following characteristics over a long period of time and to a marked degree, which adversely affects educational performance.
    - An inability to learn which cannot be explained by intellectual, sensory, and health factors;
    - An inability to build or maintain satisfactory interpersonal relationships with peers and teachers;
    - Inappropriate types of behavior or feelings under normal circumstances;
    - A general pervasive mood of unhappiness or depression; or
    - A tendency to develop physical symptoms or fears associated with personal or school problems.
- The term includes children who are schizophrenic or autistic. The term does not include children who are socially maladjusted unless it is determined that

they are seriously emotionally disturbed. (Federal Register, 42 (163), August 23, 1977).

This definition specifies three conditions that must be met:

a) **chronicity** ("over a long period of time");

b) **severity** ("to a marked degree"); and

c) **difficulty in school** ("adversely affects educational performance"),

and it lists five types of problems that qualify. But in fact, the definition is extremely vague and leaves much to the subjective opinion of the authorities (usually teachers) surrounding the child. How does one operationalize such terms as satisfactory interpersonal relationships, normal, inappropriate, and pervasive?

The Council for Children with Behavior Disorders has officially adopted the position that the phrase "behaviorally disordered" is more appropriate than the phrase seriously emotionally disturbed. This is because; it does not suggest any particular theory or causation, includes students generally with problem behaviors, and it is less stigmatizing.

12.2 Identification and Measurement of Behavior Disorders

Most behavior disordered children are readily identifiable. The first process is

a) Screening – a process of eliminating children who are not likely to be handicapped and identifying those who show signs of behavioral disturbance.

b) Projective techniques – results of projective techniques and interviews do offer some information about the presence of behavior disorders.

c) Defining and measuring disordered behavior. We can analyze or measure several dimensions of children's behavior – its Frequency, Duration, Topography, Magnitude

- Frequency refers to how often a particular behavior is performed.
- Duration is the measure of how long a child engages in a given activity (eg: temper tantrums – how long it lasted).
- Topography refers to the physical shape or form of behavior (ex: pulling out hair).
- Magnitude or intensity. Behavior may be either too soft (ex. talking too softly that one cannot hear), or too hard (such as slamming the door).

12.3 Causes of Behavior Disorders

Causes of behavior disorders can be grouped into two major categories – biological and psychological.

12.3.1 Biological Factors

- Neurochemical imbalance
- Pre and postnatal infection's
- Chromosomal disorders
- Auditory impairments
- Central nervous system dysfunction

12.3.2 Psychological Factors

- Influence of home :
  - Parents are inconsistent disciplinarians
  - Use harsh and excessive punishment
  - Show little love and affection
  - Childrearing practices
  - Parent-child relationship
- Influence of school
  - Inappropriate expectations
  - Inconsistent management
  - Experiences in school setting
  - Relation between child and teacher
  - School discipline.

12.4 Classification of Children's Behavior Disorders

12.4.1 The DSM-III-R

Diagnostic and statistical manual of mental disorders revised

One system of classifying behavior disorders is the Diagnostic and Statistical Manual of Mental Disorders (Revised) (DSM-III-R) developed by the American Psychiatric Association (1987). The DSM-III-R is an elaborate and vast classification system consisting of 230 separate diagnostic categories, or labels, to identify the various types of disordered behavior noted in clinical practice. Because of its more precise language, its use of more examples, and the greater amount of information it requires about the person being diagnosed, the DSM-IIM represents an improvement in clinical classification over earlier versions from 1952 and 1968. The DSM-III-R classification system is used quite regularly in mental health professions; however, it suffers from a lack of reliability. Even with the more precise language, it is not uncommon for one psychiatrist or psychologist to classify a child in one category and a second examiner to place the same child in a completely different category (Epstein, Derwiler, & Reitzj 1985).

But an even greater problem is that putting a child in a given category provides no guidelines for treatment. Knowing that a child has been diagnosed as fitting a certain category in the DSM-III-R provides a teacher with virtually no useful information on what intervention or therapy is needed.

12.4.2 Quay's Statistical Classification

Another well-known classification system was developed by Quay and his co-workers (Quay, 1975,1986). Quay collected a wide range of data – including behavior ratings by parents and teachers, life histories, and children's own responses on questionnaires – for hundreds of behavior disordered children. When all this information was analyzed statistically, the researchers found that children's behavior disorders tend to appear in groups, or clusters. Children showed some of the behaviors in a given cluster had a high likelihood of also showing the other traits and behaviors in that cluster. Quay calls the four types:

a) Conduct disorder

b) Personality disorder

c) Immaturity, and

d) Socialized aggression.

a) Children described as having a conduct disorder are likely to be disobedient and/or disruptive, get into fights, be bossy, and have temper tantrums.

b) A personality disorder in children is identified by social withdrawal, anxiety, depression, feelings of inferiority, guilt, shyness, and unhappiness

c) Immaturity is characterized by a short attention span, extreme passivity, daydreaming, preference for younger playmates, and clumsiness.

d) Socialized aggression, is marked by truancy, gang membership, theft, and a feeling of pride in belonging to a delinquent subculture

Table- 12.1: Classification of disturbed children by negative variants of six levels of learning competence

Too little		Optimal		Too much
Disturbances in sensory perception	Excessive daydreaming Poor memory Short attention span In a world all his or her own	Attention	Selective attention	Fixation on particular stimuli
Immobilization	Sluggishness Passivity Drowsiness Clumsiness Depression	Response	Hyperactivity Restlessness	Self stimulation
Failure to develop speech	Failure to use language for communication	Response	Extremely talkative	Uses profanity verbally abusive
Self-injurious Lawlessness Destructiveness	Disruptiveness Attention seeking Irresponsibility Disobedience	Order	Overly conforming	Resistance to change Compulsive
Bizarre or stereo typed behavior Bizarre interests	Anxiety Preoccupation Doesn't know how to have fun Behaves like an adult Shyness	Exploratory	Plunges into activities	Tries to do every thing at once
Preoccupation with inanimate objects Extreme self-isolation Inability to relate to people	Social withdrawal Alienates others Aloofness Prefers younger playmates Acts bossy Secretiveness Fighting Temper tantrums	Social	Hypersensitivity Jealousy Overly dependent	Inability to function alone
Blunted, uneven or fragmented intellectual development	Lacks self care skills Lacks basic school skills Laziness in school Dislike for school Lacks vocational skills	Mastery	Pre-occupation with academics	OverIntellectualing

Source: From Frank M. Hewett and Frank D. Taylor (1980).

Although Quay's system has proven quite reliable -the same four clusters of behavior and personality traits have been found in many samples of behavior disordered children (Quay, 1986) -it does not provide treatment information. Therefore, usefulness is limited primarily to describing the major types of children's behavior disorders for purposes of research and communication.

12.4.3 Learning Competence

Hewett and his colleagues have developed a classification scheme based on "levels of learning competence" (Hewett, 1964, 1968; Hewett & Forness, 1977; Hewett & Taylor, 1980). Hewett and Taylor (1980) describe an actual episode that led them to seek better ways of classifying behavior disorders.

Hewett's classification system includes six levels of learning competence.

1. **The attention level** has to do with children making contact with their environment
2. **The response level**, with active motor and verbal participation
3. **The order level** is concerned with teaching children to follow instructions and routines
4. **The exploratory level** has children accurately and thoroughly investigate their environment
5. **The social level** focuses on interactions with others; and
6. **The mastery level** involves skills related to self-care, academics, and vocational interests. Table below shows how the classification scheme views behavior problems along a continuum of too little to too much in respect to the six levels of learning competence.

Hewett and Taylor (1980) contend that this classification system is both descriptive and functional, that classifying a child's behavior problem within the system "provides a direct link to the setting of curriculum goals".

12.4.4 Degree of Severity

Another method of classifying children with behavior disorders is by degree of severity (Carizio, 1990). Olson, Algozzine, and Schmid (1980) found that teachers of emotionally handicapped children regularly identified only two levels, or degrees, of behavioral disturbance: mild and severe. Children who were viewed as mildly emotionally disturbed were those who could respond to interventions provided in regular classrooms by regular class teachers, with the support of guidance counselors or consulting teachers. Those considered severely disturbed were children who needed intensive treatment programs and residential placement.

Classification by degree of severity, however, is primarily after the fact. Important decisions as to type of programming and environment for delivery should be based on an objective assessment of the child's individual needs, rather than on someone's opinion that the child is either mildly or severely disturbed.

12.5 Characteristics of Children with Behavior Disorders

Having looked at some of the characteristics of behavior disordered children, we can discuss these children's intellectual ability and academic achievement as well as the two general types of behavior they display.

- Aggression/acting out and
- Social withdrawal

12.5.1 Aggressive/Acting Out Behavior

The most common pattern of behavior exhibited by children with behavior disorders is one of aggression and acting out, or externalizing behavior disorders. Hops, Beickel, and Walker (1976) list the following behaviors as characteristic of the acting-out child in the classroom.

• Is out of seat	• Does not comply with adult commands or directions
• Yells out	• Argues (talks back)
• Runs around room	• Ignores other teachers
• Disturbs peers	• Distorts the truth
• Hits or fights	• Has temper tantrums
• Ignores teacher	• Is excluded from activities by peers
• Complains	• Does not follow directions
• Fights excessively	• Does not complete assignments
• Steals	
• Destroys property	

Even though all children sometimes cry, hit others, and refuse to comply with requests of parents and teachers, children with behavior disorders do so frequently. Also, behavior disordered children's aggressive behavior often occurs with little or no provocation. Aggression takes many forms – verbal abuse toward adults and other children, destructiveness and vandalism, physical attacks on others. These children seem to be in continuous conflict with those around them. Their own aggressive outbursts often cause others to strike back in attempts to punish them. It is no wonder children with behavior disorders are seldom liked by others and find it difficult to establish friendships.

As many children with behavior disorders grow older, their aggressive behavior causes conflict in the community, leading to run-ins with law enforcement officials and arrests for criminal offenses. Teenage delinquency is a serious problem today; youth under the age of 18 are responsible for a large number of each year's criminal arrests. To add to the problem, as mentioned earlier, the incidence of serious and violent crimes committed by juveniles is increasing (Cavan & Ferdinand, 1975; U.S. Department of Commerce, 1990).

12.5.2 Withdrawn Behavior

Some behavior disordered children are anything but aggressive. Their problem is the opposite – too little social interaction with others. They are said to have internalizing behavior disorders. Although children who consistently act immature and withdrawn do not present the threat to others that aggressive children do, their behavior still creates a serious impediment to development.

- These children seldom play with others their own age.
- They usually do not have the necessary social skills to make friends and have fun
- They often retreat into daydreams and fantasies.
- Some are fearful of things without reason, frequently complain of being sick or hurt
- Go into deep bouts of depression.

Obviously, these behavior patterns limit the child's chances to take part in and learn from the school and leisure activities in which normal children participate.

Because children with internalizing problems may be less disturbing to others, there is the danger of their not being identified. Happily, for the mildly or moderately disturbed child who is withdrawn and immature and who is fortunate enough to have competent teachers and other school professionals responsible for her development, the outlook is fairly good. Carefully outlining the social skills the child should learn and gradually and systematically arranging opportunities for and rewarding those behaviors often prove successful. Cartledge and Milbrn (1986), Stepehns (1978), and Strain, Guralnick, and Walker (1986) offer information on teaching children social skills.

It is apparent that a child's behavior pattern at school is the result of a complex interaction of –

1. The behavior pattern the child has been taught at home, including attitudes toward school,
2. The experiences the child has had with different teachers in the school setting, and
3. The relationship between the child and his/her current teacher(s).

Trying to determine in what proportion the child's behavior pattern is attributable to each of these learning sources is an impossible and unnecessary task. Deviant child behavior can be changed very effectively without knowing the original causes for its acquisition and development.

12.6 Intervention Models for Children with Behavior Disorders

There are several different approaches to educating emotionally disturbed children, each with its own definitions, purposes of treatment, and types of intervention. Based on the work of Rhodes and his colleagues (Rhodes & Head, 1974; Rhodes & Tracy, 1972a, 1972b), Kauffman (1989) lists six categories of models.

12.6.1 Biogenic

This model suggests that deviant behavior is a physical disorder with genetic or medical causes. It implies that these causes must be cured to treat the emotional disturbance. Treatment may be medical or nutritional.

12.6.2 Psychodynamic

Based on the idea that a disordered personality develops out of the interaction of experience and internal mental processes (ego, id, and superego) that are out of balance, this model relies on psychotherapy and creative projects for the child (and often the parents) rather than academic remediation.

12.6.3 Psychoeducational

This model is concerned with "unconscious motivations and underlying conflicts (hallmarks of psychodynamic models) yet also stresses the realistic demands of everyday functioning in school, home, and community" (Kauffman, 1989). Intervention focuses on therapeutic discussions such as life-space interviews to allow children to understand their behavior rationally and plan to change it (Rich, Beck, & Coleman, 1982).

12.6.4 Humanistic

This model suggests that the disturbed child is not in touch with her own feelings and cannot find self-fulfillment in traditional educational settings. Treatment takes place in an open, personalized setting where the teacher serves as a nondirective, nonauthoritarian "resource and catalyst" for the child's learning.

12.6.5 Ecological

This model stresses the interaction of the child with the people around him and with social institutions. Treatment involves teaching the child to function within the family, school, neighbourhood, and larger community.

12.6.6 Behavioral

This model assumes that the child has learned disordered behavior and has not learned appropriate responses. To treat the behavior disorder, a teacher uses applied behavior analysis techniques to teach the child appropriate responses and eliminate inappropriate ones.

12.7 Instructional Practices and Teacher Skills

12.7.1 Teaching Self-Management Skills

Teaching self-control or self-management skills to children can help children with behavior disorders. Self-management skills can be taught as a social skill consisting of five elements:

- Self-selection and definition of target behavior.
- Self-observation and recording of the target behavior.
- Specification of the procedures for changing the behavior.
- Implementation of those procedures.
- Evaluation of the self-control effort.

12.7.2 Teacher Skills

Teacher must be:

- Effective and creative
- Able to adapt curriculum materials and activities to individual needs.
- Special training to manage such children.

12.7.3 Improving Social Skills

- Greater interaction with friends
- Replace maladaptive behaviors with socially appropriate responses
- Focus on contributing factors that can be altered.
- Emphasis on present and future not past
- Using community resources.

12.7.4 Management and Instruction

Procedures for managing are:

- Contingency contract
- Ignoring disruptive behavior (extinction)
- Reinforcing any behavior except the undesirable response (differential reinforcement).
- Time out: removing child from reward for a brief time following inappropriate behavior.
- Over correction: Requiring the child to make restitution beyond the damaging effects.
- Token economy: gaining tokens for appropriate behavior and loosing tokens for inappropriate behavior.

12.7.5 Group Process

The power of peer group can be an effective means of producing positive changes in students with behavior disorders. Implementing group process model helps children learn to accept responsibility for their actions.

12.7.6 Affective Traits

The teacher of behavior disordered children must be able to establish healthy child-teacher relationships. Having an empathetic relationship with the child and communicating directly and honestly, ability to understand the nonverbal uses are often keys to understanding needs of emotionally disturbed children.

❖ ❖ ❖

Autism Spectrum Disorder

Communication is an active process by which individuals exchange information and convey ideas. Language, a set of codes adopted by a specific community, is the means by which an individual communicates his/her thoughts, ideas and/or feelings through vocal/ non-vocal modality. Communication impairment can occur when an individual lacks the ability to use the language codes. There are many types of communication impairments; the most common among them in children is a condition known as 'Autism'.

Autism is a disorder characterized by impairments in communication and social development. The condition is highly variable and may be accompanied by certain behavioral features as well as severe learning difficulties. The varied manifestations of this condition make assessment and intervention a challenging task for speech-language pathologists / therapists

This is probably the unheard soliloquize of a special child with 'Autism'. The child understands himself much better than anybody else so also the mother. Mothers of such children are often reported to have commented about their child being 'special', but are unable to convince the 'society' about his/her 'special' skills and finally end up with the Herculean task of seeing a metamorphosis in her child. Do we take pride in the child for whatever he/she is or are we prejudiced towards the 'special' child?? Time is ripe to introspect and understand ourselves so that we play a fair game with these children.

13.1 Defining Autism

Autism and related disorders are a phenomenologically related set of neuropsychiatry disorders. These conditions are characterized by patterns of both delay and deviance in multiple facets of development. Although many explanations for the social, cognitive and linguistic symptoms of autism have been explored, the exact mechanism by which it operates is still not understood. Typically however, the onset is in the first few months of life.

Table-13.1: DSM-IV-TR Definition of Autism

A. A total of six (or more) items from (1), (2), and (3), with at least two from (1) and one from each (2) and (3) must be exhibited to identify autism.

1. Qualitative impairment in social interaction, as manifested by atleast two of the following:
   a) Marked impairment in the use of multiple non-verbal behaviours, such as eye-to-eye gaze, facial expression, body postures, and gestures to regulate social interaction.
   b) Failure to develop peer relationships appropriate to developmental level.
   c) A lack of spontaneous seeking to share enjoyment, interests or achievements with other people (e.g. by a lack of showing, bringing, or pointing out objects of interest).
   d) Lack of social or emotional reciprocity.
2. Qualitative impairments in communication as manifested by at least one of the following:
   a) Delay in, or total lack of, the development of spoken language (not accompanied) by an attempt to compensate through alternative modes of communication such as gesture or mime.
   b) In individuals with adequate speech, marked impairment in the ability to initiate or sustain a conversation with others.
   c) Stereotyped and repetitive use of language or idiosyncratic language.
   d) Lack of varied, spontaneous make-believe play or social imitative play appropriate to developmental level.
3. Restricted, repetitive and stereotyped patterns of behaviour, interests and activities as manifested by at least one of the following:
   a) Encompassing preoccupation with one or more stereotyped and restricted patterns of interest that is abnormal either in intensity or focus.
   b) Apparently inflexible adherence to specific, non-functional routines or rituals.
   c) Stereotyped and repetitive motor mannerisms (e.g. hand or finger flapping or twisting, or complex whole body movements)
   d) Persistent preoccupation with parts of objects.

B. Delays or abnormal functioning in at least one of the following areas, with onset prior to age of 3 years: (1) social interaction, (2) language as used in social communication, (3) symbolic or imaginative play.

C. The disturbance is not better accounted for by Retts Disorder or Childhood Disintegrative Disorder.

13.2 Specific Difficulties Experienced by Children with Autism

The knowledge of specific difficulties experienced by individuals with autism is helpful in planning intervention program for them. The Association of Head Teachers of Autistic Children and Adults (1985), has described the specific difficulties of children with autism in detail.

13.2.1 Impaired Relationships and Self-image

13.2.1.1 Lack of Self-image

- Suffers a lack of personal identity and an impairment of his own self-image.
- He is "asocial" tending to remain isolated, occupying himself with his own obsessional or ritualistic activity and having an impaired sense of his own appropriate personal territory.
- Being unaware of himself, his actions and his effects on others he is likely to display a lack of inhibition in his general behavior

13.2.1.2 Difficulty in relating to Other People

- Impairment of the awareness of other people and their needs
- An inappropriate social response to, and communication with others.
- An impairment of the ability to recognise human characteristics

13.2.1.3 Difficulty in Perception of Meaningful Relationships

- Impaired ability to see sequences of growth, time, action, etc.
- Impaired ability to see similarities or differences, like and unlike.
- Impaired ability to see a whole picture or a whole anything.
- Impaired ability to relate properties, eg. fire will burn.
- Impaired ability to generalise or transfer learning.
- Lack of awareness of the reality of what cannot be seen, an impaired ability to separate reality from fantasy.
- Impaired awareness of the relationship of objects to each other to themselves and to other people, e.g. As seen in an inability to comprehend the use of preposition.
- Lack of judgement.
- Inability to be selective in the processing of information.

13.2.1.4 Difficulty in relating to Outside Stimuli

- Impairment of motivation, lacking the desire to learn new skills and the desire to please.
- Impairment of the sense of touch, smell, taste.
- Impairment of the use of sight where he may be fascinated by visual stimuli such as lights or bright lights, and be uninterested in the rest of his environment.
- Inappropriate reaction to sounds.
- Inappropriate emotional response.
- Lack of awareness of real danger and a phobic response to harmless objects.
- Lack of awareness of cause and effect.
- Inappropriate reaction to change.

13.2.2 Deficiency in Adaptive Behaviours

a) Ritualistic, compulsive, obsessional behaviours.

b) Extreme irrational fears or phobias.

c) Rigidity of thought and action – this manifests itself in pre-occupation with sameness and difficulty with change.

d) Poor perception of reality – There is often confusion between inner and outer worlds.

e) Extreme Anxiety States, or "High Arousal".

13.2.3 Impairment in Language and Communication Skills

13.2.3.1 Cognitive Skills

a) Difficulty in language

b) Patchy development of skills – No normal development of cognitive skills. Having a particular skill does not imply that 'earlier' skills will be present.

c) Specific difficulties in problem solving.

d) Play may be stuck at early stages of development.

e) Tend to have poor imitation skills.

f) Difficulty in directing attention to certain meaningful features in the environment.

g) Motivation and self-directed action are often lacking

h) Time and causality are difficulty ideas to autistic children

i) Poor sequencing ability.

13.2.4 Deficiency in Perceptual-Motor Skills

a) Lack of body awareness, body control and perceptual control.

As implied in the specific difficulties discussed above, autism is a complex learning disorder. In order to help children with autism a multidisciplinary approach is essential. The specialists from the field of psychiatric paediatrics, clinical psychology, Special Education, physiotherapy, speech and language therapy should plan a well coordinated programme helping them. Autism is viewed from different disciplinary point of viewed in isolation. But for planning and executing intervention programme there is a need to understand autism from multidisciplinary perspective.

13.3 Causes of Autism

Recent research report and overwhelming evidences suggest that autism is a neurological rather than a psychological disability. Yet, traditionally lack of interaction with cold and unresponsive parents and certain biological factors in genetics, pregnancy, birth, neurological and biochemical development is speculated to lead to autism.

Autism and related disorders are a phenomenologically related set of neuropsychiatric disorders. These conditions are characterized by patterns of both delay and deviance in multiple facets of development. Typically, however, their onset is in the first few months of life. Although many explanations for the social, cognitive and linguistic symptoms of autism have been explored, the exact mechanism by which it operates is still not understood. Yet, the following causes have been speculated.

a) Lack of interaction with cold and unresponsive parents.

b) Biological factors such as those related to pregnancy and birth, genetics, neurology and biochemistry.

- Neurochemical imbalance
- Pre-postnatal infection
- Chromosomal disorders
- Auditory impairments
- Central nervous system dysfunction

13.4 Characteristics of Autistic Children

Newsom (1976) has described six frequently observed characteristics of children with autism.

1. *Apparent sensory deficit:* We may move directly in front of the child, smile and talk to him, yet he will act as if no one is there.
2. *Severe affect isolation:* Attempts to love and cuddle and show affection to the child encounter a profound lack of interest on the child's part.
3. *Self-stimulation:* These children exhibit repetitive stereotyped acts, such as rocking their bodies when sitting, twirling around, flapping their hands at the wrists or humming.
4. *Tantrums and self-mutilatory behavior:* The child sometimes bites himself to bleed, he beats his head against wall, beats his face with fists. Sometimes the child's aggression will be directed outward against parents.
5. *Echolalic and psychotic speech:* These children are mute, i.e., they do not speak or utter only simple sounds. These children repeat what you speak to them. This echolalic speech may be delayed at other times.
6. *Behavior deficiencies:* An 5 or 10 year old child may behave like a one year old child. He may not play with toys, but put them in his mouth and tap repetitively with his fingers.

Majority of case studies have revealed that children with autism have

- onset before 30 months of age
- normal physical development.
- good cognitive potential
- disturbances in:
  - developmental rates and sequences in the areas of motor, social-adaptive and cognitive skills.
  - responses to sensory stimuli. Hypo- or hyper- sensitivity in audition, vision, touch, motor, smell and taste.
  - "speech-language, cognition and nonverbal communication, including mutism, echolalia, failure to use abstract terms, pronominal reversals and atypical vocabulary development.
  - the capacity to appropriately relate to people, events and objects including lack of social behavior, affection and appropriate play.

  - Emotion with interruption of the idiosyncratic or pervasive use of objects.

- Self-stimulatory behavior
- Obsessive desire for the maintenance of sameness
- Extreme autistic aloneness and withdrawal tendency.
- Language abnormalities

Language is a complex communication activity, which is used as a tool for expression of feelings and emotions. This social act of language requires coordinated functioning of many faculties including intelligence, thought, reasoning, neurological and motor skills. There is much impairment in language associated with the condition of autism. The most common among them are:

- Impaired verbal comprehension and expression
- Poor understanding of questions
- Echolalia (repetition of messages-immediate, delayed and/or mitigated)
- Impairments in use of abstract concepts including emotions
- Stereotyped verbal utterances
- Impaired skills in reading, writing and mathematics

Fig.-13.1: Austistic Children

13.5 Identification of Autistic Children

Diagnosis should include assessment and evaluation of child's developmental, communication and social skills.

13.5.1 Developmental Screening

NICHD lists 5 major behaviors that signal further evaluation.

- Does not babble or coo by 12 months
- Does not gesture (point, wave or grasp) by 12 months
- Does not say single words by 16 months
- Does not say 2 word phrases by 12 months
- Has loss of language and social skills.

13.5.2 Medical Tests

- Hearing and visual
- EEG
- Metabolic screening (e.g., lead)
- MRI
- Genetic testing

13.5.3 Therapy Evaluation

- Verbal and nonverbal assessment
- Direct observation
- Play based assessment
- Functional assessment

13.6 Intervention Programmes for Autistic Children

13.6.1 Communication Intervention in Autism

As we are traditionally oralists, emphasizing oral/vocal mode of communication is primary. The initial attempts for promoting better communication concentrate on speech training and modification of existing speech in mute as well as verbal autistic children.

Facilitation of speech production and comprehension has been classically attempted through play therapy and behavioural approaches using developmental aspects of speech, language of communication. The children attend daily therapy sessions of specific (45–60 minutes) durations and parents are advised and trained to follow these up at home during the rest of the day.

The approach is highly individualistic based on functional analysis of each child's speech/language and communication behaviour.

13.6.2 Play Therapy for Language Development

Play behaviours through games, toys and other materials are employed to assist and promote language development in children. The rationale is that the language development depends upon the child's capacity to acquire an understanding of some level of symbolic representation and that this capacity in the child is closely related to the learning of how to play. Play involves besides fun, certain set of rules and regulations, orderly and meaningful sequences with the use of signals, signs and symbols. Even the earliest games mother/caretaker plays with the child contain all these important components. Ex: "Hide and seek games like peek-a-boo in English.

In play therapy, the therapist observes the child at play and/or encourages child's elaboration of games. Symbolic play i.e. the play with gradually increasing meaningful sequences and rule-governed play encouraged in children.

Similarly, co-operative/interactive play permitting close physical and social contacts with people (beginning with the clinician) encouraged to promote socialization, communication and language development. Parents are also encouraged to observe this relaxed play situation in the clinical set up and to follow up the same at home and build up interpersonal interaction and relationships.

13.6.3 Behavioural Approaches for Speech/ Language/ Verbal Training

Behavioural approaches are based upon reinforcement of appropriate behaviours. The eye contact, appropriate sitting, imitation, social behaviour and so on are positively reinforced while tantrums, screaming are punished or ignored.

Stringent control procedures form a major component of behaviour programs particularly during the early phases of training. Emphasis initially is placed upon promoting/ facilitating prerequisite behaviours for learning such as appropriate sitting skills, eye contact, attention paying and compliance.

Programs for speech behaviour focus on the ability to imitate speech and are commonly referred to as verbal imitation skills/training.

13.6.4 Verbal Training in Mute-Nonverbal Children

In teaching imitation skills, attempts are made to establish speech occasional vocalizations. All vocalizations are reinforced, if the overall rate of vocalization is low so that the frequency is increased. Once the rate of vocalization is sufficiently high, criteria for reinforcements are changed to include different dimensions (variety of sounds, time lapse, similarity criteria. etc). Consistently according to the model presented, the imitation of a 2nd speech sound begins and discrimination training is initiated.

Additional vocalizations are targeted until a generalized imitative ability is demonstrated. Subsequently, attempts are made to connect meaning to the speech behaviours taught and to teach the functional uses of words and phrases. The implicit assumption is that children learn to speak by attempting and repeating the speech of others and by being rewarded for increasingly closer approximations to adult speech.

There are several descriptions of behaviour approaches to speech training given. To cite one is Lovaas et. al. (1979). He illustrates the training program using the following steps involving parents as therapists.

1. Initially sitting on a chair for up to a minute at a time.
2. Visually fixating on the therapists face for 2 seconds or so.
3. Nonverbal imitation training: touching shoes, clapping hands, touching table, then, on to increasingly elaborate imitations of the therapists' actions.
4. Training receptive language: Beginning with the same behaviours the child has learnt in nonverbal imitation, child is given verbal clues fading out the visual clues. Ex: sit on the chair, look at me, raise your hands, touch your shoe, clap your hands, etc.
5. Verbal imitation training: Where children are taught to imitate vocalizations of therapists/ parents starting with single vowels as / a/ and consonants as / ma/ and so on to build up expressive language.

Behavioural approaches have not only been used for the training of speech imitation skills for sounds or to the teaching of a series of stereotyped answers to common questions, but they are also useful for establishing and expanding a functional repertoire of verbal behaviour. Through attempts to connect meaning to imitative vocalizations, labeling responses have been taught. Children learn to repeat names of objects and actions presented with appropriate stimulus material (objects pictures) and questions such as what is this ? What is the girl doing? Do you want? etc. (Verbal prompts are faded gradually until the child is able to name objects and actions through the use of single words, and phrases such as this is a pen; the girl is running). Thus, names objects and events and requests description of events and narration, etc have been possible with frequent prompts.

The child, however, is first made to comprehend by following commands requiring the child to pick up objects or to point to objects, pictures when presented with a verbal label. Rudimentary conversational skills are also developed through such efforts.

Research and clinical experience suggests that speech training is a time-consuming procedure. Initial training on prerequisite skills such as sitting/ eye contact, attention, cooperation and compliance would take a lot of time after which speech training is attempted.

Lovaas (1977) reported that 30 days of continuous training at the rate of 7 hours/ day were required to establish vocal imitation skills for speech sounds alone in 2 mute autistic children.

Generalization outside therapy set up has also been a persistent problem with these children. This can be helped to a certain extent through parental involvement in therapy and extension of the same in home environments.

13.6.5 Speech / Language Training in Partially Verbal /Echolalic Children

Teaching verbal imitation to echolalic children is less time consuming. Their inadequacy lies in failing to respond to commands and use of utterances often in an inappropriate context. Consequently, teaching speech imitation skill does not depend upon establishing novel behaviour but rather on a shift in stimulus control. Poor stimulus control is apparent when commands are repeated rather than (carried out) complied or when words or phrases cannot be deliberately imitated even when they are highly frequent items within a much learned delayed echolalic repertoire. Teaching appropriate speech to echolalic children involves training discriminations between appropriate and inappropriate speech imitation through reinforcement strategies.

The discriminations are taught through various techniques as punishment, prompting and prompt fading, time-out, verbal instructions such as 'don't echo' etc. to inhibit echoic responses and to promote context-appropriate repetitions.

Among the many methods available for psychological treatment and education of people with autism, Applied Behaviour Analysis (ABA) has proved to be an effective method. ABA methods are very effective in reducing inappropriate behaviour and in increasing communication learning and socially appropriate behaviour. They help in understanding their learning style. Children above 3 years of age should have school based, individualised Special Education.

13.6.6 Developmental, Individual Difference Relationship-based Model (DIR)

Relatively new intervention technique for children with ASD is the Developmental, Individual Difference Relationship-based model (DIR).

The treatment programme based on such a comprehensive model should include the following principles and strategies.

- follow individual education plan
- build on the child's interests
- functional academics
- provide scope for predictable schedule
- systematic task analysis and appropriate chaining
- enabling the child to focus attention in highly structured activities
- regular reinforcement of behaviour
- parental training and sustained involvement
- provide counselling to parents by following self-help group models which can offer inspiration, hope, encouragement support to them.
- Target specific deficits in academic learning, language imitation, attention, motivation, compliance and initiative of interaction.
- include behavioural methods, communication, occupational and physical therapy as well as social play intervention and include socially useful productive work.

Attention Deficit Hyperactivity Disorders (ADHD)

ADHD is one of the most commonly diagnosed behavioral disorders of childhood. The disorder is estimated to affect between 3 to 7, out of every 100 school-aged children [American Psychiatric Association (APA), 2000]. This makes ADHD a major health concern. The disorder does not affect only children. In many cases, problems continue through adolescence and adulthood.

The core symptoms of ADHD are developmentally inappropriate levels of inattention, hyperactivity, and impulsivity. These problems are persistent and usually cause difficulties in one or more major life areas: home, school, work, or social relationships. Clinicians base their diagnosis on the presence of the core characteristics and the problems they cause.

Not all children and youth have the same type of ADHD. Because the disorder varies among individuals, children with ADHD won't all have the same problems. Some may be hyperactive. Others may be under-active. Some may have great problems with attention. Others may be mildly inattentive but overly impulsive. Still others may have significant problems in all three areas (attention, hyperactivity, and impulsivity).

Thus, there are three subtypes of AD/HD:

A) Predominantly Inattentive Type

B) Predominantly Hyperactive-Impulsive Type

C) Combined Type (inattention, hyperactivity-impulsivity)

Of course, from time to time, practically every person can be a bit absent-minded, restless, fidgety, or impulsive. So why are these same patterns of behavior considered normal for some people and symptoms of a disorder in others? It's partly a matter of degree. With ADHD, these behaviors occur far more than occasionally. They are the rule and not the exception.

14.1 Definitions of ADHD

- **Dental Dictionary**

  ADHD is a childhood neurologic disorder that manifests itself as excessive movement, irritability, immaturity, and an inability to concentrate or control impulses. It affects learning and skill acquisition.

- **Medicine Encyclopedia**

  ADHD is a developmental disorder characterized by distractibility, hyperactivity, impulsive behaviours, and the inability to remain focused on tasks or activities.

- **Genetics Encyclopedia**

  ADHD is a condition characterized by inattention and/or impulsivity and hyperactivity that begins in children prior to the age of seven. Their inattention leads to daydreaming, distractibility, and difficulties sustaining effort on a single task for a prolonged period of time. Children with ADHD show academic underachievement and conduct problems. As they grow older, they are at risk for low self-esteem, poor peer relationships, conflict with parents, delinquency, smoking, and substance abuse.

- **Education Encyclopedia**

  ADHD is a behavioral disorder with a strong hereditary component, which likely results from neurological dysfunction.

A 1998 study by Russell A. Barkley stated that ADHD is a deficit in behavior inhibition, which sets the stage for problems in regulating behavior. Students with ADHD may experience problems in

- Working memory
- Delayed inner speech
- Problems controlling emotions and arousal
- Difficulty analyzing problems and communicating solutions to others.

Hence students with ADHD may find it difficult to stay focused on tasks such as school work – tasks that require sustained attention and concentration yet are not intrinsically interesting. In addition, the majority of individuals with ADHD experience significant problems in peer relations and demonstrate a higher incidence of substance abuse than that of the general population.

Children with ADHD have short attention spans and are easily bored and frustrated with tasks. Although they may be quite intelligent, their lack of focus frequently results in poor grades and difficulties in school. ADHD children act impulsively, taking action first and thinking later. They are constantly moving, running, climbing, squirming, and fidgeting, but often have trouble with gross and fine motor skills. As a result, they may be physically clumsy and backward. Their clumsiness may extend to the social arena, where they are sometimes shunned due to their impulsive and intrusive behavior.

14.2 Causes of ADHD

ADHD is a very complex, neurobiochemical disorder. Researchers do not know ADHD's exact causes, as is the case with many mental and physical health conditions. Recent technological advances in brain study are providing strong clues as to both the presence of ADHD and its causes. In people with the disorder, these studies show that certain brain areas have less activity and blood flow and that certain brain structures are slightly smaller. These differences in brain activity and structure are mainly evident in the prefrontal cortex, the basal ganglia, and the cerebellum (Castellanos & Swanson, 2002). These areas are known to help us inhibit behavior, sustain attention, and control mood.

There is also strong evidence to suggest that certain chemicals in the brain – called neurotransmitters – play a large role in ADHD-type behaviors. Neurotransmitters help brain cells communicate with each other. The neurotransmitter that seems to be most involved with ADHD is called dopamine. Dopamine is widely used throughout the brain. Scientists have discovered a genetic basis for part of the dopamine problem that exists in some individuals with ADHD. Scientists also think that the neurotransmitter called norepinephrine is involved to some extent. Other neurotransmitters are being studied as well (Castellanos & Swanson, 2002).

When neurotransmitters don't work the way they are supposed to, brain systems function inefficiently. Problems result. With ADHD, these are manifested to the world as inattention, hyperactivity, impulsivity, and related behaviors.

Children with ADHD are often blamed for their behavior. However, it's not a matter of their choosing not to behave. It's a matter of "can't behave without the right help." ADHD interferes with a person's ability to behave appropriately.

Parents and teachers do not cause ADHD. Still, there are many things that both parents and teachers can do to help a child or teen manage his or her ADHD-related difficulties. Before we look at what needs to be done, however, let us look at what ADHD is and how it is diagnosed.

14.3 Characteristics of Children with ADHD

ADHD is considered a mental health disorder. Only a licensed professional, such as a pediatrician, psychologist, neurologist, psychiatrist, or clinical social worker, can make the diagnosis that a child, teen, or adult has ADHD. These professionals use the Diagnostic and Statistical Manual of Mental Disorders, Fourth Edition, Text Revised (DSM-IV-TR) as a guide (APA, 2000).

Over the last 10 years, public awareness about ADHD has led to more children and adults being diagnosed with the disorder. Some people have expressed concern that the condition is being overdiagnosed. The American Medical Association (AMA) took a serious look into these claims.

In order to be diagnosed with ADHD, children and youth must meet the specific diagnostic criteria set forth in the DSM-IV-TR. These criteria are primarily associated with the main features of the disability: inattention, hyperactivity, and impulsivity. Let's take a closer look at the specific types of behavior that must be evident in ADHD.

14.3.1 Inattention Characteristics

Attention is a process. When we pay attention:

- we initiate (direct our attention to where it is needed or desired at the moment);
- we sustain (pay attention for as long as needed);
- we inhibit (avoid focusing on something that removes our attention from where it needs to be); and finally
- we shift (move our attention to other things as needed).

Children with ADHD can pay attention. Their problems have to do with what they are paying attention to, for how long, and under what circumstances. It's not enough to say that a child has a problem paying attention. We need to know where the process is breaking down for the child so that appropriate individualized remedies can be created.

With ADHD, we see three common areas of inattention problems:

- sustaining attention long enough, especially to boring, tedious, or repetitious tasks;
- resisting distractions, especially to things that are more interesting or that fill in the gaps when sustained attention quits; and
- not paying sufficient attention, especially to details and organization.

These attention difficulties result in incomplete assignments, careless errors, and messy work. Children with ADHD often tune out activities that are dull, uninteresting, or unstimulating. Their performance is inconsistent both at home and in school. Social situations are affected by frequent shifts or losing track of conversations, not listening to others, and not following directions to games or rules (APA, 2000).

Symptoms of inattention, as listed in the DSM-IV-TR, are:

- often fails to give close attention to details or makes careless mistakes in schoolwork, work, or other activities;
- often has difficulty sustaining attention in tasks or play activities;
- often does not seem to listen when spoken to directly;
- often does not follow instructions and fails to finish schoolwork, chores, or duties in the workplace (not due to oppositional behavior or failure to understand instructions);
- often has difficulty organizing tasks and activities;
- often avoids, dislikes, or is reluctant to engage in tasks that require sustained mental effort (such as schoolwork or homework);
- often loses things necessary for tasks or activities (e.g., toys, school assignments, pencils, books, or tools);
- is often easily distracted by extraneous stimuli;
- is often forgetful in daily activities. (APA, 2000)

14.3.2 Hyperactivity Characteristics

Excessive activity is the most visible sign of ADHD. Studies show that these children are more active than those without the disorder, even during sleep. The greatest differences are usually seen in school settings (Barkley, 2000).

Many parents find their toddlers and preschoolers quite active. Care must be given before labeling a young one as hyperactive. At this developmental stage, a comparison should be made between the child and his or her same-age peers without ADHD. In young children, usually the hyperactivity of ADHD will come across as "always on the go" or "motor driven." You may see behaviors such as darting out of the house or into the street, excessive climbing, and less time spent with any one toy. In elementary years, children with ADHD will be more fidgety and squirmy than their same-age peers who do not have the disorder. They also are up and out of their seats more. Adolescents and adults feel more restless and bothered by quiet activities. At all ages, excessive and loud talking may be apparent. (APA, 2000)

Symptoms of hyperactivity, as listed in the DSM-IV-TR*, are:

- often fidgets with hands or feet or squirms in seat;
- often leaves seat in classroom or in other situations in which remaining seated is expected;
- often runs about or climbs excessively in situations in which it is inappropriate (in adolescents or adults, may be limited to subjective feelings of restlessness);
- often has difficulty playing or engaging in leisure activities quietly;
- is often "on the go" or often acts as if "driven by a motor;"
- often talks excessively. (APA, 2000)

14.3.3 Impulsivity Characteristics

Children and youth with ADHD often act without fully considering the circumstances or the consequences. Actually, thinking about the potential outcomes of their actions before the fact often does not even cross their minds. Their neurobiologically caused problem with impulsivity makes it hard to delay gratification. Waiting even a little while is too much for their biological drive to have it now.

The impulsivity leads these children to speak out of turn, interrupt others, and engage in what looks like risk-taking behavior. The child may run across the street without looking or climb to the top of very tall trees. Although such behavior is risky, the child is not so much a risk-taker as a child who has great difficulty controlling impulse and anticipating consequences. Often, the child is surprised to discover that he or she has gotten into a dangerous situation and has no idea of how to get out of it. Some studies show that these children are more accident prone, particularly those youth who are somewhat stubborn or defiant (Barkley, 2000).

Symptoms of impulsivity, as listed in the DSM-IV-TR (APA, 2000), are:

- often blurts out answers before questions have been completed;
- often has difficulty awaiting turn;
- often interrupts or intrudes on others (e.g., butts into conversations or games).

For a diagnosis of predominantly inattentive type of ADHD, six or more of the inattention symptoms must be present. For a diagnosis of hyperactive/impulsive type, six or more of the hyperactivity or impulsivity symptoms must be present (see lists on this page). For a diagnosis of combined type, six or more symptoms of inattention, plus six or more symptoms of hyperactivity or impulsivity, must be present.

The word often appears before each symptom of inattention, hyperactivity, and impulsivity in the DSM-IV-TR. In order to be considered a symptom of ADHD, a behavior can't be "a once in a while" problem. Nor can it be a problem that pops up all of a sudden. According to the DSM-IV-TR, the following must be true:

— There must be clear evidence of significant difficulty in two or more settings (e.g., at home, in school, with peers, or at work).

— Symptoms of inattention, hyperactivity, or impulsivity must be present at least six months.

— Some of these symptoms have to cause problems before age seven.

— The symptoms have to be developmentally inappropriate.

"Developmentally inappropriate" is an important point. If you look again at the symptom list for the three main features of ADHD, you will notice that some of these behaviors may be fairly normal at certain ages. For instance, no one expects a two year old to keep track of toys or to stay seated for very long. So, losing things or not being able to stay in a chair for long would not be considered symptoms of ADHD at that age. These same behaviors in a ten year old, however, would be developmentally inappropriate. We don't expect a ten year old to constantly lose things. We do expect a ten year old to be able to stay seated during a half-hour of class or a family dinner.

ADHD is determined by the number of symptoms present and the extent of the difficulty these cause. Also, the number of symptoms and the problems they cause may change across the lifespan. In a small number of cases, ADHD does go away in adolescence or adult years. However, in most cases, the problems shift. A hyperactive-impulsive fourteen year old may be able to stay seated longer than he or she could at age nine. While problems caused by hyperactivity-impulsivity seem to lessen with age, other ADHD-related symptoms usually become more problematic. For instance, demands for longer periods of sustained attention increase with age. So, for example, even though a fourteen year old may sit still during a lengthy reading assignment, he or she may be bothered by an inability to concentrate.

14.4 Diagnosis of ADHD

The American Academy of Pediatrics (2000) recommends that clinicians collect the following information when evaluating a child for ADHD.

— A thorough medical and family history.

— A medical examination for general health and neurologic status.

— A comprehensive interview with the parents, teachers, and child.

— Standardized behavior rating scales, including ADHD-specific ones completed by parents, teacher(s), and the child when appropriate. (Know that people with ADHD typically are not great at accurately reporting symptoms of the disorder, because it causes them to have poor insight into their own behavior.)

— Observation of the child.

— A variety of psychological tests to measure IQ and social and emotional adjustment. These tests also help to determine the presence of specific learning disabilities, which can co-occur with ADHD.

Once the practitioner completes the evaluation, he or she makes one of three determinations:

- The child does or does not have ADHD.
- The child does not have ADHD, but either has another disorder(s) or other factors that have created the difficulties.
- The child has ADHD and another disorder (called a coexisting condition).

To make the first determination – that the child has or does not have AD/HD – the clinician considers his or her findings in relation to the criteria of the DSM-IV-TR mentioned earlier.

To make the second determination – that the child's difficulties are caused by another disorder or other factors -the professional first considers the disorders that have symptoms similar to ADHD. You should be aware that some mental health disorders have their onset after puberty, but early warning signs, which are very similar to ADHD symptoms, may be present. Thus, it is possible for a diagnosis to change as the child develops and other disorders become more apparent. It is also possible for a child or youth to have more than one disorder, or co-occuring disorders.

14.5 Symptoms of ADHD in School Performance

One of the most critical areas in which to offer support is in the school arena. This is where most children with ADHD experience the greatest difficulty. That is because schools require great skill in the areas where students with ADHD are the weakest: attention, executive function, and memory. Although ADHD does not interfere with the ability to learn, it does wreak havoc on performance. Behavior problems, which usually get the most attention, may actually be by-products of the school environment and ADHD. These usually occur when tasks are too long, too hard, or lack interest. Many behavior problems can be avoided or lessened by adapting the school setting to fit the needs of the student.

In the school arena, ADHD is an educational performance problem. When little or nothing is done to help children with ADHD improve their performance, over time they will show academic achievement problems. This underachievement is not the result of an inability to learn. It is caused by the cumulative effects of missing important blocks of information and skill development that build from lesson to lesson and from one school year to the next. (It should be noted that a number of students with ADHD also have learning disabilities, and these do interfere with the ability to learn.)

Generally, ADHD will affect the student in one or more of the following performance areas:

- starting tasks,
- staying on task,
- completing tasks,
- making transitions,
- interacting with others,
- following through on directions,
- producing work at consistently normal levels, and/or
- organizing multi-step tasks.

Those teaching or designing programs for students with ADHD need to pinpoint where each student's difficulties occur. Otherwise, valuable intervention resources may be spent in areas where they are not critical.

For example, one child with ADHD may have difficulty starting a task because the directions are not clear. Another student may fully understand the directions but forget to follow all of them. Another may have difficulty making transitions and, as a result, get stuck in the space where one task ends and another begins. With the first child, intervention needs to focus upon making directions clear and in helping the child to understand those directions. The second child would need guidance to follow all the directions. The third child would need help in making transitions from one activity to another.

The sooner educational interventions begin the better. They should be started when educational performance problems become evident and should not be delayed because the child is still holding his or her own on achievement tests.

In the elementary years, ADHD usually causes these problems:

— off-task behavior,

— incomplete or lost assignments,

— disorganization,

— sloppy work or messy handwriting,

— not following directions,

— errors in accuracy,

— inconsistent performance,

— disruptive behavior or spacey, daydreaming behavior, and/or

— social interaction difficulties.

Around middle school and into high school and beyond, most of these problems continue. However, additional ones arise. That is because adolescents are expected to be much more independent and self-directed. They receive less supervision. Demands for concentration and more sophisticated thinking and problem solving increase. ADHD makes it hard to meet those demands.

Given the additional problems that seem to arise in middle school and beyond, it's not unusual to see a student who's gotten by in earlier grades academically around puberty.

The thinking difficulties associated with ADHD do not have to do with intellectual ability. Instead, they arise out of problems with concentration, memory, and cognitive organization. Typically, ADHD-related memory problems arise in two areas:

❖ **working memory** – which helps the student keep one thing in mind while working on another, and

❖ **retrieval** – being able to locate on demand information that has been learned and stored in memory.

Many students also show problems in:

- time management,
- prioritizing work,

- reading comprehension,
- note taking,
- study skills, and
- completing multi-step tasks.

Clearly, a student with ADHD can have difficulty in any number of academic areas and with critical academic skills. Thus, it is extremely important that the school and parents work together to design an appropriate educational program for the student.

14.6 Treatment of ADHD

The recommended multi-modal treatment approach consists of four core interventions:

1. patient, parent, and teacher education about the disorder;
2. medication (usually from the class of drugs called stimulants);
3. behavioral therapy; and
4. other environmental supports, including an appropriate school program.

14.7 Educational Interventions for Children with ADHD

In addition to the core interventions described, there are a number of other educational interventions that can potentially help students with ADHD. Some of the more common interventions, modifications, and adaptations, are as follows:

14.7.1 Select a Supportive Teacher

Try to place the student with teachers who are positive, upbeat, flexible, and highly organized problem-solvers. Teachers who praise liberally and who are willing to "go the extra mile" to help students succeed can be enormously beneficial to students with ADHD.

14.7.2 Adapt Curriculum and Instruction

— Provide more direct instruction and as much one-on-one instruction as possible.

— Use guided instruction.

— Teach and practice organization and study skills in every subject area.

— Lecture less.

— Design lessons so that students have to actively respond -get up, move around, go to the board, move in their seats.

— Design highly motivating and enriching curriculum with ample opportunity for hands-on activities and movement.

— Eliminate repetition from tasks or use more novel ways to practice.

— Design tasks of low to moderate frustration levels.

— Use computers in instruction.

— Challenge but don't overwhelm.

— Change evaluation methods to suit the child's learning styles and strengths.

14.7.3 Provide Supports to Promote On-Task Behavior

❖ Pair the student with a study buddy or learning partner who is an exemplary student.

❖ Provide frequent feedback.

❖ Structure tasks.

❖ Monitor independent work.

❖ Schedule difficult subjects at the student's most productive time.

❖ Use mentoring and peer tutoring.

❖ Provide frequent and regularly scheduled breaks.

❖ Set timers for specific tasks.

❖ Call attention to schedule changes.

❖ Maintain frequent communication between home and school.

❖ Do daily/weekly progress reports.

❖ Teach conflict resolution and peer mediation skills.

14.7.4 Provide Supports to Promote Executive Function

- To support planning:

  ❖ Teach the student to use assignment pads, day planners or time schedules, task organizers and outlines.

  ❖ Teach study skills and practice them frequently and in all subjects.

- To increase organization:
  - Allow time during school day for locker and backpack organization.
  - Allow time for student to organize materials and assignments for homework.
  - Have the student create a master notebook -a 3-ring binder where the student organizes (rather than stuffs) papers.
  - Limit number of folders used; have the student use hole-punched paper and clearly label all binders on spines; monitor notebooks.
  - Have daily and weekly organization and clean up routines.
  - Provide frequent checks of work and systems for organization.
- To improve follow through:
  - Create work completion routines.
  - Provide opportunities for self-correction.
  - Accept late work.
  - Give partial credit for work partially completed.
- To improve self-control:
  - Prepare the student for transitions.
  - Display rules.
  - Give behavior prompts.
  - Have clear consequences.
  - Provide the student with time to de-stress.
  - Allow doodling or other appropriate, mindless motor movement.
  - Use activity as a reward.
  - Provide more supervision.

14.7.5 Memory Boosters

- To assist with working memory:
  - Focus on one concept at a time.
  - List all steps.
  - Write all work down.

- Use reading guides and plot summaries.
- Teach note-taking skills – let the student use a study buddy or teacher-prepared notes to fill in gaps.
- List all key points on board.
- Provide summaries, study guides, outlines, and lists.
- Let the student use the computer.

* To assist with memory retrieval:
  - Teach the student memory strategies (grouping, chunking, mnemonic devices).
  - Practice sorting main ideas and details.
  - Teach information and organization skills.
  - Make necessary test accommodations (allow open book tests; use word banks; use other memory cues; test in preferred modality – e.g., orally, fill in blank; give frequent quizzes instead of lengthy tests).

14.7.6 Attention Getters and Keepers

* For problems beginning tasks:
  - Repeat directions.
  - Increase task structure.
  - Highlight or color code directions and other important parts.
  - Teach the student keyword underlining skills.
  - Summarize key information.
  - Give visual cues.
  - Have the class start together.
* For problems sticking with and finishing tasks:
  - Add interest and activity to tasks.
  - Divide larger tasks into easily completed segments.
  - Shorten overall tasks.
  - Allow the student choice in tasks.
  - Limit lecture time.
  - Call on the student often.

For parents, teachers, and children challenged by this disorder, ADHD can be a truly unique experience. While some days the struggles seem insurmountable, it's important to realize that when ADHD is properly managed children with ADHD can turn some of their liabilities into assets, and they can minimize the others.

Meanwhile, there is help and hope available. Parent support groups exist in every state. Others like the Learning Disabilities Association and Parent's Anonymous may also be useful depending on your individual circumstances. Visit the Websites of these groups, where you'll find information on activities and contact numbers of similar groups in your area.

Orthopedical Impairment

15.1 Physical Impairment and Neurological Impairments

A human body is the best creation of nature. Every movement we make depends on the co-ordinated interaction of the muscles, bones, ligaments and tendons that make up musculo-skeleton system. The 206 major bones that form the skeleton are the body's supporting workmen, but they do much more than they provide simple support. The skull and spine protect the brain and spinal cord, while the rib cage and pelvis shield the other vital organs. These elegantly engineered intersections of joints permit the wide range of movements of which we are capable. The bones also serve as living storehouses for minerals, constantly releasing and reabsorbing calcium and other essential elements and inside certain bones lies the red marrow that manufacture most of our new blood cells.

For like other parts of the body, the bone and muscular system are subjected to a variety of ills, due to malnutrition, sickness, stresses, infections or any accidents by which bones and muscles are prone to various injuries and problems, which will lead to impairment. Such deficiency or deformation which in turn relate to bone or muscle is termed as orthopaedical impairment.

15.1.1 Definitions of Orthopedic Impairment

The word orthopedics was synthesized by Nicholos Andry from the Greek roots 'orthos' and 'paidios'.

Orthos means straight and paidios means child, which means the prevention of deformed adults lies in the development of straight children.

Orthopedically impairment refers to defects in size and structure of bones and joints with deviation in muscle strength, co-ordination and control.

According to Whitehouse conference: "The crippled child, in orthopedic sense is a child that has defect which causes a deformity or an interference with normal function of bones , muscles or joints. The condition may be congenital or due to disease or accident; it may be aggravated by neglect or by ignorance."

"An orthopedic handicap means a condition of malformation, malfunction due to loss of bones, muscles or body tissue which requires Special Education or related services.

According to Public Law 94 – 142 "Orthopedically impaired means, a severe orthopedic impairment which adversely affects a child's educational performance. The term includes impairments caused by congenital anomaly [E.g.: club foot], impairments caused by disease (E.g.: poliomyelitis, bone tuberculosis etc.,) and impairments from other causes [E.g.: cerebral palsy, amputation and fractures or burns which cause contractures]".

"Crippled children are those who suffer from a defect. That is accompanied by one or another type of deformity that inhibits the normal exercise of his/her muscles, joints or bones".

From the above mentioned definitions it is clear that orthopedically impaired children are those who have the defects in size and structure of bones and joints with deviation in muscle strength, co-ordination or control.

Orthopaedic and neurologic impairments are frequently described in terms of the affected parts of the body. The term *Plegia* is often used in combination to indicate the location of limb involvement.

Quadriplegia – all four limbs (both arms and legs) are affected; movement of the trunk and face may also be impaired.

Paraplegia – Motor impairment of the legs only.

Hemiplegia – only one side of the body is affected; for example, the left arm and the left leg may be impaired.

Diplegia – major involvement of the legs, with less severe involvement of the arms.

A Hemiplegia Arm, body, leg affected on one side	B Diplegia: Legs affected more than arms	C Quadriplegia Whole body affected
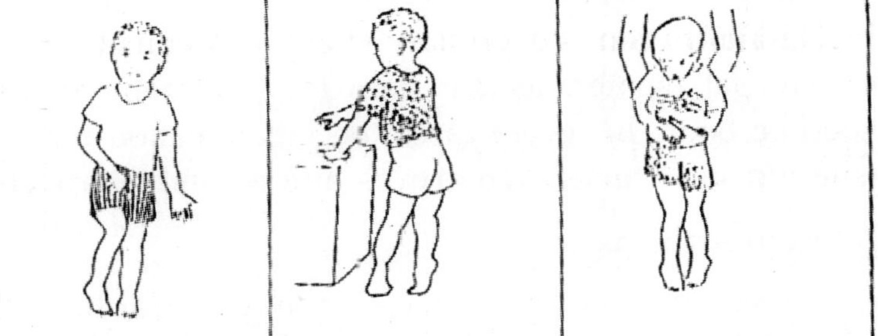		
Arm turned in and bent Hand fisted, Leg turned in and bent, Tiptoe standing.	Arms slightly clumsy, Legs pressed together and turned in Tiptoe standing	Poor head control Arms turned in & bent Legs pressed together Tiptoe standing.

Less common forms of involvement include:

Monoplegia – only one limb is affected

Triplegia – three limbs are affected

Double hemipleiga – major involvement of the arms, with less severe involvement of the legs.

15.1.2 Types of Orthopedical Impairments

Some of the major types of orthopedical disorders are:

1. Arthritis or Rheumatism
   a) Rheumatoid Arthritis
   b) Osteo-arthritis
2. Club foot
3. Scolisis
4. Poliomyelitis
5. Osteogenesis imperfecta
6. Rickets.
7. Osteoporisis

15.1.2.1 Arthritis or Rheumatism

The terms arthritis or rheumatism are commonly used to describe pain, swelling and stiffness of joints; Arthritis literally means inflammation of joints, rheumatism means pain and stiffness in the muscles, bones, joints and tendons.

Arthritis reveals two major types:

a) Rhematoid arthritis,

b) Osteo arthritis.

a) Rheumatoid Arthritis

Inflammation is a primary event in rheumatoid arthritis typically starting in the synobial membrane that lines the joints and spreading to the cartilage and underline bone. In severe cases the inflammation may spread to other connective tissue and some times even to eyes, arteries and internal organs.

b) Osteo Arthritis

Osteoarthritis is the most common type of arthritis. It is most commonly found among children with disabilities. Here the cartilage around the joint is damaged, the space between bones becomes smaller and looses its lubrication and movement becomes painful and impossible Osteoarthritis is also called degenerate joint disease.

15.1.2.2 Club Foot

The club foot is another type of deformity. It accounts for 26% of congenitally crippled children. Club foot means one or both the feet turned or the wrong angle of the ankle. This can be completely cured and later noted that the person fully recovers and leads a normal life.

15.1.2.3 Scoliosis

Scoliosis is the lateral curvature of the spine due to which the person might bend on one side. The curvature may progress with age. In very severe cases it may cause heart and lung problems and limitation of movement.

15.1.2.4 Poliomyelitis

The poliomyelitis is a most common neuromotor disease noted in a large number of children. Polio is caused by polio virus which attacks the nerve cells in the spinal cord leading to paralised muscles, pain and deformity. This disease does not affect intellectual functioning or the ability to learn.

15.1.2.5 Osteogenesis Imperfecta

This disease appears to be congenital and is known as brittle bones. Here bones are formed imperfectly and break very easily. It hinders bone growth both in length and thickness, and dwarfism and deafness may occur.

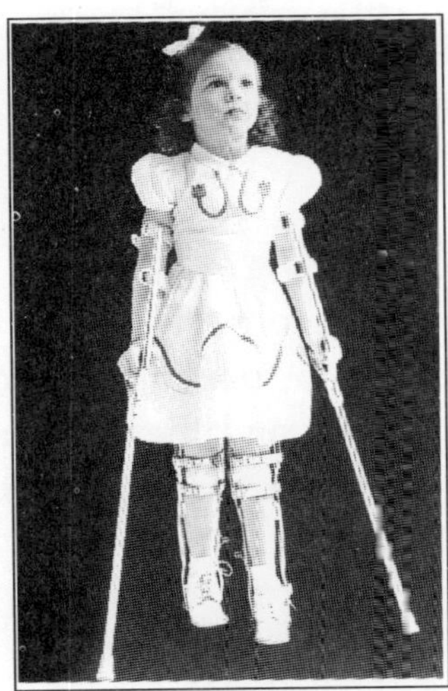

Fig.-15.1: Poliomyelitis

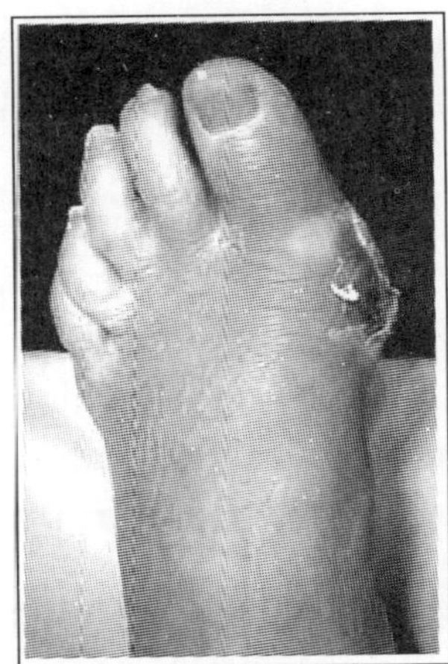

Fig.-15.2: Osteomyelitis

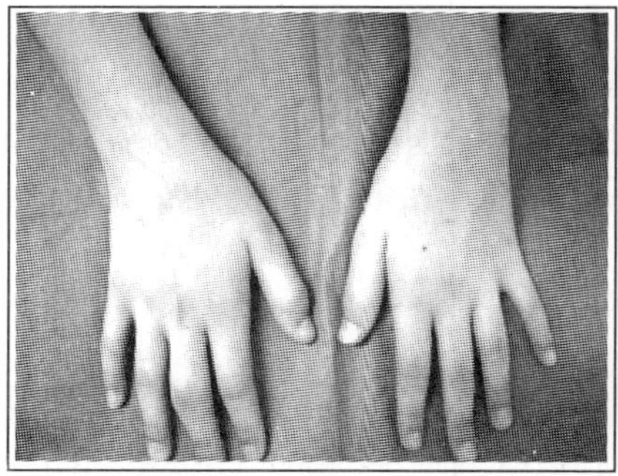

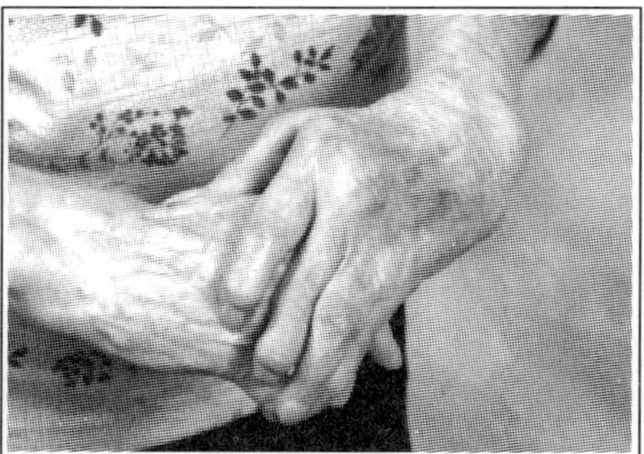

Fig.-15.3: Rheumatoid Arthritis

15.1.2.6 Rickets

Rickets in case of children is a condition in which bones fail to harden because of shortage of vitamin D in the diet and by inadequate exposure to sunlight. Rickets in case of children is called nutritional ricket and usually occurs in children about one year old. The general health is impaired; the predominant signs are a large head, retarded skeletal growth, enlarged epiphysis, curvature of long bones and deformity of chest. Rickets in case of adults is called osteomalacia, which is also caused by Vitamin D deficiency. Increased susceptibility to bone fracture is the main symptom in adult. It is more common among pregnant women and older people.

15.1.2.7 Osteoporosis

It is a serious and very common condition in which skeletal bones may lose strength to such a degree that they break with little or no trauma. Hip, wrist and spinal bones are those most likely to fracture.

15.1.3 Causes of Orthopedic Impairment

The causative factors of all types of impairments are many. But a thorough knowledge of some main causative factors is necessary for planning a programme for them. The deformities may be congenital or acquired and they may reflect an underlying abnormality of bone, joint or soft tissue. The essential material which leads to orthopaedic impairment is bone.

15.1.3.1 Congenital Deformities

Congenital deformities or malformations are present at birth, though they may not be recognised until later. They vary from severe malformations that are incompatible with life and may be found in stillborn infants, to minor abnormalities of structure that have no practical significances.

The congenital abnormality of development may be caused by

a) genetic abnormality

b) environment abnormality,

c) combined genetic and environmental abnormalities.

a) Genetic Causes

It includes mutation of a whole chromosome, as in Down's syndrome (Mongolism) and mutation of a small part of a chromosome or of a single gene, as in achondroplasia. The defect is not necessarily always inherited from an affected parent it may arise from a mutation in the germ cell.

b) Environmental Causes

These causes are not well understood. Experiments in animals have shown that many different types of environmental influence dietetic, hormonal, chemical, physical or infective –may cause abnormalities of development, and the system of the body that is mainly affected depends upon the timing of the environmental 'insult'; The specific agents whose influence in man are well attested include radiation, the virus of rubella, and certain drugs (notably aminopterin & thalidamids).

c) Combined Genetic and Environmental Factors

These seem to be the usual cause of the more common congenital malformation in man. It is thought probable that developing embryos react differently to environmental influences. Some have a natural resistance whereas others are susceptible. A malformation is therefore likely to arise when an environmental "insult' is inflicted upon cells that have a genetically determined lack of resistance to it.

E.g. Congenital dislocation of the hip, congenital club foot, spinabifida, congenital scoliosis, osteogenesis, imperfecta, cervical rib, certain types of osteoarthritis (especially of the hips), ankylosing spondylitis.

15.1.3.2 Acquired Deformities

Acquired deformities may be classified in two groups: those in which deformity arises at a joint, and those in which it arises in a bone.

a) Deformity arising at a joint

Deformity may be said to exist at a joint when the joint cannot be placed voluntarily in the neutral anatomical position.

Causes

The causes for this deformity are,

- Dislocation or subluxation
- Muscle imbalance.
- Feathering or contracture of muscles or tendons
- Contracture of soft tissues
- Arthritis
- Posture
- Unknown causes.

b) Deformity arising in a bone

Deformity exists in a bone when it is out of its normal anatomical alignment.

Causes

There are three causes of deformity arising in bone.

- Fracture
- Bending
- Uneven epiphysial growth.

E.g.

— Polio in a non-immunized child may result in the loss of use of limbs.

— Meningitis can cause deafness or blindness.

— Accidents in the home or street or child battering may produce physical or sensory defects or even cerebral palsy.

15.1.4 Characteristics of Orthopedic Impaired Children

15.1.4.1 Physical Characteristics

- Involuntary contraction of muscles when they are suddenly stretched,
- Lack of voluntary control of fingers or toes and they will be on constant motion.
- Lack of control all over the body, unable to co-ordinate the movement of two or three parts of the body.

  For *e.g.*While playing, difficulty in moving hands & legs simultaneously / or moving hand or bend up the body to a particular direction.

- Widespread continuous muscle tension or stiffness.
- Rhythmic, involuntary, uncontrollable motions limited to certain groups.
- Generalized seizure with tensing of muscles and/or twitching and tremour with loss of consciousness
- Brief lapse of consciousness (3–10 second), some times rhythmic 3 seconds blinking.
- Sudden generalised jerk or loss of tone without detectable alteration of consciousness.
- Rhythmic movement of one part of body, stationary or progressing to other parts.
- One or both feet turned downward and outward at ankle.
- Lateral curvature of spine, body thrown out of alignment resulting in growth and deformities.
- Congenital amputation or malformations of the extremities (lacks hands or legs or fingers or toes or some deformity from birth)
- Deviations in the running pattern -such as failure to alternate sides automatically, jerkiness, whipping of the leg or the foot in or out.
- Deviations in standing or sitting patterns, such as weight shifted more to one side than the other or one part of the body twisted (e.g.: the trunk) with regard to the rest of the body.
- Throwing or catching deviations, such as loss of balance while throwing or catching, inability to control the object, inability to adjust to different speeds or heights incatching the object.
- Loss of limb or extremities for one or the other reason (by accident)

15.1.4.2 Psychological Characteristics

- They are passive, less persistent, having shorter attention span, engage themselves in less exploration and display less motivation.
- They are more dependent on adults and have high anxiety and frustration.
- They are tender minded and somewhat tense.
- Social relationships constitute a problem area for many crippled youngsters as they feel inferior and depressed.

- They possess a poor ego, and unconscious guilt feelings.
- They have the strong sense of fear and lack confidence in their abilities.

Depending on these characteristics the orthopedically impaired child can be identified.

15.1.5 Identification of Orthopedic Impaired Children

— Look at cumulative records of children to see if there is any evidence of a crippling disease for a specific child.

— *One legged race* – Ask the children to hop a certain distance on the right foot and then return hopping on the left foot.

— *Side ways race* – Have the children run sideways, keeping their feet at right angles to the direction in which they are running.

— *Backwards race* – Mark two lines on the gym floor. Have the children walk on one line and race backwards, until they have crossed the second line.

— *Ball throwing games* – Ask the boys and girls to choose games they like that involve throwing and catching a ball. These and other similar activities will get the children into action. So you can observe them.

— Give a standardized test, pre-test of vision, hearing and motor co-ordination.

— After the above testing, these must be referred to a doctor or specialist for final identification.

Orthopaedically impaired children are identified by orthopaedic surgeons regarding degree of disability.

15.1.6 Diagnostic Tools

1. History
2. Physical examination
3. General orthopaedic examination
4. Local orthopaedic examination
5. X-ray examination
6. Laboratory studies
7. Special tests:
   a) Biopsy
   b) Joint aspiration
   c) Myelograhy
   d) Electro Myography
8. Consultation

15.1.7 Treatment of Orthopedic Disorders

Orthopedic treatment falls into 3 categories.

1. No treatment – Simply reassurance or advice.
2. Non-Operative treatment.
3. Operative treatment.

15.1.7.1 No Treatment

In every case these three possibilities of treatment should be considered one by one, in the order given. At least half of the patients attending orthopaedic outpatient clinics (excluding cases of fractures) do not require treatment; all that they need is reassurance and advice. In many cases the sole reason for the patients' attendance is that he fears that he may have cancer, tuberculoses, impending paralysis or other serious disease. If he can be reassured that there is no evidence of serious disease, he goes away satisfied and his symptoms immediately become less disturbing.

15.1.7.2 Non-Operative Treatment

Some methods of non-operative treatment are as follows.

a) **Rest:** Rest has been one of the main ways of orthopedic treatment, complete rest demands recumbency in bed or immobilisation of the diseased part in plaster.

b) **Support:** E.g. Steel – Reinforced tumber corsets, spinal braces, cervical collars wrist supports, walking calipers, below knee stretch with ankle strips and devices to control drop foot.

c) **Physio therapy:** This approach is particularly rewarding in the rehabilitation of patients after injury or after operation and in diseases such as polio myelitis, cerebral palsy, hemiplegia and peripheral nerve palsies.

   - Active exercises
   - Hydrotherapy
   - Passive point movements

d) **Local injections** – It has 2 groups.

   1. osteoarthritis or rheumatoid arthritis, in which the substance is directly injected into the affected joint with rigid aseptic precautions.

2. Extra-articular lesions of the type often ascribed to chronic strain as exemplited by tennis elbow tendonitis above the shoulder and certain types of back pain.

e) **Drugs:** Drugs have rather a small place in orthopaedic practice. Those used may be placed in 7 categories.

i) Antibacterial agents
ii) Analgesics
iii) Sedatives
iv) Anti-inflammatory drugs
v) Hormone like drugs
vi) Specific drugs
vii) Cytotoxic drugs

f) **Manipulation**

- Manipulation for correction of deformity.
- Manipulation to improve the range of movements at stiff joints.
- Manipulation for relief of chronic pain in or about a joint.

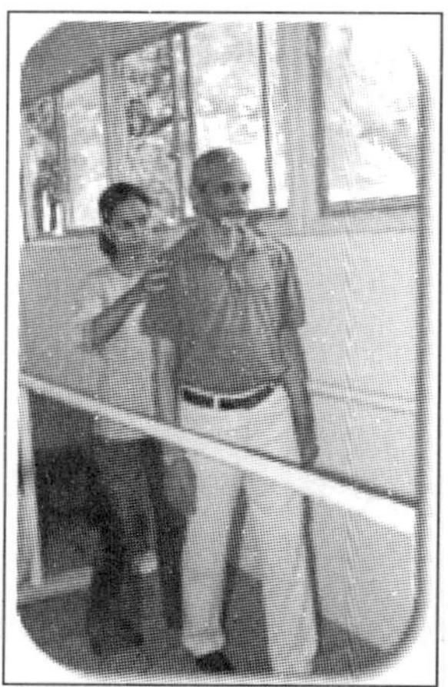

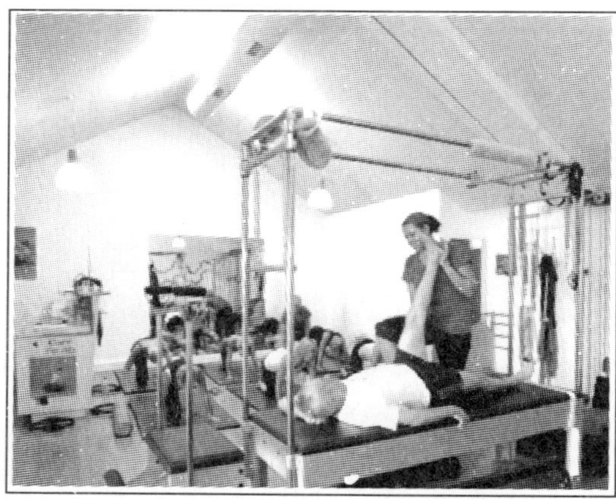

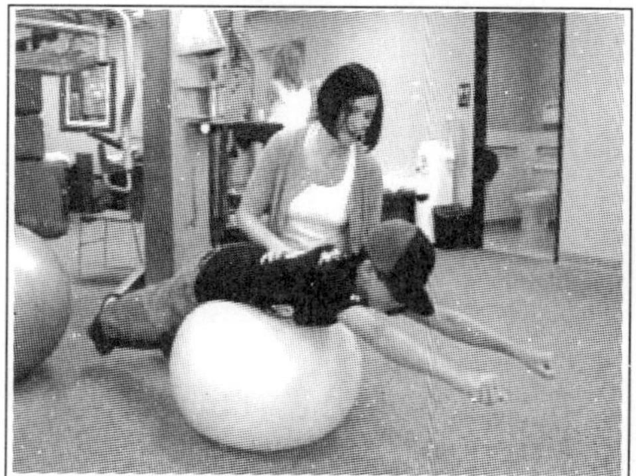

Fig.-15.4: Physiotherapy for Orthopedically Impaired

g) Therapy

- Radiotherapy
- Electrical stimulation of muscles
- Electrophysical agents

  i) Local heat   ii) Ultrasound waves
- Cryotherapy
- Interferantial therapy and transcutaneous nerve stimulation

15.1.7.3 Operative Treatment

Some of the most important operations are,

a) **Synovectomy:** It is the operation for removal of the inflammed lining of a joint while leaving the capsule intact.

   E.g.: Some types of chronic infective arthritis, early rheumatoid arthritis.

b) **Osteostamy:** It is the operation of cutting a bone or creating a surgical fracture. It has almost supplanted osteoclasis (forcible bending or incomplete breaking of a bone) E.g.: To correct deformities of the long bones in children with rickets.

c) **Arthrodesis:** The operation of orthrodesis of joint fusion, is still widely used, though since the advent of reliable techniques of joint reconstruction, joint is usually slight, and patients readily adopt themselves to it. Even when two or three joints are fused, function may be surprisingly good, depending upon the particular joints affected.

   Arthrodesis is indicated mainly in the following conditions.

   i) Advanced osteoarthritis or rheumatoid arthritis with disabling pain especially when confined to a single joint.

   ii) Quiescent tuberculosis arthritis.

15.1.7.4 Prosthetic Services

Prosthetic orthotics and adaptive devices for daily living

a) Prosthesis is an artificial replacement for a missing body part. E.g.: An artificial hand or leg.

b) An orthosis is a device that replaces a function no longer present in a part of a person's body.

E.g.: A brace or a device that allows a person to hold a utensil even though he cannot grasp the utensil with his hand,

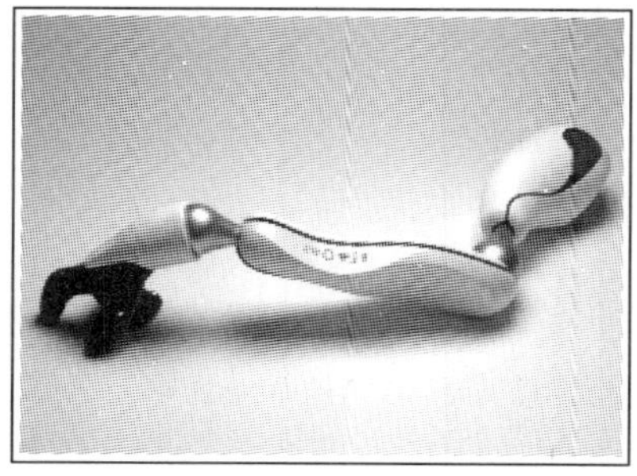

Fig.-15.5: Artificial Arm

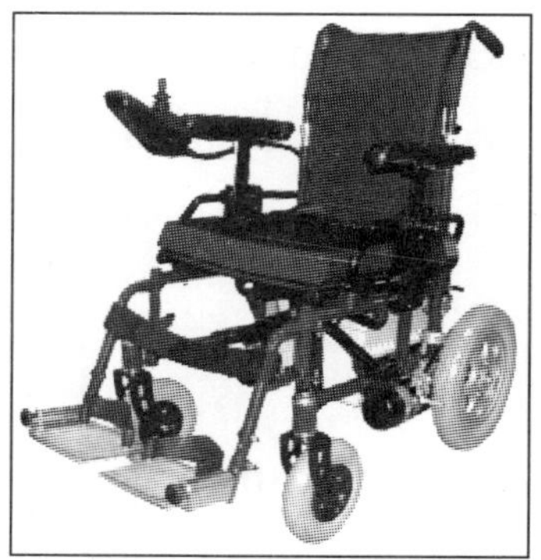

Fig.-15.6: Wheel Chair

Fixing artifical limbs

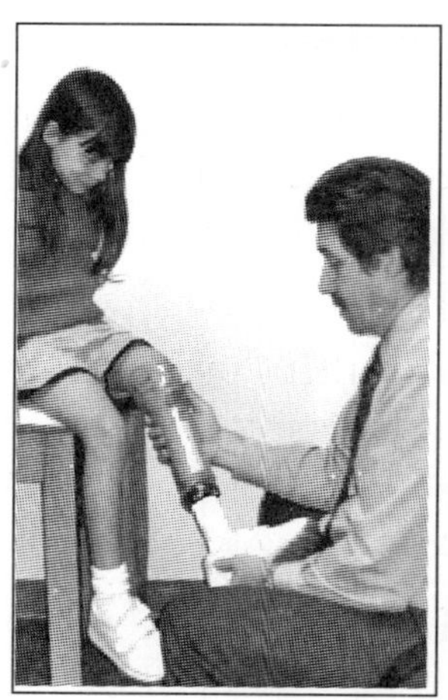

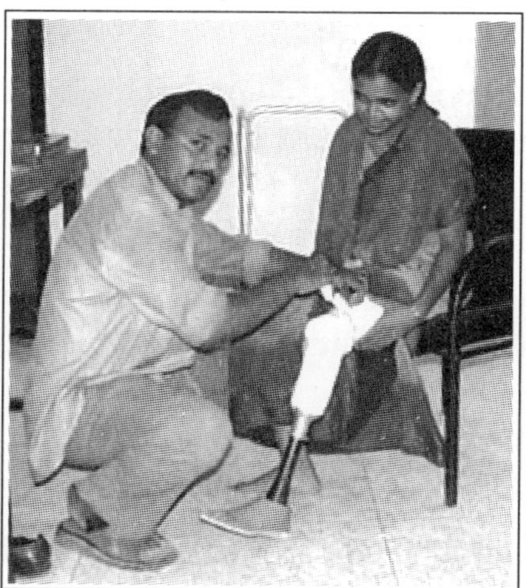

Fig.-15.7: Fixing Artifical Limbs

c) Adaptive devices for daily living include a variety of adaptations of ordinary items found in the home, office, or a school that make performing the tasks required for self-care and employment easier for the person who has a physical disability.

   E.g.: A device to aid bathing or hand washing.

The most important principles to keep in mind here are use of residual function, simplicity and reliability. A prosthesis or orthasis allows the individual to use some residual function of his remaining body parts.

E.g.: 1. An artificial hand is operated by the muscles of the arm, shoulder or back.

2. A person with complete absence of arms must be taught to use his leg to feed himself, put on his clothes, and manipulate objects with his feet. A person with lower body paralysis uses his arm to get around in wheel chair.

A few common orthotic and adaptive devices that are helpful to persons with various physical disabilities are as follows.

— A short ramp on steps to enable children in wheel chairs or crutches to enter the building.

— Addition of a hand bar by the side of a water tap, in a toilet.

— Removal of desks to make room for the wheel chair to move.

— Modification of furniture to provide for the comfort of the child with braces.

— Rubber mats over slippery sections of the floor within the classroom.

— Problem of children having poor hand coordination can be solved by taping paper to the desk, devising some means of keeping pencils and crayons from rolling to the floor, providing holders for books.

— Page turner operated with a toggle switch.

— Head pointer to operate a typewriter.

— Recorder to replace writing, calculator with printout tape.

— Eating aids, tactile writing paper, pencil grips, lap trays.

— Larger and / or weighted objects for manipulation.

— Environmental adjustment in the classroom would include storage for crutches, rounded corners, play areas.

The classroom furniture may be modified into

a) Adjusting seats to turn to side so that the child with braces can sit more easily.

b) Providing foot rests.

The intellectual development of these children should be accelerated by using meaningful, purposeful and interesting materials familiar to the child.

15.1.7 Educational Provisions for Orthopedically Impaired Children

The "National Policy on Education 1986" has formulated objectives to integrate the physically handicapped with general community as equal partners, to prepare them for normal growth and to enable them to face the life with courage and confidence.

15.1.7.1 Integrated Education

The term integration signifies the process of interaction of disabled children and normal children in the same educational setting. The child's success in an integrated education system appears efficient when the teacher's functions include,

— Diagnosis of deprived experience and provision of what is essential.

— Developmental guidance.

— Coordination of habitation.

— Promotion of integrated activities.

— Maintenance of reality standards and discipline.

The education of crippled children should be extensive so that their whole personality can be developed. The following measures should be observed while educating them.

1. **Selection of curriculum:** Special curriculum should be designed for the crippled children keeping in view their physical disabilities. It will be more beneficial to structure the syllabi according to the nature and severity of the impairment.

2. **Provision of emotional adjustment and security:** The emotional and social adjustment of these children should be taken care of. The activities and atmosphere should be so organised through which their inferiority complex can be removed and feelings of self-confidence and self-direction can be aroused within them.

3. **Motivation and determination**: Teacher should motivate these children in a manner by which self-determination can be promoted which may enable them to fulfill the aims of education of life.

4. **Development of physical efficiency**: These children should be given such an educational programme by which they may win over even their physical handicap. Vocational training should be given by trained personals in Special Education institutes which may develop physical efficiency in them.

5. **Opening of special schools**: For severely orthopaedically handicapped children special schools should be established. Separate hostels facilities should be provided for both boys and girls. The strength of the boys' hostel should be 50 and that of the girls about 50.

6. **The Rehabilitation Council of India** a statutory body under the Ministry of Social Justice and Empowerment was set up by an Act of parliament in1992 to regulate and standardize the training of professionals, personnel in Special Education , and in offering number of courses all over the country.

One such institution run by RCI is,

a) National institute for the Orthopaedically Handicapped, Kolkata.

15.1.7.2 Role of a Teacher

- The teachers and experts, in co-operation with parents may take action to provide relevant aid for mobility of the limbs.
- The teacher must accept these children and avoid taunts of the expense of the child's disability.
- The teacher should encourage peer interaction on the basis of mutual respect, help and co-operation.
- In the classroom, suitable adjustment in view of disability may be made in seating arrangements.
- The most important function of the teacher is to help the child to accept his handicap to prevent the psychological crippling.
- Teacher should take care of these children in providing adequate opportunities to participate in games and recreational activities suiting their needs.
- The teacher should possess personal friendliness, patience and warmth interest.

The orthopaedically impaired children are just normal children except for their physical deformity. Therefore education of orthopaedically impaired children is of paramount importance for the development of the country. Generally the mental ability of these children will be fairly good. They can be given intellectual work rather than play and recreational programmes. In our country a few provisions have been made for their education which have to be followed up with right spirit and perspective, Their difficulties should be removed by giving them individual attention. Their emotional disturbances can be removed by the proper behaviour of friends, teachers and members of the family.

15.2 Cerebral Palsy

Cerebral palsy is actually a group of neuromuscular disorders that result from damage to the central nervous system (the brain and spinal cord) before, during or after birth. Cerebral palsy is one of the most prevalent physical impairments in children of school age. It is a long term condition resulting from a lesion in the brain or an abnormality of brain growth that causes a variety of disorders of movements and posture. "Virtually hundreds of diseases may affect the developing brain and lead to cerebral palsy" (Batshaw and Perret 1986).

Cerebral palsy can be treated but not cured; the impairment usually does not get progressively worse as a child ages. Cerebral palsy is not fatal, it is not contagious, and, in the great majority of cases is not inherited.

15.2.1 Characteristics of Children with Cerebral Palsy

a) Children with cerebral palsy have disturbances of voluntary motor functions. These disturbances may include paralysis, extreme weakness, lack of co-ordination, involuntary convulsions, and other motor disorders.

b) Children with cerebral palsy may have little or no control over their arms, legs, or speech, depending on the type and degree of impairment.

c) They may also have impaired vision or hearing.

d) Intellectual impairments.

e) A child with only mild motor impairment may experience severe developmental delays whereas a student with severe motor impairments may be intellectually gifted.

Fig.-15.8: Steven Hawking a Physicist on his Multipurpose Chair

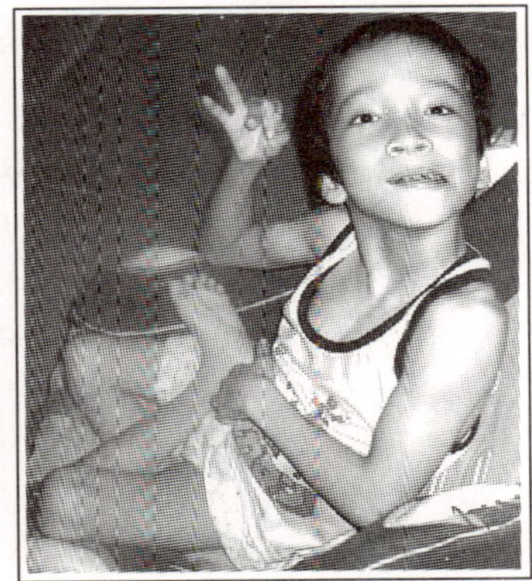

Fig.-15.9: Children with Cerebral Palsy

Table-15.1: Guidelines for Determining Level of Impairments

Severe handicap

- Total dependence in meeting physical needs.
- Poor head control
- Deformities, present or potential, that limit function or produce pain.
- Perceptual and/or sensory – integrative deficits that prevent achievement of academic and age-appropriate motor skills.

Moderate handicap

- Independence in meeting physical needs
- Functional head control
- Deformities, present potential, that limit independent function or produce pain.
- Perceptual and/or sensory integrative deficits that interfere with achievement of academic and age-appropriate motor skills.

Mild handicap

- Independence in meeting physical needs
- Potential to improve quality of motor and/or perceptual skills with therapy intervention.
- Potential for regression in quality of motor and perceptual skills without intervention.

15.2.2 Causes of Cerebral Palsy

The causes of cerebral palsy are varied and not clearly known. It has often been attributed to occurrence of injuries, accidents, or illness that are –

— Prenatal (before birth)

— Perinatal (at or near time of birth)

— Postnatal (soon after birth)

An extensive study of children with cerebral palsy found that the factors most likely to be associated with cerebral palsy were mental retardation of mother, premature birth, low birth weight, and a delay of five minutes or more before the baby's first cry.

15.2.3 Types of Cerebral Palsy

Cerebral palsy is divided into three major types of cerebral palsy according

a) To muscle tone – Hypertonia or hypotonia.

b) Quality of motor involvement – Atherosis or Ataxia.

c) Mixed type – A severe condition.

15.2.3.1 Hypertonia – commonly called Spasticity

It is characterized by tense, contracted muscles. Their movements are jerky, exaggerated, and poorly co-ordinated. They are unable to grasp objects with their fingers. When they try to control their movements, they may become even jerkier. If they are able to walk, it may be with a scissors gait, standing on the toes with knees bent and pointed inward. Deformities of the spine, hip dislocation, and contractures of the hand, elbow, foot, and knee are common.

15.2.3.2 Hypotonia

It is characterized by weak, floppy muscles, particularly in the neck and trunk. These children have low levels of motor activity, are slow to make balancing responses, and may not walk until 30 months of age. Severe hypotonic children may use external support to achieve and maintain an upright position.

15.2.3.3 Atherosis

This condition occurs in about 20% of all cases of cerebral palsy. Children with athetoid cerebral palsy make large, irregular, twisting movements they cannot control. When they are at rest or at sleep, there is little or no abnormal motion. These children may not be able to control the muscles of their lips, tongue, and throat.

They make awkward movements while moving. Extreme difficulty in expressive oral language, mobility, and activities of daily living often accompanies this from of cerebral palsy.

15.2.3.4 Ataxia

Children with ataxic cerebral palsy have a poor sense of balance and hand use. They may appear to be dizzy while walking and may fall easily if not supported. Their movements tend to be jumpy and unsteady, with exaggerated motion patterns that often "overshoot" the intended objects. They seem to be constantly attempting to overcome the effect of gravity and to stabilize their bodies.

15.2.3.5 Rigidity and Tremor

Rigidity and tremor are addition but much less common types of cerebral palsy. Children with this type of cerebral palsy display extreme stiffness in the affected limbs; they may be fixed and immobile for long periods. Tremor cerebral palsy, also rare, is marked by rhythmic, uncontrollable movements. The tremors may actually increase when the children attempt to control their actions.

15.2.4 Management of Cerebral Palsy

Cerebral palsy is the result of not just a brain with a bit missing, but a reorganized brain, working to its own rules. Because cerebral palsy is such a complex condition, it is most effectively managed through interdisciplinary approach through the cooperative involvement of physicians, teachers, physical therapists, occupational therapists, communication specialists, counselors, and parents and others who work directly with children and families. Regular exercise and careful positioning in school settings help the child with cerebral palsy to move as fully and comfortably as possible and prevent or minimize progressive damage to muscles and limbs.

Interdisciplinary team of professionals and parents should work toward achieving four general goals in the educational program of a student with a physical impairment.

- — Physical independence, including mastery of daily living skills.
- — Self-awareness and social maturation
- — Academic growth
- — Career education, including constructive leisure activities.

Physical therapists use specialized knowledge to plan and oversee a child's program in making correct and useful movements. They may prescribe specific exercises to help a child increase control of muscles and use specialized equipment such as braces effectively.

Occupational therapists are concerned with child's participation in activities, especially those that will be useful in self-help, employment, recreation, communication, and other aspects of daily living.

15.2.4.1 Positioning, Seating, and Mobility Devices

Importance of positioning

The positioning of a physically disabled child can often have significant effects on how the child is perceived and accepted by others. Simple adjustments contribute to improved appearance and greater comfort and increased health for the disabled child (Wright & Bigge, 1991).

- Good positioning results in alignment and proximal support of the body.
- Stability positively affects use of the upper body.
- Stability promotes feelings of physical security and safety.
- Good positioning can reduce deformity.
- Positions must be changed frequently.

Proper Seating

Proper seating helps combat poor circulation, muscle tightness, and pressure sores, and contributes to digestion, respiration, and physical development. Be attentive to the following:

- *Pelvic position;* hips as far back in the chair as possible and weight distributed evenly on both sides of the buttocks.
- *Foot support:* both feet level and supported on the floor or wheelchair pedals.
- *Shoulder/upper trunk support:* seat belt, pummel or leg separator, and/or shoulder and chest straps may be necessary for upright positions.

Mobility

Many students are unable to move freely from place to place without the assistance of a mobility device. Mobility devices should be selected with the following variables in mind (Clarke, 1988):

- Motor capabilities
- Physical strength and endurance
- Cost of the device

- Physical layout of the home, school, and community
- Educational and therapy goals

15.2.4.2 Environmental Modifications

Teachers frequently find it necessary to modify the environment to enable a student with physical and health impairments to participate more fully in the classroom. An environmental modification may involve adapting the equipment or materials used for a given task or changing the manner in which the task is done (Sowers, Jenkins, & Powers, 1988). Wright and Bigge (1991) describe four types of environmental modifications: (1) changes in location of materials and equipment, (2) work surface modifications, (3) object modifications, and (4) manipulation aids.

Although barrier-free architecture is the most publicly visible type of environmental modification for making community buildings and services more accessible, some of the most functional adaptations require little or no cost.

— Changing desk and tabletops to appropriate heights for students who are very short or who use wheelchairs.

— Providing a wooden pointer to enable a student to reach the upper buttons on an elevator control panel.

— Installing paper-cup dispensers near water fountains so they can be used by students in wheelchairs.

— Moving a class or activity to an accessible part of a school building so that a student with a physical impairment can be included.

15.2.4.3 Adaptive Devices and Assistive Technology

Both "low technology" adaptive devices and "high tech" assistive equipment is used by children with physical and health impairments in many everyday activities. Special eating utensils, such as forks and spoons with custom-designed handles or straps, may enable children to feed themselves more independently. Simple switches are common parts of homemade environmental control systems to enable persons with disabilities to operate electric appliances such as a TV, stereo, computer, or electric wheelchair (Levin & Scherfenberg, 1987; Wright & Momari, 1985).

New technological aids for communication are used increasingly with children whose physical impairments prevent them from speaking clearly. For students who are able to speak but have limited motor function, there are voice input/output products that enable them to access computers (Esposito & Campbell,

1987). Such developments allow students with physical impairments to communicate expressively and receptively with others and to take part in a wide range of instructional programs.

15.3 Epilepsy

15.3.1 Introduction

From the earliest time, men of all races and levels of civilization have been afflicted with a variety of sudden and recurring attacks of cerebral origin, characterized by partial or complete loss of consciousness, with or without attending psychomotor disturbances. These attacks have been called the falling disease, fits, convulsions, seizures and epilepsy.

Long ago this disease was regarded as a sacred disease coming as some divine torture. Afterwards this disease was attributed to influences of some evil spirit which had entered into the skull of the patient. Now this is generally known as 'epilepsy' which has been coined from Greek word 'epilepsia1 which means seizure or a fit.

15.3.2 Meaning of Epilepsy

Over a half century ago, Hughlings Jackson, the great English neurologist, defined epilepsy as "The name for occasional, sudden, excessive rapid and local discharges of grey matter".

Epilepsy in general refers to the disorder of the nervous system. This disorder disturbs the rhythm in the activity of the nerves in the brain. There is abnormal electrical activity in the brain. This condition may result from an underlying lesion caused by scar tissue from a head injury, a tumour or an interruption in blood supply to the brain. A wide variety of psychological, physical and sensory factors are thought to trigger seizures in susceptible persons. For ex. fatigue, excitement, anger, surprise, hyperventilation, hormonal changes, withdrawal from drugs, alcohol, or exposure to certain patterns of light, sound or touch.

15.3.3 Nature of Epilepsy

— Convulsions or seizures are the main symptoms in all type of epilepsy.

— Between seizures – that is most of the time – the brain functions normally.

— Duration and intensity of fits depends upon the nature of disorder in a particular portion of the brain.

— The disorder can occur at any stage of life, but frequent in childhood.

— Both male and female are equally affected.

— All types of children, average, brilliant and dull may be afflicted with it.

15.3.4 Types and Characteristics of Epilepsy

It is important for teachers, school healthcare personnel, and perhaps classmates to be aware that a child is affected by a convulsive disorder so they can be prepared to deal with a seizure if one should occur in school. There are several classifications of seizures, three of which are relatively common.

They are:

A) Generalized tonic-clonic (grandmal) seizure.

B) Absence (petitmal) seizure.

C) Complex partial (psychomotor) seizure.

15.3.4.1 Generalized Tonic-clonic (Grandmal) Seizure

This is the most serious type of convulsive seizure, alarming to school personnel and other students.

Characteristics of Epilepsy

- Individual looses consciousness, collapses.
- He may shout or produce a gurgling sound, saliva may escape from lips.
- Muscles become rigid; there are jerky movements of arms and legs.
- Individual may bite the tongue or loose bladder control.
- Breathing is often labored, jaws are clenched, and eyes become wide open.
- The seizure lasts for about 2-5 minutes.

Afterwards the individual may be very tired and want to sleep for a short time.

This type of seizure can be frightening unless the teacher knows exactly what to do. The Epilepsy Foundation of America suggests the following steps in the event of a generalized tonic – clonic seizure:

❖ Remain clam. Students tend to assume the same emotional reaction as their teacher. The seizure itself is painless to the students.

❖ Do not try to restrain the student. Nothing can be done to stop a seizure once it has begun. It must run its course.

- Help the student lie down, and put something under the student's head.
- Clear the area around the student so that he is not injured on hard, sharp or hot objects. Try not to interfere with the student's movements in any way.
- Remove glasses and loosen tight clothing.
- Do not force anything between teeth. Under no circumstances, hard object such as spoon, pen or pencil should be put in the student's mouth.
- After the seizure, turn the student's head to one side. This keeps his airway clear and allows saliva to drain away.
- Do not offer the student anything to drink until he is fully awake.
- It is not generally necessary to call a physician unless the attack is immediately followed by another major seizure or unless the seizure lasts more than 10 minutes.
- When the seizure is over, let the student rest.
- Inform the student's parents of the seizure.

15.3.4.2 Absence Seizure (Petitmal)

Characteristics

- Absence seizures are generally short in duration, lasting from 3 to 30 seconds.
- Common in children and may occur between 50 and 200 times a day if untreated.
- Student may become pale and stare into space.
- Eyelids may twitch or the student may demonstrate slightly jerky movement.
- Absence seizures have a tendency to disappear before or near puberty but may be replaced by other types.

Often a student who experiences absence seizures may be accused of being a daydreamer because he loses contact with what is happening in the classroom during the seizure. The significant problem of this kind is that it often goes undiagnosed.

Teacher can play an important role in identification and should watch for a number of signs that might otherwise elude detection for some time. Repeated occurrences of two or more of following signs may indicate the presence of this form of epilepsy.

- Head dropping
- Daydreaming or lack of attentiveness
- Slight jerky movements of arms or shoulders.
- Eyes rolling upward or twitching.
- A seeming inability to hear complete sentences or direction.
- Dropping things frequently.

If any combination of these signs is observed, parents or school nurse are contacted to ensure that a proper medical examination is obtained. Absence seizure can be brought under control with medication

15.3.4.3 Complex Partial Seizures

Complex partial seizures affect not only the motor system but also mental processes. Behaviour during the seizure varies from person to person, but for any individual, generally the same behaviour occurs during each seizure.

Characteristics

- Individual may chew or smack lips or appear to be confused.
- Purposeless activities like rubbing the arms or legs, walk around aimlessly are carried out.
- He may demonstrate a sudden arrest of activity along with staring.
- Some individuals experience fear, anger or rage.
- It usually last from 2–5 minutes and the individual is not aware of his unusual behaviour.
- He will not remember what happened and wants o sleep.
- This seizure may occur weekly, monthly, or only once or twice a year.

A teacher who observes any of these behaviours should contact the school nurse and the student's parents. The teacher should keep dangerous objects out of the child's way and except in emergencies, should not try to physically restrain him.

Sometimes there may also be attacks similar to seizure attacks but are not seizure attacks. They are called hysteria attacks. Though both seemed to be same, they are entirely different from one another. The treatment also differs; one should be able to distinguish these attacks by knowing their characteristics.

Table-15.2: Difference between Epilepsy and Hysteria

Sl.No.	*Feature*	*Epilepsy*	*Hysteria*
1.	Consciousness	Complete loss	Inconsistent
2.	Environment	Any place, any circumstance	Indoors, especially home, with people present
3.	Onset	Sudden	Often gradual
4.	Pattern	Stereotyped	Variable
5.	Screaming	At onset	During attack
6.	Talking	Rare	Often
7.	Urination	Often	Rate
8.	Biting	Tongue	Lips, hands, even others
9.	Injury	Often	Rare
10.	Duration	Few min	Many min

15.3.3 Treatment of Epilepsy

When epilepsy occurs due to some brain injury, brain surgery may be useful. The disordered portion of the brain due to excessive use of intoxicant may also be removed through surgery. Many of the newly discovered drugs like ethosuximide, phenyle thylacetylurea, carbarnazepina, chlordiazepoxide and diazepam are found to be effective with many cases of epilepsy. The patient should take medicine regularly for 5 years after the last attack. Failure to take medication attacks them, again. Depending upon the body weight, the dosage of the medicine is adjusted.

In recent years some of the advanced preventive techniques like pocket size radio device are proving quite effective in preventing as well as controlling epileptic seizures. The person is warned so that he may be able to find a place to rest or to take appropriate medication.

15.3.4 Management of Epileptic Patients

Parents, family members and teachers play an important role in handling the epileptic patients. The following care should be taken to keep them away from dangers:

- Food should be taken from time to time; he should not be hungry for a long time.
- He should have sufficient sleep.

- He should never be allowed to watch T.V. from far/near.
- Since he may have attacks at any time, he should not be allowed to drive or travel alone.
- He may do any type of work but one who works with machineries should b careful.
- He can take any type of food.
- He should be monitored with regular medicines.
- Proper orientation of the patient to his disorder is very much needed.

15.3.5 Educational Implications

All the three types of seizures can cause severe educational problems. Generalized tonic-clonic epilepsy is probably the most serious because of the possibility of bodily injury and because it is so widely misunderstood. Absence seizure can seriously limit a student's achievement because he or she misses the material being covered during a seizure and may be labeled a behaviour problem. Although complex partial seizures are relatively uncommon in children, they impose serious limitations on school achievement and adjustment.

Special curricular modifications are not necessary for students with epilepsy. Their academic programme and materials are the same. But several factors should be considered by the teacher.

— If a seizure occurs, a teacher may turn the incident into a learning experience for the entire class. Explain what a seizure is, that it is not contagious, and that it is nothing to be afraid of. Teach the class understanding of the student so that classmates continue to accept the student as one among them. Over reaction by the teacher can have a negative effect on the student with epilepsy and on other students in the class.

— A teacher may want to discuss the condition with the student and the student's parents to obtain more information concerning how the student feels about the condition and any individual aspects that need to be considered.

— A teacher should not lower the level of expectation of the student with epilepsy.

— A teacher should inform special or substitute teachers that there is a student in the class with epilepsy and should record in writing what to do in the event of seizure.

— School personnel and other teachers should be educated about the nature of epilepsy and procedures to be employed in the event of a seizure.

— Student with a seizure should participate in school sports, games and other activities. The teacher must consult the parents and physician to determine if there are any activities that must be specifically avoided.

— A teacher should obtain information from state and national agencies concerned with epilepsy. Free information is available from the Epilepsy Foundation of America. Students can be assigned specific responsibilities so that care of the student with epilepsy becomes a routine matter and it will not be a disturbing experience.

15.3.6 Conclusion

There are many misconceptions concerning epilepsy, including the presumption of mental retardation, brain injury or insanity. The greatest limitation imposed by epilepsy is not the condition itself but the antiquated attitudes and consistent rejection in a society. Today, the majority of children with convulsive disorder can be helped with medication. Drugs can sharply reduce or even eliminate seizures in many cases. All children with convulsive disorders benefit from a realistic understanding of their condition and from accepting attitudes on the part of teachers and classmates.

Glossary

Absence seizure A type of epileptic seizure in which the individual loses consciousness, usually for less than half a minute; can occur very frequently in children.

Acceleration An educational approach that provides a child with learning experiences usually given to older children; most often used with gifted and talented children.

Accommodation The adjustment of the eye for seeing at different distances, accomplished by muscles that change the shape of the lens to bring an image clear focus on the retina.

Acquired immune deficiency syndrome (AIDS) A fatal illness in which the body's immune system breaks down. At present there is no known cure for AIDS or a vaccine for the virus that causes it (see human immunodeficiency virus).

Adaptive device Any piece of equipment designed to improve the function of a body part. Examples include standing tables and special spoons that can be used by people with weak hands or poor muscle control.

Adventitious A handicap that develops at any time after birth, from disease, trauma, or any other cause; most frequently used with sensory or physical impairments. Contrasts with congenital handicap.

Advocate Anyone who pleads the cause of a handicapped person or group of handicapped people, especially in legal or administrative proceedings or public forums.

Amblyopia Dimness of sight without apparent change in the eye's structures; can lead to blindness in the affected eye if not corrected.

American Sign Language (ASL) A visual-gestural language with its own rules of syntax, semantics, and pragmatics; does not correspond to written or spoken English. ASL is the language of the deaf culture in the United States and Canada.

Anoxia A lack of oxygen severe enough to cause tissue damage; can cause permanent brain damage and mental retardation.

Aphasia Loss of speech functions; often, but not always, refers to inability to speak because of brain lesions.

Applied behavior analysis "The science in which procedures derived from the principles of behavior are systematically applied to improve socially significant behavior to a meaningful degree and to demonstrate experimentally that the procedures employed were responsible for the improvement in behavior" (Cooper, Heron, & Heward, 1987, p. 14).

Aqueous humor Fluid that occupies the space between the lens and the cornea of the eye.

Articulation The production of distinct language sounds by the vocal organs.

Asthma A chronic respiratory condition characterized by repeated episodes of wheezing, coughing, and difficulty breathing.

Astigmatism A defect of vision usually caused by irregularities in the cornea; results in blurred vision and difficulties in focusing. Can usually be corrected by lenses.

Ataxia Poor sense of balance and body position and lack of coordination of the voluntary muscles; characteristic of one type of cerebral palsy.

Athetosis A type of cerebral palsy characterized by large, irregular, uncontrollable twisting motions. The muscles may be tense and rigid or loose and flaccid. Often accompanied by difficulty with oral language.

At risk A term used to refer to children who are not currently identified as handicapped or disabled but who are considered to have a greater-than-usual chance of developing a handicap. Physicians use the terms at risk or high risk to refer to pregnancies with a greater-than-normal probability of producing a baby with handicaps.

Attention Deficit Disorder (ADD) See attention deficit-hyperactivity disorder (ADHD).

Attention Deficit-Hyperactivity Disorder (ADHD) Diagnostic category of The American Psychiatric Association for a condition in which a child exhibits developmentally inappropriate inattention, impulsivity, and hyperactivity.

Audiogram Graph of the faintest level of sound a person can hear in each ear at least 50% of the time at each of several frequencies, including the entire frequency range of normal speech.

Audiologist A professional who specializes in the evaluation of hearing ability and the treatment of impaired hearing.

Audiology The science of hearing.

Audiometer A device that generates sounds at specific frequencies and intensities; used to examine hearing.

Auditory canal (external acoustic meatus) Slightly amplifies and transports sound waves from the external ear to the middle ear.

Auditory training A program that works on listening skills to teach hearing impaired persons to make as much use as possible of their residual hearing.

Augmentative communication Nonspeech communication used to supplement whatever naturally acquired speech may be present; may be aided (e.g., computer -based speaking system) or unaided (e.g., signing or gestures), depending upon the individual's cognitive and motor abilities.

Auricle External part of the ear; collects sound waves into the auditory canal.

Autism A severe behavior disorder usually characterized by extreme withdrawal and lack of language and communication skills. Lack of affect, self-stimulation, self-abuse, and aggressive behavior are also common in autistic children.

Baseline A measure of the level or amount of behavior prior to implementation of an instructional procedure that is to be evaluated. Baseline data are used as an objective measure against which to compare and evaluate the results obtained during instruction.

Behavior modification The systematic application of procedures derived from the principles of behavior (e.g., reinforcement) in order to achieve desired changes in behavior.

Behavior observation audiometry A method of hearing assessment in which an infant's reactions to sounds are observed; a sound is presented at an increasing level of intensity until a response, such as head turning, eye blinking, or cessation of play, is reliably observed.

Behavioral disorder A handicapping condition characterized by behavior that differs markedly and chronically from current social or cultural norms and adversely affects educational performance.

Behavioral contract A written agreement between two parties in which one agrees to complete a specified task (e.g., a child agrees to complete a homework assignment by the next morning) and in return the other party agrees to provide a specific reward (e.g., the teacher allows the child to have 10 minutes of free time) upon completion of the task.

Bilingual Special Education Using die child's home language and home culture along with English in an individually designed program of Special Education.

Binocular vision Vision using both eyes working together to perceive a single entity.

Blind Having either no vision or only light perception; learning occurs through other senses.

Blind, legally See legally blind.

Braille A system of writing letters, numbers, and other language symbols with combination of six raised dots. A blind person reads the dots with his or her fingertips.

Cataract A reduction or loss of vision that occurs when the crystalline lens of the eye becomes cloudy or opaque.

Catheter A tube inserted into a body to permit injections or withdrawal of fluids or to keep a passageway open; often refers to a tube inserted into the bladder to remove urine from a person who does not have effective bladder control.

Cerebral palsy Motor impairment caused by brain damage, which is usually inflicted during the prenatal period or during the birth process. Can involve a wide variety of symptoms (see ataxia, athetosis, rigidity, spasticity, and tremor) and range from mild to severe. Neither curable nor progressive.

Chorion Villus Sampling (CVS) A new procedure for prenatal diagnosis of chromosomal abnormalities that can be conducted during the first 8 to 10 weeks of pregnancy; fetal cells are removed from the chorionic tissue, which surrounds the fetus, and directly analyzed.

Cleft palate A congenital split in the palate that results in an excessive nasal quality of the voice. Can often be repaired by surgery or dental appliance.

Cochlea Main receptor organ for hearing located in the inner ear; tiny hairs within the cochlea transform mechanical energy into neural impulses that then travel through the auditory nerve to the brain.

Communication The process by which individuals interact with, transmit, and receive messages by any means, including sounds, symbols, and gestures.

Complex partial seizure A type of epileptic seizure in which an individual goes through a period of inappropriate activity but is not aware of that activity.

Conduct disorder A group of behavior disorders including disobedience, disruptiveness, fighting, and tantrums, as identified by Quay (1975).

Conductive hearing loss Hearing loss caused by obstructions in the outer or middle ear or malformations that interfere with the conduction of sound waves to the inner ear. Can often be corrected surgically or medically.

Congenital Any condition that is present at birth. Contrasts with adventitious handicap.

Continuum of services The range of different placement and instructional options that a school district can use to serve handicapped children. Typically depicted as a pyramid, ranging from the least restrictive placement (regular classroom) at the bottom to the most restrictive placement (institution or hospital) at the top.

Convulsive disorder See epilepsy.

Cornea The transparent part of the eyeball that admits light to the interior.

Cri-du-chat syndrome A chromosomal abnormality resulting from deletion of material from the fifth pair of chromosomes. It usually results in severe retardation. Its name is French for "cat cry," named for the high-pitched crying of the child due to a related larynx dysfunction.

Cued speech Method of supplementing oral communication by adding cues in the form of eight different hand signals in four different locations near the chin.

Cultural-familial mental retardation Any case of mental retardation for which an organic cause cannot be found; suggests that retardation can be caused by a poor social and cultural environment. (See psychosocial disadvantage.)

Cultural pluralism The value and practice of respecting, fostering, and encouraging the cultural and ethnic differences that make up society.

Culture The established knowledge, ideas, values, and skills shared by a society; its program of survival and adaptation to its environment.

Curriculum-based assessment Evaluation of a student's progress in terms of his performance on the skills that comprise the curriculum of the local school.

Cystic fibrosis Inherited disorder that causes a dysfunction of the pancreas, mucus, salivary, and sweat glands.

Cystic fibrosis causes severe, long-term respiratory difficulties. No cure is currently available.

Deafness Inability to use hearing to understand speech, even with a hearing aid.

Decibel (dB) The unit of measure for the relative intensity of sound on a scale beginning at zero. Zero dB refers to the faintest sound a person with normal hearing can detect.

Deinstitutionalization The social movement to transfer disabled persons, especially persons with mental retardation, from large institutions to smaller, community-based residences and work settings.

Diabetes See juvenile diabetes mellitus.

Diabetic retinopathy Type of vision impairment caused by hemorrhages on the retina and other disorders of blood circulation in people with diabetes.

Dialect A variety within a specific language; can involve variation in pronunciation, word choice, word order, and inflected forms.

Differential reinforcement of other behavior A behavior modification technique in which any behavior except the targeted maladaptive response is reinforced; results in a reduction of the inappropriate behavior.

Diplegia Paralysis that affects the legs more often than the arms.

Disability Technically, refers to the reduced function or loss of a particular body part or organ. In practice, disability is often used interchangeably with handicap.

Double hemiplegia Paralysis of the arms, with less severe involvement of the legs.

Down syndrome A chromosomal anomaly that often causes moderate to severe mental retardation, along with certain physical characteristics such as a large tongue, heart problems, poor muscle tone, and a broad, flat bridge of the nose.

Due process Set of legal steps and proceedings carried out according to established rules and principles; designed to protect an individual's constitutional and legal rights.

Duration (of behavior) Measure of how long a person engages in a given activity.

Dyslexia A disturbance in the ability to read or learn to read.

Echolalia The repetition of what other people say as if echoing them; characteristic of some children with delayed development, autism, and communication disorders.

Electroencephalograph (EEG) Device that detects and records brain wave patterns.

Endogenous Refers to an inherited cause of a disability or impairment.

Enrichment Educational approach that provides a child with extra learning experiences that the standard curriculum would not normally include. Most often used with gifted and talented children.

Epilepsy Convulsive disorder characterized by sudden seizures (see generalized tonic-clonic seizure, complex partial seizure, and absence seizure); can usually be controlled with medication, although the drugs may have undesirable side effects; may be temporary or lifelong.

Equal protection Legal concept included in the 14th Amendment to the Constitution of the United States, stipulating that no state may deny any person equality or liberty because of that person's classification according to race, nationality, or religion. Several major court cases leading to the passage of P.L. 94-142 found that handicapped children were not provided equal protection if they were denied access to an appropriate education solely because they were handicapped.

Etiology The cause(s) of disability, impairment, or disease. Includes genetic, physiological, and environmental or psychological factors.

Evoked-response audiometry Method of testing hearing by measuring the electrical activity generated by the auditory nerve in response to auditory stimulation. Often used to measure the hearing of infants and children considered difficult to test.

Exceptional children Children whose performance deviates from the norm, either below or above, to the extent that Special Education programming is needed.

Exogenous Refers to a cause of a disability or impairment that stems from factors outside the body such as disease, toxicity, or injury.

Extinction A behavior modification procedure in which reinforcement for a previously reinforced behavior is withheld. For example, a teacher may ignore a child's disruptive behavior instead of scolding. If the actual reinforcers that are maintaining the behavior are identified and withheld, the behavior will gradually decrease in rate until it no longer, or seldom, occurs.

Fetal Alcohol Syndrome (FAS) A condition sometimes found in the infants of alcoholic mothers; can involve low birth weight, developmental delay, and cardiac, limb, and other physical defects.

Field of vision The expanse of space visible with both eyes looking straight ahead, measured in degrees; 180 degrees is considered normal.

Fluency The rate and smoothness with which a movement is made. In communication, the rate and ease of speech; the most common speech fluency disorder is stuttering.

Fragile-X syndrome Chromosomal abnormality associated with mild to severe mental retardation. Thought to be the most common known cause of inherited mental retardation. Affects males more often and more severely than females; behavioral characteristics can be autistic-like. Diagnosis can be confirmed by studies of the X chromosome.

Generalization Performing a behavior under conditions other than those under which the behavior was originally learned. Stimulus generality occurs when a person performs a behavior in the presence of relevant stimuli (people, settings, instructional materials) other than those that were present originally. For instance, stimulus generality occurs when a child who has learned to label baseballs and beach balls as "ball" identifies a basketball as "ball." Response generality occurs when a person performs relevant behaviors that were never directly trained but are similar to the original trained behavior. For example, a child may be taught to say, "Hello, how are you?" and "Hi, nice to see you," as greetings. If the child combines the two to say, "Hi, how are you?" response, generality has taken place.

Generalized tonic-clonic seizure The most severe type of epileptic seizure, in which the individual has violent convulsions, loses consciousness.

Genetic counseling A discussion between a specially trained medical counselor and persons who are considering having a child about the chances of having a child with a disability, based on the prospective parents' genetic backgrounds.

Glaucoma An eye disease characterized by abnormally high pressure inside the eyeball. If left untreated, it can cause total blindness, but if detected early most cases can be averted.

Grand mal seizure See generalized tonic-clonic seizure.

Group home A residential arrangement for adults with disabilities, most often persons with mental retardation, in which several residents live together in a house with non-handicapped supervisors.

Handicap The problems a person with a disability or behavioral characteristic considered unusual by society encounters when interacting with the environment

Handicapism Prejudice or discrimination based solely on a person's disability, without regard for individual characteristics.

Hard of hearing Level of hearing loss that makes it difficult, although not impossible, to comprehend speech through the sense of hearing alone.

Hearing impaired Describes anyone who has a hearing loss significant enough to require Special Education, training, and/or adaptations; includes both deaf and hard-of-hearing conditions.

Hemiplegia Paralysis of both the arm and the leg on the same side of the body.

Hemophilia An inherited deficiency in blood-clotting ability, which can cause serious internal bleeding.

Hertz (Hz) A unit of sound frequency equal to one cycle per second; used to measure pitch.

Human Immunodeficiency Virus (HIV) The virus that causes Acquired Immune Deficiency Syndrome (AIDS).

Hydrocephalus A condition present at birth or developing soon afterward; involves an enlarged head caused by cerebral spinal fluid accumulating in the cranial cavity; often causes brain damage and severe retardation. Sometimes treated successfully with a shunt.

Hyperactive Describes excessive motor activity or restlessness.

Hyperopia Farsightedness; condition in which the image comes to a focus behind the retina instead of on it, causing difficulty in seeing near objects.

Hypertonia Muscle tone that is too high; tense, contracted muscles.

Hypotonia Muscle tone that is too low; weak, floppy muscles.

Immaturity Group of behavior disorders, including short attention span, extreme passivity, daydreaming, preference for younger playmates, and clumsiness, as identified by Quay (1975).

Impedance audiometry Procedure for testing middle ear function by inserting a small probe and pump to detect sound reflected by the eardrum.

Incidence The percentage of people who, at some time in their lives, will be identified as having a specific condition. Often reported as the number of cases of a given condition per 1,000 people.

Individualized Education Program (IEP) Written document required by PL. 94-142 for every child with a disability; includes statements of present performance, annual goals, short-term instructional objectives, specific educational services needed, relevant dates, regular education program participation, and evaluation procedures; must be signed by parents as well as educational personnel.

Individualized Family Services Plan (IFSP) A requirement of P.L 99-457, Education of the Handicapped Act Amendments of 1986, for the coordination of early intervention services for handicapped infants and toddlers. Similar to the IEP that is required for all school-age handicapped children.

Inflection Change in pitch or loudness of the voice to indicate mood or emphasis.

Inservice training Educational program designed to provide practicing professionals (such as teachers, administrators, physical therapists) with additional knowledge and skills.

Interdisciplinary team Group of professionals from different disciplines (e.g., education, psychology, speech and language, medicine) who work together to plan and implement a handicapped child's individualized education program (IEP)'

Interindividual differences Differences between two or more people in one skill or set of skills.

Intervention All the efforts made on behalf of children and adults with disabilities; may be preventive, remedial, or compensatory.

Iris The opaque, colored portion of the eye that contracts and expands to change the size of the pupil.

Kinesics The study of bodily movement, particularly as it relates to and affects communication.

Language A system of vocal symbols (sounds) that give a group of people who understand the language a way to communicate. Nonverbal languages, such as American Sign Language, use movements and physical symbols instead of sounds.

Least Restrictive Environment (LRE) The educational setting in which a child with disabilities can receive an appropriate education and which is most like the regular classroom.

Legally blind Visual acuity of 20/200 or less in the better eye after the best possible correction with glasses or contact lenses, or vision restricted to a field off 20 degrees or less. Acuity of 20/200 means the eye can see clearly at 20 feet; the normal eye can see at 200 feet.

Lens The clear pan of the eye that focuses rays of light on the retina.

Longitudinal study A research study that follows one subject or group of objects over an extended period of time, usually several years.

Low-incidence disability A disability that occurs relatively infrequently in the general population; in particular, used to refer to vision and hearing impairments, severe mental retardation, severe behavior disorders such as autism, and multiple handicaps.

Low vision Vision so limited that Special Educational services are required; nonetheless, permits learning through the visual channel.

Macular degeneration A deterioration of the central part of the retina, with difficulty in seeing details clearly.

Magnitude (of behavior) The force with which a response is emitted.

Mainstreaming The return to the regular classroom, for all or part of the school day, of children with disabilities previously educated exclusively in segregated settings.

Meningitis An inflammation of the membranes covering the brain and spinal cord; can cause problems with sight and hearing and/or mental retardation.

Meningocele Type of spina bifida in which the covering of the spinal cord protrudes through an opening in the vertebrae, but the cord itself and the nerve roots are enclosed.

Mental retardation "Significantly subaverage general intellectual functioning resulting in or associated with deficits in adaptive behavior and manifested during the developmental period" (Grossman, 1983, p. 11).

Microcephalus A condition characterized by an abnormally small skull with resulting brain damage and mental retardation.

Minimal brain dysfunction A once-popular term used to describe the learning disability of children with no actual (clinical) evidence of brain damage.

Mobility The ability to move safely and efficiently from one point to another.

Model program A program that implements and evaluates new procedures or techniques in order to serve as a basis for development of other similar programs.

Monoplegia Paralysis affecting one limb.

Morpheme The smallest element of a language that carries meaning.

Multicultural education An educational approach in which the curriculum and instructional methods for all children instill an awareness, acceptance, and appreciation of cultural diversity.

Multifactored assessment Assessment and evaluation of a handicapped child with a variety of test instruments and observation procedures. Required by P.L 94-142 when assessment is for educational placement of a child who is to receive Special Education services. Prevents the misdiagnosing and misplacing a student as the result of considering only one test score.

Muscular dystrophy A group of diseases that gradually weakens muscle tissue; usually becomes evident by the age of 4 or 5.

Myelomeningocele A protrusion on the back of a child with spinal bifida, consisting of a sac of nerve tissue bulging through a cleft in the spine.

Myopia Nearsightedness; results when light is focused on a point in front of the retina, resulting in a blurred image for distant objects.

Neurologic impairment Any physical disability caused by damage to the central nervous system (brain, spinal cord, ganglia, and nerves).

Normal curve A mathematically derived curve depicting the probability or distribution of a given variable (such as a physical trait or test score) in the general population. Indicates that approximately 68.26% of the population will fall within one standard deviation above and below the mean; approximately 27.18% will fall between one and two standard deviations either above or below the mean; and less than 3% will achieve more extreme scores of more than two standard deviations in either direction.

Normalization The principle of allowing each person's life to be as normal as possible in all aspects, including residence, schooling, work, recreational activities, and overall independence. Similarities between disabled and nondis-abled people of the same age are emphasized.

Nystagmus A rapid, involuntary, rhythmic movement of the eyes that may cause difficulty in reading or fixating on an object.

Occupational therapist A professional who programs and/or delivers instructional activities and materials to help children and adults with disabilities learn to participate in useful activities.

Ocular mobility The eye's ability to move.

Operant conditioning audiometry Method of measuring hearing by conditioning the subject to make an observable response to sound. For example, a child may be taught to drop a block into a box each time a light and a loud tone is presented. Once this response is conditioned, the light is no longer presented and the volume and pitch of the tone are gradually decreased. When the child no longer drops the block into the box, the audiologist knows the child cannot hear the tone. This procedure is used to test the hearing of nonverbal children and adults.

Optic nerve The nerve that carries impulses from the eye to the brain.

Oral An approach to education of deaf children that stresses learning to speak the essential element of integration into the hearing world.

Orientation The ability to establish one's position in relation to the environment

Orthopedic impairment Any disability caused by disorders to the musculoskeletal system.

Ossicles Three small bones (hammer, anvil, and stirrup) that transmit sound energy from the middle ear to the inner ear.

Osteogenesis imperfecta A hereditary condition in which the bones do not grow normally and break easily; sometimes called brittle bones.

Otitis media An infection or inflammation of the middle ear that can cause a conductive hearing loss.

Overcorrection A behavior modification procedure in which the learner must repair the effects of his undesirable behavior and mend the environment in even better shape than it was prior to the misbehavior. Used to decrease the rate of undesirable behaviors.

Paraplegia Paralysis of the lower part of the body, including both legs; usually results from injury to or disease of the spinal cord.

Paraprofessionals (in education) Trained classroom aides who assist teachers; may include parents.

Perceptual handicap A term formerly used to describe some conditions now included under learning disability; usually referred to problems with no known physical cause.

Perinatal Occurring at or immediately after birth.

Peripheral vision Vision at the outer limits of the field of vision.

Personality disorder A group of behavior disorders, including social withdrawal, anxiety, depression, feelings of inferiority, guilt, shyness, and unhappiness, as identified by Quay (1975).

Petit mal seizure See absence seizure.

Phenylketonuria (PKU) An inherited metabolic disease that can cause severe retardation; can now be detected at birth and the detrimental effects prevented with a special diet.

Phonemes The smallest unit of sound that can be identified in a spoken language. There are 45 phonemes, or sound families, in the English language.

Photophobia Extreme sensitivity of the eyes to light; occurs most notably in albino children.

Physical therapist A professional trained to help people with disabilities, develop and maintain muscular and orthopedic capability and make correct and useful movement.

Positive reinforcement Presentation of a stimulus or event immediately after a behavior has been emitted, which has the effect of increasing the occurrence of that behavior in the future.

Postlingual Occurring after the development of language; usually used to classify hearing losses that begin after a person has learned to speak.

Postnatal Occurring after birth.

Pragmatics Study of the rules that govern how language is used in a communication context.

Precision teaching An instructional approach that involves pinpointing the behaviors to be changed; measuring the initial frequency of those behaviors; setting an aim, or goal, for the child's improvement; using direct, daily measurements to monitor progress made under an instructional program; graphing results of those measurements; and changing the program if progress is not adequate.

Prelingual Describes a hearing impairment that develops before a child has acquired speech and language.

Prenatal Occurring before birth.

Prenatal asphyxia A lack of oxygen during the birth process usually caused by interruption of respiration; can cause unconsciousness and/or brain damage.

Prevalence The number of people who have a certain condition at any given time.

Projective tests Psychological tests that require a person to respond to a standardized task or set of stimuli (e.g., draw a picture or interpret an ink blot); responses are thought to be a projection of the test-taker's personality and are scored according to the given test's scoring manual to produce a personality profile.

Prosthesis Any device used to replace a missing or impaired body part.

Psychomotor seizure See complex partial seizure.

Psychosocial disadvantage Category of causation for mental retardation that requires evidence of subnormal intellectual functioning in at least one parent and one or more siblings (when there are siblings). Typically associated with impoverished environments involving poor housing, inadequate diets, and inadequate medical care. The term is used, often synonymously with cultural-familial retardation, when no organic cause can be identified.

Pupil The circular hole in the center of the iris of the eye, which contracts and expands to let light pass through.

Quadriplegia Paralysis of all four limbs.

Rate (of behavior) A measure of how often a particular action is performed; usually reported as the number of responses per minute.

Refraction The bending or deflection of light rays from a straight path as they pass from one medium (e.g., air) into another (e.g., the eye). Used by eye specialists in assessing and correcting vision.

Regular Education Initiative (REI) A perspective that all students with mild disabilities, as well as some with moderate disabilities, can and should be educated in regular classrooms under the primary responsibility of the general education program.

Rehabilitation A social service program designed to teach a newly disabled person basic skills needed for independence.

Reinforcement See positive reinforcement.

Related services Developmental, corrective, and other supportive services required for a child with disabilities to benefit from Special Education. Includes special transportation services, speech and language pathology, audiology, psychological services, physical and occupational therapy, school health services, counseling and medical services for diagnostic and evaluation purposes, rehabilitation counseling, social work services, and parent counseling and training.

Remediation An educational program designed to teach a person to overcome a disability through training and education.

Residual hearing The remaining hearing, however slight, of a hearing impaired person.

Resource room Classroom in which Special Education students spend part of the school day and receive individualized Special Education services.

Retina A sheet of nerve tissue at the back of the eye on which an image is focused.

Retinitis Pigmentosa (RP) An eye disease in which the retina gradually degenerates and atrophies, causing the field of vision to become progressively more narrow.

Retinopathy of Prematurity (ROP) A condition characterized by an abnormally dense growth of blood vessels and scar tissue in the eye, often causing visual field loss and retinal detachment Usually caused by high levels of oxygen administered to premature infants in incubators. Also called retrolental fibroplasia (RLF).

Retrolental Fibroplasia (RLF) See retinopathy of prematurity.

Rigidity A type of cerebral palsy characterized by increased muscle tone, minimal muscle elasticity, and little or no stretch reflex.

Rubella German measles; when contracted by a woman during the first trimester of pregnancy; may cause visual impairments, hearing impairments, mental retardation, and/or other birth defects in me child.

Schizophrenic Describes a severe behavior disorder characterized by loss of contact with one's surroundings and inappropriate affect and actions.

Screening A procedure in which groups of children are examined and/or tested in an effort to identify high-risk children; identified children are then referred for more intensive examination and assessment.

Self-contained class A special classroom, usually located within a regular public school building that includes only exceptional children.

Semantics The study of meaning in language.

Sensorineural hearing loss A hearing loss caused by damage to the auditory nerve or the inner ear.

Severe handicaps Term used to refer to challenges faced by students with severe and profound mental retardation, autism, and/or physical/sensory impairments combined with marked developmental delay. Persons with severe handicaps exhibit extreme deficits in intellectual functioning and need systematic instruction for basic skills such as self-care and communicating with others.

Sheltered workshop A structured work environment where persons with disabilities receive employment training and perform work for pay. May provide transitional services for some individuals (i.e., short-term training for competitive employment in the community) and permanent work settings for others.

Shunt Tube inserted in the body to divert fluid from one body part to another; often implanted in people with hydrocephalus to remove extra cerebrospinal fluid from the head and send it directly into the heart or intestines.

Social validity A desirable characteristic of the objectives, procedures, and results of instruction, indicating their appropriateness for the learner. For example, the goal of riding a bus independently would have social validity for learners residing in most cities, but not for those in small towns or rural areas.

Socialized aggression A group of behavior disorders, including truancy, gang membership, theft, and delinquency, as identified by Quay (1975).

Spasticity A type of cerebral palsy characterized by tense, contracted muscles.

Special Education The individually planned and systematically monitored arrangement of physical settings, special equipment and materials, teaching procedures, and other interventions designed to help learners widi special needs achieve the greatest possible personal self-sufficiency and success in school and community.

Speech A system of using bream and muscles to create specific sounds for communicating.

Speechreading Process of understanding a spoken message by observing die speaker's lips in combination widi information gained from facial expressions, gestures, and die context or situation.

Spina bifida A congenital malformation of die spine in which die vertebrae mat normally protea die spine do not develop fully; may involve loss of sensation and severe muscle weakness in die lower part of die body.

Spina bifida occulta A type of spina bifida diat usually does not cause serious disability. Although the vertebrae do not close, there is no protrusion of die spinal cord and membranes.

Standard deviation A unit used to measure die amount by which a particular score varies from die mean of all scores in the norm sample.

Stereotype An overgeneralized or inaccurate attitude held toward all members of a particular group, on the basis of a common characteristic such as age, sex, race, or disability.

Stereotypic (stereotyped) behavior Repetitive nonfunctional movements (e.g., hand flapping, rocking), characteristic of autism and other severe handicaps.

Stimulus control Occurs when a behavior is emitted more often in the presence of a particular stimulus than it is in the absence of that stimulus.

Strabismus A condition in which one eye cannot attain binocular vision with the other eye because of imbalanced muscles.

Stuttering A complex fluency disorder of speech, affecting the smooth flow of words; may involve repetition of sounds or words, prolonged sounds, facial grimaces, muscle tension, and other physical behaviors.

Supported employment An approach to helping persons with disabilities find, learn, and maintain paid employment at regular worksites in the community. A supported employment specialist assists the disabled worker in performing the job, gradually reducing the amount of on-the-job assistance as the employee's work performance improves over time.

Syntax The system of rules governing the meaningful arrangement of words in a language.

Task analysis Breaking a complex skill or chain of behaviors into smaller, teachable units.

Tay-Sachs disease A progressive nervous system disorder causing profound mental retardation, deafness, blindness, paralysis, and seizures. Usually fatal by age 5. Caused by a recessive gene; blood test can identify carrier; analysis of enzymes in fetal cells provides prenatal diagnosis.

Time-out A behavior management technique that involves removing the opportunity for reinforcement for a specific period of time following an inappropriate behavior; results in a reduction of the inappropriate behavior.

Token economy System of reinforcing various behaviors by delivering tokens (e.gi, stars, points, poker chips) when specified behaviors are emitted. Tokens are accumulated and turned in for the individual's choice of items on a "menu" of backup reinforcers (e.g., a sticker, hall monitor for a day).

Topography (of behavior) The physical shape or form of a response.

Total communication An approach to education of deaf students that combines oral speech, sign language, and finger spelling.

Tremor A type of cerebral palsy characterized by regular, strong, uncontrolled movements. May cause less overall difficulty in movement. Paralysis of any three limbs; relatively rare.

Turner's syndrome A sex chromosomal disorder in females, resulting from an absence of one of the X chromosomes. Although not usually a cause of mental retardation, it is often associated with learning problems. It also causes lack of secondary sex characteristics, sterility, and short stature.

Tymphonic membrane (eardrum) Located in the middle ear, the eardrum moves in and out to variations in sound pressure, changing acoustical energy to sound energy.

Usher's syndrome An inherited combination of visual and hearing impairments. Usually, the person is born with a profound hearing loss and loses vision gradually in adulthood because of retinitis pigmentosa, which affects the visual field.

Visual acuity The ability to clearly distinguish forms or discriminate details at a specified distance.

Visual efficiency A term used to describe how effectively a person uses his vision. Includes such factors as control of eye movements, near and distant visual acuity, and speed and quality of visual processing.

Vitreous humor The jellylike fluid that fills most of the interior of the eyeball.

Vocational rehabilitation A program designed to help adults with disabilities, obtain and hold employment.

Work activity center A sheltered work and activity program for persons with severe disabilities; teaches concentration and persistence, along with basic life skills, for little or no pay.

References

Achenbach T.M., Howull, C.T. Quay, H.C. & Conners, C.K. (1991). National survey of problems and competencies among four to sixteen year olds monographs of society for research in child Development, Serial No. 225. (Vol.56, No.3).

American Association on Mental Retardation, Ad HOC Committee on terminology and classification. (1992). Mental retardation (9th ed.) Washington DC, Author.

American Psychiatric Association (1994). Diagnostic and statistical manual of mental disorders (4th ed.) Washington DC. Author.

Ashman Adrian and Elkins John. "Educating children with special needs". Australia: prentice Hall Pvt. Ltd., 1994. PP 515-518.

Auerbach J., Benjamin J., Faroy M., Geuer V., and Ebstein R. (2001). DRDH related to infant attention and information processing. A link to ADHD? Psychiatric Genetics 11, 31-35.

Barkley R.A. (1998). Attention – deficit hyperactivity disorder: A hand book for diagnosis and treatment. New York: Guilford.

Barkley, R. (2000). Taking charge of AD/HD: The complete, authoritative guide for parents (Rev.ed), New York: Guilford.

Barr W.B. (2000). Epilepsy. In A. Kazdin (Ed), Encyclopedia of psychology. Washington DC, and New York: American Psychological Association and Oxford University Press.

Bender W. (1998). Learning disabilities (3rd ed.) Boston : Allyn and Bacon.

Blackhurst A.E. (1997, May/June). Perspectives on technology in Special Education. Teaching exceptional children. pp41-47.

Border, E. (1973). Developmental dyslexia. Developmental medicine and child neurology, 15:663-87.

Bos C.S., Vaughn S. (2002). Strategies for teaching students with learning and behavioral problems (5th ed.) Boston: Ally & Bacon.

Boyles N.S., and Cantadino D. (1997). The learning differences source book. Los Angeles : Lowell House.

Brophy J. (1996). Teaching problem students. New York: Gullford.

Castellanos, F.S., Swanson, I.M. (2002). Biological underpinnings of ADHD. In S. Sandberg (Ed) Hyperactivity and attention disorders of childhood (2nd ed). Cambridge, England, Cambridge University Press.

Castles, A., & Colt heart, M. (1993). Varieties of developmental dyslexia. Coguition, 47 (2): 149-180.

Coleman James C. "Abnormal Psychology and Modern life". Scott Foresman and Company. 1984. PP.478.

Coleman M.C. and Webber J. (2002). Emotional and behavioral disorders (4th ed). Boston: Allyn & Bacon.

Collins et al., (2003). Learning disabled brains. Journal of Clinical and Experimental Neuropsychology, 25(7): 1011-1034.

Critchley, M., and Critchley, EA. (1978). Dyslexia defined. Spring field, Charles C. Thomas, 149.

Davis G.A., Rimm S.B. (2004). Education of the gifted and talented (5th ed.) Boston: Allyn & Bacon.

Drew CJ, Logan Dr, Hardman ML, (1984). Mental regardation a life cycle approach. Times Mirror / Mosby College publishing, 3rd ed., p.26.

Fallon M.A., and Watts E. (2001). Portflio assessment and use. Teacher education and Special Education . 24, 50-57.

Friend M., and Bursyck W.D. (2002). Including students with special needs (3rd Ed.) Boston: Allyn & Bacon.

From Frank M. Hewett and Frank D. Taylor (1980). The emotionally disturbed child in the classroom: the orchestration of success, 2nd Edn., Allyn and Bacon, Icn.

Gaskins I, Downer M, Gaskins R. (1986). Introduction to the Benchmark school word identification/vocabulary development program. Media, PA. Benchmark school.

Gearheart Bill R, Weishahn Mel W, Gearheart Card J. "The Exceptional student in the Regular classroom". New York: Merrill Publishing Company. 1992. PP. 255-259.

Govinda Rao, L. (2008). "Perspectives on Special Education" 2 Volumes, Neelkamal Publications Pvt. Ltd., New Delhi, Hyderabad.

Govt. of India (1992). Scheme of Integrated Education of disabled children, Ministry of Human Resource Development, New Delhi.

Hallahan D.P., and Kauffman J.M. (2000). Exceptional learners (8th ed.) Boston : Allyn & Bacon.

Hallahan D.P., Kauffman J.M. (2003) Exceptional learners (9th ed.) Boston : Allyn & Bacon.

Hammill D.D. (2004). What we know about correlates of reading. Exceptional children. 70, 453-468.

Hertzog N.B. (1998) Gifted education specialized. Teaching exceptional children. Jan/Feb; pp39-43.

Heward W.L. (2000) Introduction to Special Education (6th ed.) Upper Saddle River, NJ: Merrill.

Heward William L, and Orlansky Michael D. (1992). "Exceptional children". New York: Merrill Publishing Company. PP 387-390.

Hinshelwood, J. (1917). Congenital word-blindness. HK Lewis & Co., Ltd.

IGNOU – MHRD (2006). Hand book of inclusive education – Government of India project.

Jenkins J, O'Cohnor R. (2003). Cooperative learning for students with learning disabilities.

Johnson, DJ., and Myklebust, HR. (1967). Learning disabilities: Educational principles and practices. New York, Grune and Stratton.

Kauffman, J.M. and Hallahan, D.P. (2005). Special Education. Boston: Allyn & Bacon.

Koestler, F. (1976). The unseen minority: A social history of blindness in the United States. New York, McKsay.

Lane K.L., Greshman, F.M., and O'Shavghessy T.E. (2002). Interventions for children with or without risk for emotional and behavioured disorders. Boston: Allyn & Bacon.

Lerner, J. (2002). Learning disabilities. (8th ed) Boston: Houghton Mifflin.

Lewis, V. (2002). Development and disability. (2nd ed) Malden, MA: Blackwell.

Lovett M, Lacerenza L, Bordern S, Palma M. (2000). Components of effective remediation for developmental reading disabilities. Journal of Educational Psychology, 92:263-83.

Lyon et al., (2003). A definition of dyslexia. Ann Dyslexia, 53:1-14.

Lyytinen, et al., (2007). Reading and reading disorders. In Hoff, Erika, Blackwell Handbook of Language Development, Blackwell, pp.454-474.

Mangal S.K. "Abnormal Psychology". New Delhi : Sterling Publishers, 1981.PP 139- 141.

MHRD (2008). Department of school education and literacy, Government of India : Conference volume 3 & 5.

Moyer J.R., & Darding J.C. (1978). Practical task analysis for teachers. Teaching exceptional children. 11, 16-18.

Orton, ST. (1928) : Specific reading disability – strephosymbolia. Journal of the American Medical Association. 90(14): 1095-1099.

Page James D. "Abnormal Psychology". New Delhi : Tata KcGraw Hill Publishing Company Ltd. 1947. PP 335-352.

Pierangelo, R., & Giuliani G. (2002). Assessment in Special Education . Boston : Allyn & Bacon.

Polloway E.A., Patton J.R., Smith T.E.C. & Buck G.H. (1997). Mental retardation and learning disabilities: Conceptual and applied issues. Journal of Learning Disabilities, 30, 297-308.

Pueschel, S.M., Scola P.S., Weidenman, L.E., & Bernier, J.C. (1995). The special child. Baltimore: Paul H. Brookes.

Reed V.A. (2005). Introduction to children with language disorders (2nd ed.) Boston: Allyn & Bacon.

Samuelsson S., Lundberg I., & Herkner B. (2004). ADHD and reading disability in male adults. Journal of Learning Disabilities. 37, 155-168.

SCERT (2007). Gearing up for inclusive education New Delhi.

Spafford, C.S., Grosser G.S., & Daurich B. (2005). Dyslexia and reading difficulties. (2nd Ed.) Boston: Allyn & Bacon.

SSA Karnataka (2007-2008). Annual report.

Stahl S, Heuback K. (2005). Fluency oriented reading instruction. Journal of Literacy Res, 37: 25-60.

Stanovich, KE. (1988). Explaining the differences between the dyslexic and the garden – variety poor reader. Journal of Learning disabilities, 21(10): 590-604.

Strichart S.S., & Mahgrum C.T. (2002). Teaching study skills and strategies to students with learning disabilities. Attention deficit disorders or special needs (3rd ed.) Boston: Allyn & Bacon.

Swanson H, Hoskyn M, Lee C. (1999). Interventions for students with learning disabilities. Guilford. New York.

Terman D.L., Larner M.B., Stevenson C.S., & Behrman R.E. (1996). Special Education for students with disabilities.

Thomson, ME. (1990). Developmental dyslexia : Its nature, assessment and remediation, ed 3, London, Whyrr Publisher.

Torgesen and Mathes (2000). A basic guide to understanding, assessing and teaching phonological awareness. Austin, Tx: Pro.Ed.

Torgesen J.D. (1995 Dec). Prevention and remediation of reading disabilities. Progress report (NICHD Grant HD 30988). Bethesdu MD: National Institute of Child Health & Human Development.

U.S. Department of Education (2000). To assure a free and appropriate public education of all children with disabilities. Washington DC: U.S. Office of Education.

Vaughn and Klingner. (2004). Teaching reading comprehension to students with learning disabilities. In handbook of language and literacy : Development and disorders, ed. C Stone, E Silliman, B.Ehren, KK Apel, pp.541-55. New York : Guilford.

Wagher M.W. & Blackorby J. (1996). Transition from high school to work or college : How Special Education students fare. Future of Children, 6(1): 103-120.

Westling D.L. & Fox L. (2002). Teaching students with severe disabilities (2nd ed.) Upper Suddle River, NJ: Prentice Hall.

Whalen C. (2002). Attention deficit hyperactivity disorder. In A. Kazdin (Ed.) Encyclopedia of psychology. Washington, DC & New York: American Psychological Association and Oxford University Press.

Winner E. (1996). Gifted children. Myths and Realities. New York: Basic Books.

Wong B.Y.L. & Dohahue M. (Eds.) (2002). The social dimension of learning disabilities. Mahawah, NJ: Erilbaum.

Yesseldyke James E. and Algozzine Bob. (1998). Special Education – A Practical Approach for Teachers. Kanishka Publishers, New Delhi.

Zigler E.F. (2002). Looking back 40 years and seeing the person with mental retardation as a whole person. In H.N. Switzky (Ed.) personality and motivational difference in persons with mental retardation. Mahwah, NJ: Erlbaum.

❖ ❖ ❖

Index

Author Index

Subject Index

S

T

U

V

W